Multiple Intelligences
A Collection

Edited by
Robin Fogarty & James Bellanca

IRI/Skylight Training and Publishing, Inc.
Arlington Heights, Illinois

Multiple Intelligences: A Collection

Published by IRI/Skylight Training and Publishing, Inc.
2626 S. Clearbrook Dr.
Arlington Heights, IL 60005
800-348-4474, 847-290-6600
Fax 847-290-6609
info@iriskylight.com
http://www.iriskylight.com

Creative Director: Robin Fogarty
Managing Editor: Julia Noblitt
Editors: Amy Wolgemuth, Sabine Vorkoeper
Type Compositor and Formatter: Donna Ramirez
Book Designers: Michael Melasi, Bruce Leckie
Production Coordinators: David Stockman, Maggie Trinkle

LCCCN 95-75389
ISBN 0-932935-91-5

1348E-8-98V
Item number 1313
06 05 04 03 02 01 00 99 98   15 14 13 12 11 10 9 8 7 6 5

9/15/05

Table of Contents

Multiple Intelligences
A Collection

I t's not *how smart you are*, but rather, *how you are smart* that counts, says Howard Gardner in his theory of multiple intelligences (MI). Since his seminal piece, *Frames of Mind: The Theory of Multiple Intelligences,* hit the education scene in 1983, Gardner's seven ways of viewing the world have had a major impact on the educational community's perception of human intelligence.

Embracing ideas derived primarily from neurobiology and complemented by fields such as psychology, anthropology, philosophy, and history, Gardner posits a theory of seven distinct "frames of mind" or intelligences. In addition to the widely accepted verbal/linguistic and mathematical/logical intelligences, Gardner's intelligences include the visual/spatial, bodily/kinesthetic, musical/rhythmic, interpersonal, and intrapersonal.

Reviewing "evidence from a large and unrelated group of sources: studies of prodigies, gifted individuals, brain-damaged patients, *idiots savants,* normal children, normal adults, experts in different lines of work, and individuals from diverse cultures" (Gardner, 1993, p. 9), Gardner convincingly argues for an alternative look at human intellectual competences.

As a concise resource of Gardner's theory and the impact of its implications for schooling around the globe, *Multiple Intelligences: A Collection* is designed for educators in every sphere of the school arena, as well as for parents, parent councils, board members, trustees, and community leaders in urban, suburban, and rural areas.

Divided into five clearly defined sections, this collection offers a comprehensive synopsis of Gardner's work—from theory to practice. The first section, "About Howard Gardner," uncovers the man behind the theory as an eclectic student/master of both the arts and cognitive psychology. Once introduced to the personage of Howard Gardner, section two, "From Theory. . . ," expounds the creative genius of his theory of multiple intelligences. From Gardner's early papers and his later work, readers get an indepth look at the thinking behind the theory.

The third section, ". . . to Practice," explores the practical applications of these esoteric underpinnings. This section describes five MI "best practices" and examines the overall impact of Gardner's theory on the contemporary classroom.

Expanding on the practical applications of MI, section four, "For All Children," focuses on three authors' positions on the usefulness of the multiple intelligences approach for all children regardless of background or label. This section reinforces Gardner's idea that all children possess multiple intelligences, from the "learning disabled" to the "gifted."

The collection concludes with an exciting array of essays and commentaries on the numerous uses of multiple intelligences theory. The ideas presented in the final section, "Special Applications," span the spectrum from goal setting to technology integration to innovative assessment alternatives.

Multiple Intelligences: A Collection offers the novice a comprehensive, concise, and pragmatic picture of Howard Gardner's theory of multiple intelligences. For the student of Gardner's work, it provides an indepth look at the many facets of multiple intelligences theory, featuring a broad range of voices—from the tower of academic research to the field of academic practice. This sweeping collection is an invaluable resource for anyone interested in the mystery of the human mind and an expanded view of human intellectual capacities.

REFERENCE

Gardner, H. (1983). *Frames of mind: The theory of multiple intelligences.* New York: Basic Books.

About Howard Gardner

Who is the man behind the theory of multiple intelligences? How did Howard Gardner, Professor of Education at Harvard Graduate School of Education, codirector of Harvard Project Zero come to develop his theory? And what is Project Zero?

Profiled in interviews from resources as diverse as *Gifted Child Today, Language Arts,* and *Mid-Western Educational Researcher,* Howard Gardner emerges from the printed page as an eloquent communicator, thoroughly immersed and educated in his field and genuinely concerned for children and the future of education. His responses to the questions of Robert Kirschenbaum, David Fernie, and Jacqueline Anglin paint a rich image of the man behind the theory.

Gardner, naturally, embodies his theory of multiple intelligences. He presents that "jagged profile" of intelligences—a unique combination of seven frames of mind. The following cognitive sketch of Howard Gardner is offered merely to suggest a most interesting individual to read about.

PROFILE OF HOWARD GARDNER AND THE SEVEN INTELLIGENCES
Verbal/Linguistic: prolific writer—*Shattered Minds; Frames of Mind: The Theory of Multiple Intelligences; To Open Minds; The Unschooled Mind; Multiple Intelligences: The Theory in Practice.*

Mathematical/Logical: posits seven intelligences; defines and applies criteria; logically argues theory.

Visual/Spatial: interests in arts and arts education well documented—*Artful Scribbles: The Significance of Children's Drawings; Art, Mind, and Brain: A Cognitive Approach to Creativity.*

Bodily/Kinesthetic: enrolled in drama classes at Harvard; runs along the Charles River in Boston daily; believes an active, hands-on approach to uncovering the intelligences in children is far superior to his early thinking about a test for the seven frames.

Musical/Rhythmic: early years at the piano; some experimentation with musical composition as a youth; plays the piano, even now, as often as twice a day, with Benjamin, his young son.

Interpersonal: globetrotting speaker able to interact with diverse audiences; shows team collaboration in coauthoring materials and codirecting Project Zero.

Intrapersonal: explores his educational, family, and personal experiences in *To Open Minds* as he compares his learning environments to those he studied in China.

     This preview gives a flavor of the man behind the multiple intelligences theory. Read on to find out more about Howard Gardner.

An Interview with Howard Gardner

by Robert J. Kirschenbaum

Dr. Howard Gardner is Professor of Education at Harvard Gradu-
ate School of Education in Cambridge, Massachusetts, and co-Di-
rector of Harvard Project Zero, a research program investigating
the development of knowledge, artistic ability, and creativity in
young children. His extensive list of publications includes Artful
Scribbles: The Significance of Children's Drawings; Art, Mind,
and Brain: A Cognitive Approach to Creativity; *and* Frames of
Mind: The Theory of Multiple Intelligences, *all published by Ba-*
sic Books. His book on multiple intelligences has had an impact on
the field of gifted education because in it, Dr. Gardner criticizes the
reliance of educators and psychologists on the IQ test as a measure
of intelligence. Instead, he advocates the viewpoint that people pos-
sess seven distinct intelligences and may be very high in one or
more of them without have a high IQ score. Dr. Gardner was in-
terviewed in Boston during the Annual Conference of the Ameri-
can Educational Research Association in April, 1990.

G CT [Gifted Child Today]: *What is cognitive science and how*
does it relate to psychology and education?

Gardner: Cognitive science is a new, self-styled field that was
named about thirty years ago. While the major work has thus
far been done by psychologists and people in the field of artificial intelligence, philosophers, educators, neuroscientists, anthropologists, and linguists have also contributed to cognitive
science. It is an interdisciplinary field in which researchers are

From *Gifted Child Today,* vol. 13, no. 6, p. 26–32, November/December 1990.
© 1990 by Prufrock Press. Reprinted with permission.

intent on answering questions about mental processes, operations, and products. From my point of view, cognitive scientists are trying to answer longstanding questions about the nature of the mind by using contemporary, empirical techniques in which the computer plays an important part. For many researchers, the computer is the best model of the mind, although I don't necessarily agree with that.

GCT: Is there a cognitive approach to parenting?

Gardner: One might consider a few points. Some people orient to children's behaviors as if they were observing trained monkeys and are therefore only interested in controlling and shaping behavior. When I was in China, I discovered that people there are interested primarily in performance and show little interest in what people are thinking. From a contrasting viewpoint, we can focus on the *ideas* that children have, their conceptual development, and how they interpret and understand events and things in the world. For instance, if we examine a child's drawing, we can talk about how beautiful it is and how closely it resembles what is being drawn. Those are not particularly cognitive issues. But, if we ask what the child is thinking, how did he plan, and what was he trying to accomplish, we are asking questions that utilize a cognitive approach.

> If we ask what the child is thinking, how did he plan, and what was he trying to accomplish, we are asking questions that utilize a cognitive approach.

There are good and bad approaches to parenting. We might consider it a positive cognitive approach when parents understand that their children do not view the world and think in the same manner as they do. An inappropriate cognitive approach would be demonstrated by parents who try to rationalize everything and always give explanations for what they have done. If your two-year-old child put his hand near a stove or walked near a cliff, you wouldn't give him an explanation of the danger, you'd move him away firmly and quickly. For such a young child, that's the appropriate method of parenting. Eventually, the child should understand the reason to be careful in those situations, but at the age of two years he must be trained to stay clear of dangerous situations that his parents have identified for him.

GCT: *Aren't there scientists who say that children learn best when parents mediate their child's experiences, focus the child's attention on the relationship among objects and events, and offer explanations that emphasize cause-and-effect? Is this a cognitive approach?*

Gardner: I would call it an intellectual approach. I'm wary of the tendency for people to put the term "cognitive" in front of anything to make it seem good. I'm more interested in the underlying ideas that are being conveyed, not whether someone calls his approach cognitive or not. We live in a society in which it is appropriate for parents to offer explanations to their children for why they do things, but explanations are not desirable when a child's behavior should be stopped quickly to keep him or her out of danger.

> **I'm wary of the tendency for people to put the term "cognitive" in front of anything to make it seem good.**

GCT: *Do you think that parents can over-intellectualize situations to the point where their children become too rational and reflective?*

Gardner: Sometimes people have to act quickly and not stand there scratching their heads. Many opportunities for action only present themselves briefly and then they're gone.

GCT: *You have written about the importance of the interpersonal relationship between teacher and student in preliterate societies, and the relationship between school and community in agricultural societies. What relationship is at the core of learning in our technological society?*

Gardner: Over the last hundred years, educators have tried to introduce "objective" mechanisms into the schools. One of the reasons for standardized testing is to establish an objective criterion for determining academic placement. That way, it doesn't matter whether a teacher does or doesn't like a child when it comes to making a decision about his educational advancement. There are reasons for distancing the student from the teacher, but basically this phenomenon reflects a misunderstanding about the nature of the educational process. Education is inherently a function of the human relationship. Even though we can use all kinds of technological substitutes, when the human relationship is absent, education doesn't work. The notion that a computer can take the place of a human being as a teacher can only be offered by a person who lacks an understanding of the nature of education. A computer is useful just like a pencil is a useful tool, but nobody suggests that a pencil can take the place of a human being.

> Even though we can use all kinds of technological substitutes, when the human relationship is absent, education doesn't work.

GCT: What do you mean by the term "intelligence?"

Gardner: I pluralize the concept of intelligence. If there is one campaign that I'm on, it's to knock out the popular notion that there is a single general, or "g", factor of intelligence. In writing *Frames of Mind,* I argued against the concept of a unitary intellectual capacity or potential. Instead, I consider an intelligence as a human intellectual competence that enables one to solve problems encountered in society and to create effective products. According to my analysis, a human intelligence emerges only in an appropriate cultural context.

Most intelligence tests rely almost exclusively on the assessment of linguistic and logical skills. I posit the existence of seven relatively autonomous intelligences—linguistic, logical-mathematical, spatial, musical, body-kinesthetic, intrapersonal, and interpersonal, each with its own particular problem-solving and product-making characteristics.

Think of the last ten American presidents. While they were all smart in one way or another, they weren't smart in the same way. You can't compare the intellectual abilities of Kennedy to Reagan, or Carter to Johnson. They all had different kinds of minds and so do all the rest of us. You find out about the differences in intelligences when you go on a trip with someone and lose your way. People approach this problem differently. Some people resort to a map, others ask somebody for directions. We don't look the same way, we don't have the same types of personality traits, so only a psychologist would think we all have the same kind of intelligence.

GCT: How do you use the term "talent?"

Gardner: I use the words "talent" and "intelligence" interchangeably. For instance, one might say, "So-and-so is a very talented artist but what's really important is how smart you are." If we call human abilities talents, in the sense that Einstein was talented in science, T. S. Elliot was talented in language, and Pablo Casals was talented in music, then we can equally well say that they each were intelligent in their own domains. There is something wrong when a person is able to do some things very well, but is not considered smart if those things happen not to be connected to school success. One can view Reagan as being very talented and intelligent, or not, depending on which of his actions are being assessed. If he is being measured according to how well he was able to mobilize people to act and think a certain way and to like what he had to say, he was a genius. If he was to take an intelligence test, I would guess that he would not do very well.

> There is something wrong when a person is able to do some things very well, but is not considered smart if those things happen not to be connected to school success.

GCT: What do you mean by competence?

Gardner: I think intelligence and talent refer to the potential to think and act. However, a potential by itself is meaningless until it is expressed in a social setting. For example, two people who do not have the same potential to express themselves in music could take the same number of lessons, but one person would advance further than the other in musical competence. Competence is a term to use *after* a person has had the opportunity to be trained or to practice a skill. Potential is latent until a measure of competence is obtained. Potential, talent, and intelligence are there (so to speak) ahead of time and can only be seen once a crystallizing moment has occurred and a person's competence is then observed. Competence is also evaluated in terms of the degree of skill a person possesses at one moment and may change considerably over time, while potential changes very little over time. Still, if situations or opportunities arise that allow people to perform in new ways, then a person's talents may become evident that had previously been hidden.

GCT: How would you define giftedness?

Gardner: I define giftedness as a property of individuals who are "at promise" in an intellectual domain. I use the term "intellectual" more broadly than others. Music is an intellectual domain just as understanding other people is an intellectual domain. A person is more gifted than other people in a specific domain if he can advance more quickly in competence given the same amount of exposure to that domain. Giftedness is therefore a function of rapidity of development.

> **I define giftedness as a property of individuals who are "at promise" in an intellectual domain.**

Where I differ from other people is that I consider each intelligence to have its own type of giftedness. A person may be a gifted chess player but that says nothing about his competence in other intelligences. Giftedness is domain- and intelligence-specific. Giftedness also is unrelated to creativity. A person may advance very quickly in competence but lack originality. Creativity is doing something in a new way. People may be very creative and not gifted; it may have taken them a long time to develop competence, but then they do very original things with what they have learned. More often, people are gifted but are not very creative. They can scoot up the ladder very quickly, but once at the top they don't do anything creative.

GCT: Are gifted students better able to develop and use learning and performance strategies in developing their competencies?

Gardner: It depends on the particular case. Some gifted individuals who advance very quickly may use the same strategies as everybody else does but use them more efficiently. Other individuals may be able to come up with different strategies from the outset that are more efficient than the strategies or techniques that most people use. It's unclear whether very gifted persons can skip the use of simple strategies before learning to use complex strategies, or if they use and abandon simple strategies more quickly than others. It has to do with how our brains work. Our brains aren't all the same. For example, one child may not be able to learn to read in the ordinary way. That might mean that the child is going to have a lot of trouble learning how to read, or it might mean that the child is going to be able to read more quickly because he or she is going to develop a new strategy for reading.

> **There are no particular patterns of intelligences that tend to develop together or to be disassociated from one another.**

GCT: Is the possession of certain intelligences incompatible with the possession of others?

Gardner: No. There are no particular patterns of intelligences that tend to develop together or to be disassociated from one another. Some people may be good in music and math while others are good in music but not in math or *vice versa*. The intelligences are semi-autonomous. There's no reason why the development of one should interfere with another. There is a popular image of mathematicians that they have their heads in the clouds and are impractical, but there is no reason to believe that a mathematician can't be practical. Dr. Johnny Von Neumann, a great mathematician, was a very practical person. Sometimes the limitations inherent in working in a particular field prevent a person from having the time to develop other abilities, but so far as I can see, there are no neurological reasons why any combination of intelligences can't be developed together.

GCT: Dr. Julian Stanley has found that when a student is very high in math and moderately high in verbal ability, he or she is better at math than a student who is very high in both math and verbal areas. Do you have any explanation or comment on that?

Gardner: That's an interesting finding. One possibility is that society gives students more interesting options if they have high ability in the verbal areas. I studied visually talented students who became artists. We found that students who are very talented in art and very good in school tend to drop art since success in school is more universally rewarded. If a person is talented in art and doesn't do well in school, he or she is more likely to pursue an art career. Another possibility can be drawn from the work of Dr. Mihaly Csikszentmihalyi. He found that many children who are good in math don't enjoy doing math. It is not a time of high "flow" for them. In other words, they don't feel real connected to their work. It's a shame.

GCT: *Maybe that offers some explanation of why many of the high ability students in Dr. Stanley's Study of Mathematically Precocious Youth don't become professional mathematicians, although they often go into math-related or science fields.*

There's danger in not giving individuals enough choices in their educational and life options.

Gardner: I have grave doubts about his approach. I think it's great to give highly able children the chance to discover the extent of their ability, but I don't think children should be pushed to graduate from college at the age of 18. I think they suffer some kind of loss and it can be very dangerous. There can be casualties.

GCT: *Is there danger in mastering material too quickly or in being radically accelerated through the educational system?*

Gardner: There's danger in not giving individuals enough choices in their educational and life options. The problem is not restricted to any field and I don't want to pick on Dr. Stanley and his work with mathematically talented youth. What bothers me is the mentality of people who find a gifted child and say, "This child has tremendous potential so let's push him as far as we can. If he's not in the New York City Ballet by the age of 20, he never will be." Of course, by the age of 30 or so, dancers are all through and many thereafter live very sad lives.

In a place like China, which I've visited several times, there is almost no choice for young people in terms of their education. In our society, there are many students who end up in a field and realize at some point that it wasn't what they wanted to do but what someone else wanted them to do.

GCT: A teacher who took one of my courses told me that she was offered a full scholarship to a prestigious art school when she graduated from high school in the sixties, but her father decided she should become a teacher. When I met her she was forty years old and still was afraid to do things with her life that would meet with her father's disapproval.

Gardner: I think that Dr. Stanley is absolutely right in providing an avenue for children who have tremendous talent and want to take advanced training in math and science. It would be to their detriment to hold them back arbitrarily. But, a different mentality sometimes takes over when the focus is on the ends of development and that's always dangerous. I'm not surprised that few of the high ability math students go into mathematics as a profession because it's not at all clear that getting a high SAT-math score in seventh grade is what it takes to be a mathematician for the rest of your life. Dr. Andrew Gleason, a mathematician at Harvard, told me that he can predict which of his students will be mathematicians not by their test scores, but by whether they read math books on their own and come up with new problems.

> A different mentality sometimes takes over when the focus is on the ends of development and that's always dangerous.

GCT: Based on your observations of art training in China and the teaching of music through the Suzuki method, both of which are effective at helping young students to reach high levels of competence, what are the implications for gifted education?

Gardner: One implication of the Suzuki method is that the demonstration of high performance doesn't mean that there's something special in the person, in the brain, or in the fingers. Much of the impetus for superior performance is in the environment. The Suzuki method takes ordinary children and gives them a rich, supportive environment. Parents and older peers share in teaching the young children. Good teaching techniques such as "scaffolding" are used. This is a method in which the teacher acts as a partner to the student and together they approach a situation and decide what the problem or task is and how it is to be resolved. If the student doesn't understand what to do, the teacher highlights certain features unobtrusively and has the student work on subproblems that can be solved more easily. Having an effective educational environment is at least as important as having a lot of talent. As Dr. Benjamin Bloom concluded from his studies of exceptional adult performers in several fields, a lot of potentially gifted persons don't have the disposition and support to perform at a high level, while many exceptional performers may not have the most talent to start with, but have had excellent training.

> Having an effective educational environment is at least as important as having a lot of talent.

In Japan, they don't worry about individual differences as much as we do, but are more concerned with getting everybody to reach a certain level of competence. That's a valuable concept that Dr. Bloom has discussed extensively in his publications on Mastery Learning. Japan and the United States have the opposite attitudes from what you would expect. While we espouse egalitarian values, we believe in inborn talents and feel that a person with low test scores is considered to have little talent and therefore is not as capable of achievement as someone with high test scores. We label children as gifted if they have a high IQ score and give them special program benefits and we put students with low test scores in slow classes. Japan takes the approach that a person with less talent needs to work harder and deserves extra tutoring. That's the message from Japan.

In China, I found their approach very instructive because it challenged my ideas about what young children can be expected to do. As a scientist, it's important for me to know what can be accomplished with ordinary children. They have children performing at a level which is "off the scale" in Western terms, yet I have ambivalent feelings about how they accomplish this feat. There are two aspects of Chinese education that should be noted, however. One is that they don't test the extent to which the students can put their skills to new uses. Our observations are that the skills can be quite flexible, but if the students are not "stretched" to try new things, their performance becomes uninteresting and commonplace.

The other point is that many scientists in this country assume that children should be allowed to explore their environment freely in preschool and kindergarten before their attention is focused on skill development. China does not allow this free exploration and yet is effective in its own way because the society believes in this approach. The lesson that we seem to learn over and over again is that individuals are more "plastic" and flexible than we thought. What I didn't like about China, and what is also the basis of my concern about radical acceleration, is that they send their talented children down a path that offers few options.

> **The lesson that we seem to learn over and over again is that individuals are more "plastic" and flexible than we thought.**

Granted that most people in China live pretty restricted and depressing lives anyway, but we live in a society in which people do have choices. We can change our minds and take a second chance at something. I don't think it is right to take any group of children and say to them, "Because you're gifted in this area, we're going to push you totally in that direction."

GCT: In your book on China, you mention that you encountered some art students whose work was more creative than others. Their parents were artists who encouraged them to express themselves more creatively. Could you elaborate on this?

Gardner: The method for teaching art in China is as rigid as can be. Teachers follow certain canons or rules that have been passed on for centuries. For instance, their technique for drawing goldfish dictates how every single stroke should be made. Artists in China have had some exposure to other ways of doing things and if their children show artistic talent, they will try to guide the children away from drawing like everyone else. There is a Chinese artist named Wang Yani, a girl who was discovered at the age of four and who is the most talented young visual artist I've ever seen. Her father took her out of art class because he felt it was destroying her talent. We interviewed dozens of artists and they don't like what's going on in the schools because they want their children to be more original.

If we simply want to produce high level performers, the Chinese have an exemplary method for doing so. If we want children to acquire skills that are more generative with a deeper understanding of a field, then we have to consider other methods. The teachings of Confucius, which is the basis of thinking in China, contrasts sharply with the teachings of Socrates. Being a Westerner, I prefer Socrates, who was superficially messy in his approach to education, but who wanted people to probe into why things are the way they are. Confucius was very prescriptive in his approach to behavior. The Chinese don't ask embarrassing questions because they want everybody to behave properly and everything to look right. We don't believe that life should be so regimented, while the Chinese look askance at our relatively stochastic existence in which we constantly make choices and select alternative paths. Since the crackdown on the democratic student movement, the government has become even less tolerant of deviation.

> Some teachers just don't want children to do too good a job or it makes them feel superfluous.

GCT: Are the artists' children punished in school when they show any originality and told to do things the "right" way?

Gardner: We visited very good schools in China and I noticed that teachers would often leave the most talented students alone. Perhaps the teachers realized that these students could do not only what was expected, but were also able to go beyond the methods being taught. When students who weren't as talented started to deviate from the prescribed method, they were chastised severely. The treatment of creative children depended on the teacher just as in this country.

Some teachers just don't want children to do too good a job or it makes them feel superfluous. That's a big problem for gifted students and it's obvious that a teacher of gifted students shouldn't feel threatened by their rapid learning ability and the originality of highly creative students. I've read books about the MacArthur Fellowship winners who are highly creative in their fields. A book by Dr. June Cox describes how many of these individuals did not have a good school experience because they didn't like what they were doing in their classes. Their teachers responded angrily when they asked difficult questions. The gifted child needs to be supported in his or her pursuit of a deeper understanding of what is being taught and not restricted in exploring the contradictions and gaps in knowledge. In the absence of a mentor, somebody who tells the child that it's okay to be inquisitive and that teachers don't have all the answers, the gifted child will be unhappy and confused and might even suffer a nervous breakdown. It must be very difficult to grow up understanding things and being able to do things that most children can't do, at the same time getting the message that it's not all right to be too bright and that one should know one's place.

GCT: What other factors besides talent play a role in performance?

Gardner: How do people approach work? We use a term called "working style" to describe certain behavioral characteristics. A big part of life is work and work plays a big role in the fulfillment we get from life. Intelligences are important for work but that's not all that you need to do a good job. The effectiveness of a person is partly determined by how "planful" and careful a person is and partly by how much effort is put forth. Persistence is very important. These aspects of behavior reflect the working style. While not computational in a strict sense, they are as important as intellectual ability.

> **Intelligences are important for work but that's not all that you need to do a good job.**

GCT: Are these working style characteristics always good in any situation?

Gardner: Dr. Jerome Kagan, who studies reflectivity-impulsivity differences, has shown that a reflective approach to problems is associated with academic achievement, but he points out that sometimes you don't want to be too reflective. One of the interesting "apparent" findings in our Program Spectrum is that working style characteristics do not go across the board. Project Spectrum is a preschool program that offers a curriculum that covers most of the intelligences and allows us to assess the cognitive profile and working style of children. They may be very persevering in areas that they like or in which they have some talent, but they may avoid getting involved in areas that do not appeal to them. It's dangerous to assume that learning or working styles are predominant in any activity. A child may be an analyzing type or a "left quadrant" sort during an activity in area A but not in area B. We need to investigate the intersection of the intelligences and different types of styles and determine which styles go across the board and which ones are distributed only over certain domains.

GCT: Which intelligences do we focus on in school and which ones do we neglect?

Gardner: The schools give special recognition to the verbally talented students, those high in linguistic intelligence. As the children get older, there's more praise for students who are logical and high in logical/mathematical intelligence. The hidden curriculum revolves around social status so interpersonal intelligence is rewarded with friendship or leadership roles. It helps in getting along with teachers. There's too little attention to intrapersonal intelligence. Children are left to develop it by themselves because there is almost no help from the schools. Intrapersonal needs are unfortunately neglected in every area of education. People are very uneducated about their own cognitions. It's terribly important that people living in a complex world understand themselves, their abilities and their options.

> **The hidden curriculum revolves around social status so interpersonal intelligence is rewarded with friendship or leadership roles.**

As far as the other intelligences are concerned, it is the unusual teacher who pays much attention to them except in the context of extracurricular activities. While time in sports and the band is important, it is not viewed as a critical time for education to take place, which is when the curriculum is being taught. There are some schools, like the Key School designed by Patricia Bolanos in Indianapolis, that endorse my ideas and try to give students a diet of activities across all the intelligences every day. The school curriculum is tied together by themes that last nine weeks, at the end of which period the students are expected to present a project associated with the current theme. All the intelligences are addressed on a daily basis so the students are able to recognize where they are the most talented.

The Waldorf School of Rudolf Steiner emphasizes the arts, but the arts aren't valued much in this country. In China or Japan, artistic cultivation is important, while here artistic interests are considered effeminate or ethereal.

GCT: Do these countries use the arts to develop self-discipline as well as aesthetic awareness?

Gardner: Self-discipline is an important part of the training. Traditionally, Japan and China are more aesthetic societies than western societies. China now is hideous in many respects, but Japan continues to be one of the most aesthetic-minded societies in the world.

> Most children have "jagged profiles," having both high points and low points on a graph that show the extent of their ability in each of the intelligences.

GCT: You've reported that the preschool children you work with may be high in some intelligences but are low in others. Have you found any students who are high in most of the intelligences?

Gardner: While I'm sure there are children who are high in many areas, we haven't come across any omnibus prodigies yet. Most children have "jagged profiles," having both high points and low points on a graph that show the extent of their ability in each of the intelligences. We need to develop methods for examining each intelligence directly, which means that the tasks we give the examinee aren't unfamiliar and don't have to rely excessively on the use of language. The more effective we become in measuring each intelligence without relying on verbal responses to test questions, the more likely that most children will display this jagged profile, with very few students exhibiting all high or all low scores across the intelligences.

I'm not impressed by the fact that many tests of intelligence correlate strongly with one another because tests are very specific kinds of task situations and some people are very good test-takers. Other people are very good performers, but don't do well on tests. I would like to say to parents that there are very few children who don't have some areas of strength even if those areas aren't ones particularly cultivated by society. Parents must decide if they want their child to feel good about doing something well in one of these less valued areas and develop self-confidence, or if they would rather focus on the child's weaknesses in areas that may be valued more highly by society. Those are the options that parents can choose from. Parents may decide that their child's musical or artistic talent is not important and that their child should spend most of his time practicing how to read and write. The risk is that the child may fail to develop the one area in which he felt good about himself and replace it with low academic self-esteem and never become very good in reading and writing. However, it might turn out that with a lot of extra help and practice in the area of literacy, the child will become good enough to get good grades and have an enhanced self-image, in which case a parent may feel vindicated.

> **...the child may fail to develop the one area in which he felt good about himself and replace it with low academic self-esteem...**

GCT: You've written that "an individual in possession of an intelligence can be said to have no circumstance that prevents him from using that intelligence." You just seemed to say that a child can lose ability in an intelligence that's not utilized fully.

Gardner: That statement reflects a philosophical point I was trying to make. If, for example, a person is deaf, then musical intelligence is necessarily limited. A crippled person's bodily intelligence is limited, but there are Olympic-level athletes who have succeeded despite an infirmity. There are also disabled persons who compete in athletics amongst themselves, like the Boston marathon participants in wheelchairs. A person may be lacking in certain facets of an intelligence but excel in others. Another point is that any intelligence can be compromised severely while others function at a high level. There are persons who excel in math but have language problems inasmuch as they are low in linguistic intelligence. The main thing to understand is that our assessment of people should not be contaminated by accidental values as we examine the range of human competencies. I'm not concerned with trying to predict who's going to do well in school; the IQ enthusiasts do that pretty well. I'm interested in painting a picture of the profile of human abilities on a much broader canvas.

GCT: Researchers have found that the variety of individual learning styles is not evenly distributed in the general population. Does the same hold true for the multiple intelligences, or would we expect that 14% of the population is high in each intelligence?

Gardner: That question is moot because it depends on what are counted as the criteria for each intelligence. On the one hand, the whole population of speaking individuals can be considered linguistically intelligent since almost everyone learns fairly easily to speak compared to the effort needed to learn how to play music or perform the calculus. On the other hand, there are clearly some individuals who are much more linguistically intelligent than others. We would need to set the criterion for linguistic intelligence much higher (for example, speaking four languages or writing epic verse) in order to say there aren't more people who are linguistically talented than there are people who are musically talented.

GCT: So in any intelligence, there are always people who are more highly talented than others, but the scales or criteria by which one would measure talent are unique for each intelligence and not easily compared.

Gardner: Another point I want to make is that since we don't know all the different environments that people can be raised in, we can't possibly tell if under optimal conditions, all children would be high in at least one area. If a child was raised in a symphony hall, we would expect the child to be naturally more musically talented.

GCT: You are emphasizing the role of the environment in the development of intelligence. Some scientists who study the contributions made by hereditary and environmental influences say that 60–80% of intelligence as measured by IQ tests can be attributed to a person's genes. What do you think of those figures, which represent a view that genetic factors are more important than the environment?

Gardner: Most scientists would not try to make it an environment vs. heredity issue because that's an unsophisticated way to think about the development of ability. Most of this debate comes from studies of twins in which people try to determine the percentage of variation contributed to IQ scores by genetics in cases where the twins were reared separately. This shouldn't be of much interest to anyone except those who do the studies. They can't look at a range of environments because these situations are a quirk of fate and are not scientifically controlled.

> **There are a wide range of gifts and talents that people have and we had better think real carefully before we decide to promote one ability over others.**

GCT: *If I can turn your attention to gifted education, what do you consider its benefits and drawbacks?*

Gardner: First of all, there are a wide range of gifts and talents that people have and we had better think real carefully before we decide to promote one ability over others. Resources are limited and the fact that 90% of the programs in this country make their placement decisions on the basis of student IQ scores is not very praiseworthy. I would prefer that people put forward their gifts for examination and have competent judges determine who will receive enrichment.

GCT: *Put forward their gifts?*

Gardner: Sure. Ask a group of thirty children in a class, "Who wants to have some enrichment? Give me the reason why you deserve it and don't cite a test score. Let me see what you can do. If you can't do anything now, let me put you in a bunch of situations so I can see where you show some promise." That's what I would do.

GCT: *How can curriculum and assessment complement each other?*

Gardner: I would look much more at performance than at test scores. Rather than worrying about instrument selection, I would ask students to show me the best they have done in any area. "Tell me about the puzzles or games you have made up and play." How do they use their intelligences? Looking at instruments that have no relationship to anything meaningful in society is strictly a matter of faith. I certainly agree with Dr. Stanley that anyone who has a talent should be allowed to go as fast and as far as he wants. If someone wants to call me an elitist, that's fine. Acceleration, though, shouldn't be at the expense of developing other parts of the individual. Life is much more than one's area of strength. Much of what we learn in school comes from struggling in areas in which we don't have maximum ability. There are also many parts of society which shouldn't be cordoned off. Children come in all colors and flavors. When giftedness in certain valued areas becomes an excuse to set up positive and negative concentration camps, I'm against it.

> The crystallizing experience is a moment when a person says, "Gee, this is really me. This is where I fit in."

GCT: What are "crystallizing experiences?"

Gardner: A complex society has between 100 and 200 adult competencies that are valued either vocationally or avocationally. What's really important for any human being is to discover a few of those competencies to which one feels a sense of connection to take place. Most people either discover it serendipitously or not at all. When a person discovers something that he is really good at, it's a terrific experience. Stephen Gould, a MacArthur Fellow, was interviewed for the book *Uncommon Genius* and said, "Find out what you're good at and stick to it." He also said that it wasn't until a few years ago that he discovered what he was really good at and started to believe that he could do something better than most other people. He could tell what other people were good at doing but not himself. The crystallizing experience is a moment when a person says, "Gee, this is really me. This is where I fit in. I have a knack for this more than anything else." That gives a person extra leverage in applying his effort in the most effective manner.

GCT: What kind of childhood behaviors do you see as being antecedent to adult creativity?

Gardner: That's a big mystery, but I know that childhood creativity won't be found in an authoritarian environment. That stamps it out. We know more about how to kill creativity than how to foster it. One easy answer to the development of creativity is to put a person in an environment where there are creative people who ask questions, think aloud about situations, and reflect on their projects.

> **Creativity has more to do with personality and motivational factors than it has to do with intelligence.**

GCT: *You've observed how the expressiveness of children is dampened by age 10. This harks back to the fourth/fifth grade slump in creativity that Dr. E. Paul Torrance first commented on thirty years ago.*

Gardner: What you are talking about now is universal creativity that is evident in every child whose creative development isn't stunted by authoritarian restrictions.

GCT: *You don't see it, though, in some children of preschool age. I know children who were not brought up in a harsh environment but are very insecure and seem to have a very limited fantasy life.*

Gardner: You're right, but creative ability is very widely distributed if the environment nurtures children's imagination. We still don't know how creative expression in children, let's call it "small c," relates to "big C" in adults. It is extraordinarily complicated.

GCT: *Dr. Benjamin Bloom found in his research that creative artists considered themselves to be average in ability at a young age but they enjoyed drawing and kept doing it. When they were a little older, their peers started relating to them in terms of their artistic performance and always asked them to help on art projects in school. They weren't picked out at an early age as being very talented artistically.*

Gardner: Creativity has more to do with personality and motivational factors than it has to do with intelligence. A certain amount of intelligence is necessary to do anything, but the amount of talent is not what determines creativity.

GCT: Working style is as important as ability?

Gardner: The creative person has to be tough. People who do things by the book will knock the creative person around. If you can't take the criticism and stay committed to your goal, you end up crippled. One has to learn from one's mistakes without being overwhelmed by them. Those are characterological qualities.

I take a systemic approach to the conception of creativity. In other words, it's not all in the head. We have to consider a certain head operating in a certain domain with a certain set of judges. There are three components to creativity: a person's talents or gifts, the area of performance, and the society that judges something to be original enough to be noticed. To be creative, besides having certain abilities and personality characteristics, a person must understand the domain in which he works and where the boundaries or "points of give" are. Then, one has to do things that other people say are real good. We can't tell by ourselves how good we are. There must be a thousand people who think they are good *New Yorker* short story writers for every person who gets a story accepted by the editors. Being convinced of one's own talent isn't enough any more than having a super brain is enough. Creativity boils down to communal judgment. Giftedness is different in that regard.

GCT: How so?

Gardner: In the first place, it has more to do with what's "inside," defined as broadly as people wish. If someone can learn music very quickly, that's giftedness, and that's recognized across many cultures according to similar criteria. What's considered creative can change enormously from one culture to another, from one year to another. . . .

GCT: From one day to another.

Gardner: That's right. That's the problem with the visual arts: no one knows what's creative. Giftedness is more confidently recognized by experts than creativity at the highest level of performance by studying people like Freud, Einstein, and Picasso who, at the beginning of the modern era, changed the way we think about the world. I hypothesize that personality traits will be more similar among them than their ways of thinking, which might be more dependent on the fields they work in. I will seek parallels in the development of personality and ways of thinking across different domains of accomplishment.

Profile: Howard Gardner

by David E. Fernie

Department Editor's Note: School reform is on everyone's mind, from the would-be "Education President" to local school boards struggling to keep their schools financially afloat. Frequently, policymakers turn to easy-sounding solutions such as more testing. Into the fray steps developmental psychologist Howard Gardner with his recent book, The Unschooled Mind: How Children Think and How Schools Should Teach. *Gardner's views on testing and assessment and his implicit trust in children as learners are likely to find a sympathetic audience among many* LA *readers, some of whom may want to take him up on the challenge to try out some of his ideas and inform him of the results.*

This month's "Profile" features Howard Gardner, eminent cognitive psychologist, researcher, and educator. As a "Profile" subject in *Language Arts*, the choice of Gardner is a bit extraordinary: He is not a writer of fiction, though he is a prolific and literate writer of books; children are not the audience for his work but instead are the frequent subject; and language is not his primary focus but merely one of a nexus of interests related to human development and education.

As an academician, Gardner's scholarship profile is also extraordinary. Professor in the Harvard Graduate School of Education, Gardner is the first American to receive the University of Louisville Grawemeyer Award in Education and is a 1984 MacArthur Prize Fellow. At heart a writer of books despite an impressive spate of scholarly articles, he has authored a dozen books that span topics related to human development and edu-

From *Language Arts*, vol. 69, no. 3, p. 220–227, March 1992. © 1992 by the National Council of Teachers of English. Reprinted with permission.

cation, including the well-known *Frames of Mind: The Theory of Multiple Intelligences* (1983). These accolades and accomplishments are all the more impressive in a person just now arriving at midcareer.

In his research and writing, Gardner pursues large-scale questions: What is the nature of intelligence? What is creativity, particularly in the arts? How can we educate to achieve children's full potential? His concerns with such "big ideas" intrigue both a scholarly and a wider public audience and are of particular interest to educators and developmental-minded readers like those of *Language Arts.*

In some good children's books and fiction, writers' life experiences are either a "just-below-the-surface" presence or an explicit and central element of the text. In social science and academic writing, these biographical influences, though no less important, are usually more hidden or distant from the topic and text. This "Profile," however, benefits and draws heavily from Gardner's *To Open Minds* (1989), in which he uses the occasion of an extended visit to China to reflect upon his own American education and upon family, personal, and professional influences on his career path. (All quotes in the noninterview section of the "Profile" are from that book.) In it, he reveals a singular career path informed by a constellation of interests and influenced by, in his words, "a galaxy of mentors." Gardner's own education reflects a balance between traditional and progressive educational experiences consistent with the views expressed in this interview and in his newest book, *The Unschooled Mind: How Children Think and How Schools Should Teach* (1991). Growing up in a family of German-Jewish immigrants in Scranton, Pennsylvania, his formal public education was unremarkable; but that did not preclude his progressive self-education as an avid reader of history, biography, and literature or his creative pursuit of self-selected activities. This broader early education was marked by a musical "apprenticeship" at the piano, beginning when he was invited to play for a friend's teacher and ending precipitously when he rejected his teacher's plan for artistry:

> He [Gardner] reveals a singular career path informed by a constellation of interests and influenced by, in his words, "a galaxy of mentors."

increased hours of practice. But both in "tinkering" with musical composition and in dedicated attention to writing and editing the school newspaper, his artistic and literary impulses were evident even then.

During his undergraduate and graduate years at Harvard, he pursued a wide range of interests, intrigued by ideas and ways of thinking about them in subjects as diverse as drama, economic history, and social psychology. By his own account, Gardner may have set a record for the number of courses he audited in charting his intellectual path ("a bit like the proverbial 'kid in a candy store'").

Along the way, Gardner's ideas were shaped in mentoring opportunities with several giants in the field of psychology and education: as an undergraduate tutee of Erik Erikson, a graduate advisee of Roger Brown, and a research assistant to Jerome Bruner during the *Man: A Course of Study* (MACOS) curriculum and demonstration project. A self-described iconoclast, Gardner's scope of interests widened under their tutelage to include personality and cognitive development during these years. The work with Bruner, along with a short ("I survived for a semester") and eye-opening career as an elementary classroom teacher, informed his view of the value and challenge of a progressive education— "one in which individuals are provided with rich nourishment but not directed along one path as opposed to another."

> Gardner's ideas were shaped in mentoring opportunities with several giants in the field of psychology and education.

Between undergraduate and graduate work, Gardner spent a year in England as a Knox Fellow. His experiences there crystallized his interests in the arts and in cognitive psychology, reading Piaget by day and taking in theater and art gallery-hopping at night. This period also served as a self-imposed literary apprenticeship in which he wrote essays, articles, and most ambitiously, a 1000-page novel. Practicing the craft of writing, Gardner stretched and strengthened his writing muscles in diverse genres while learning that his voice would be found in social-scientific writing rather than in fiction.

During the years leading to adulthood and professional life, these formal and informal educational experiences had a marked impact on Gardner's writing style. In his writing, he draws from an expansive knowledge base, synthesizing ideas beyond the sometimes parochial ways in which topics are defined and thought about within particular disciplines. Quotes from Goethe and examples from quantum physics fit comfortably within the text, as science, art, and literature are infused seamlessly, whether in critiquing American education or in describing an aspect of children's development. Yet despite this scope, the logic and articulation of his arguments make his writing straightforward and accessible to a wide readership.

> The goal of Project Zero was to begin to understand and to chart through research the human development of artistic and creative abilities.

The substance of Gardner's writing, however, rests upon the empirical investigations and theory generated at the Harvard Project Zero research "shop" over the past 25 years. Founded by philosopher Nelson Goodman, the goal of Project Zero was to begin to understand and to chart through research the human development of artistic and creative abilities. In contrast, developmental psychology of the time (provoked by Piaget's work) centered on the logical and linguistic abilities characteristic of the scientist (and of the "little scientist" in the child). In beginning this novel exploration of artistic development with a few volunteer (read unpaid) graduate assistants including Gardner, Goodman quipped, "We know nothing about this, so let's call it Project Zero."

For the last twenty years, "PZ" has been codirected by Gardner and David Perkins. In the Gardner part of the shop, investigations by Gardner and his group of colleagues and research assistants have documented a nonlinear U-shaped developmental pattern in children's artistic development, with young children more like the mature artist than an older peer.

Not surprisingly, PZ investigations, though coalescing around issues of artistry and creativity, have been of wide scope, including symbolic development in various representational systems (from music to numbers to block building), the development of nonliteral language use, and the influence of media formats (such as books and television) on children's learning. The result of such an extensive network of research topics is apparent in Gardner's ability to conceptualize broadly as, for example, in the depiction of multiple and distinct domains of intelligence in *Frames of Mind*.

Commenting on the research life which has held his focus for 2 decades, Gardner explains his continuing enthusiasm:

> What makes it fun—even exquisite pleasure—is the opportunity to launch a new project: to generate a set of promising ideas; to follow a lead that might hold the clues for illuminating a mysterious process; to challenge a received truth and see if I can formulate a more adequate characterization, which will, of course, be challenged in turn and in time by someone else. (p. 88)

Gardner's research and writing up until the past few years might be best labeled as applied developmental psychology. Recently, he has turned more directly to educational issues. Now developing curricula and assessment procedures related to artistic (and other undervalued) abilities at Project Zero, the Indianapolis Key School, and at the preschool program Project Spectrum, Gardner and colleagues have turned increasingly to demonstration projects and to collaborations with schools.

Gardner and colleagues have turned increasingly to demonstration projects and to collaborations with schools.

Gardner's latest work, *The Unschooled Mind* (1991), is his most direct statement about a developmental-based and relevant education. In it and in the "written conversation" which follows, he presents an argument for what he calls "education for understanding"—a fresh synthesis of progressive education complemented by the promise held in both innovative nonschool institutions (such as children's museums) and undervalued traditions (such as the apprenticeship).

DEF: In some of your past research and writing, you've argued for an education that supports the diversity of children's abilities—their multiple intelligences. But do we make a mistake in our educational settings by emphasizing linguistic and mathematical competence, or is this merely education rightly serving society's priorities and needs?

HG: In a democracy, schools have two primary educational responsibilities: to prepare students to survive in the changing world of tomorrow and to make sure that each individual reaches his or her full potential as a human being. Neither of these goals is well-served by an education which is focused too narrowly on linguistic and logical-mathematical competence. In the first instance, we do not know for sure which capacities will be valued in the future, and so we are well-advised to develop a range of capacities in each person. As for the goal of realizing potential, individuals succeed in the world to the extent that they can develop and exploit their potentials. For those with strength in the logical and linguistic domains, school often provides appropriate and rich educational experiences; but schools have an equal duty to help those students with other kinds of strengths to recognize and develop them.

> **Individuals succeed in the world to the extent that they can develop and exploit their potentials.**

These points being made, certainly every school in the land has an obligation to develop the vital cultural skills of linguistic and mathematical literacies. It is a scandal that we do not do a better job in these areas. In contrast, Japanese schools develop a variety of human potentials, such as those in the arts, without sacrificing achievement in the linguistic and numerical spheres.

DEF: *Let's assume, then, that we haven't done such a stellar job in promoting these two intelligences? Do you worry that a call to educational pluralism, to broadening the types of intelligences to support, could actually dilute our efforts at school reform?*

HG: This is not a worry of mine. When schools are well-conceived and well-run, when they have an agreed upon set of goals and a means of achieving them, they can accomplish a great deal. A good school—and there are many in the United States and abroad—can succeed in a variety of educational spheres. And a poor school will not do well by its students, whether it is narrowly conceived or it attempts to touch all bases.

So much of our time in schools is based on noneducational activities, and much of the apparently educational work is actually time-filling rote learning and dull lecturing. If we used our time wisely and involved parents and students in the learning and assessment process, we could achieve so much more than we do today.

DEF: The title of your new book, The Unschooled Mind: How Children Think and How Schools Should Teach *(1991), is intriguing. What are the core ideas that guide the book?*

HG: The original title for the book, replaced by the publisher in its wisdom, was *Education for Understanding.* That is the real purpose of the book: to show how we can help students to understand. I define understanding simply as the capacity to apply knowledge, skills, and concepts to new situations, in ways which are appropriate to those situations. I claim that even our best schools typically fail to yield students who understand because we test students only on what they have been directly taught, rather than ask them to stretch their mental muscles in new and appropriate ways.

"In nearly every student, there is a 5-year-old mind struggling to get out and express itself."

The book is based on a developmental argument which will be novel to most readers. I believe that during the first years of life, all normal children develop very powerful theories about how the world works—the physical world and the world of other human beings. Schools (and teachers) do not appreciate the power and robustness of these ideas, so they actually pass them by for the most part. So long as we ask students simply to parrot back what they have been taught, we think they have understood. But once we remove students from the "text-test context," they approach problems very much the way they did before they entered school. Hence the provocative title, *The Unschooled Mind*—and the most provocative sentence in the book: "In nearly every student, there is a 5-year-old mind struggling to get out and express itself." I hope that this brief description is enough to stimulate some readers to read the book and to join the debate that I have launched.

DEF: In a time when teachers have taken on many roles and competing priorities, you suggest one clear, overriding goal in this book—for education to promote "deep understanding" in children. What do you mean by this? How is such a goal different from what goes on in schools today?

HG: If you want students to have deep understanding—for instance, to be able to apply historical knowledge to the elucidation of recent events, to apply Newton's laws to an accident which has happened outside their window, to be able to interpret a text or a painting along a number of different dimensions—you have set for yourself some ambitious goals. As far as I am concerned, they are the *only* goals worth pursuing, but you must realize that they are ambitious. More, they take time to achieve. If a student is to "understand deeply," he or she must immerse himself or herself in subject matter, learning to think of it and to approach it in a variety of ways. We must sacrifice coverage for uncoverage—we must embrace the belief that "less can be more."

> We must sacrifice coverage for uncoverage—we must embrace the belief that "less can be more."

In my own view, this is a worthwhile trade. I believe that in each discipline below the college level, only a limited number of rich and central concepts are deserving of much attention. Take, for example, the concepts of democracy in history, of evolution in biology, and of energy and mass in physics. I would like to see curricula centered on these topics, revisiting them over the years in a variety of ways, so that students feel at ease with them: This would be more valuable than curricula that attempt to teach students 1000 historical names or facts, or 50 physical laws and equations which are memorized for the sake of a test, whose significance is only dimly perceived, and which are forgotten by all except those who become experts in the domain.

DEF: Early on in this book, you introduce three "characters" who represent quite different and perhaps incompatible ways of learning; and in doing so, you suggest gaps between early learning, formal schooling, and the gaining of disciplinary expertise. Would you describe these images and their significance within the book?

HG: These characters are my ways of introducing the pitfalls and possibilities of an education for understanding. The "unschooled" 5-year-old has very powerful ideas and theories which he or she attempts to apply everywhere. The mind of that child is original, rich, and creative but often subscribes to explanations which are simplistic or misconceived.

> The "unschooled" 5-year-old has very powerful ideas and theories which he or she attempts to apply everywhere.

The second character is the dutiful school child. This individual attempts to master the materials in school, but because there is so much to cover and so little time to explore, the student ends up with textbook knowledge. That knowledge is readily evoked in a school context, but it is basically inert; the student cannot put it to use outside the school context. And so when asked about issues that actually require the understanding of disciplinary concepts, the student reverts to the very kinds of explanations and simplifications that characterize the young, unschooled mind.

Finally, and standing as a goal, is the mind of the expert, the individual schooled in a discipline, who is actually able to apply the approaches and ideas of a discipline in a new way. This is the person who can perform the kinds of historical or scientific or artistic analyses that I described above, using concepts appropriately and avoiding an inappropriate application of disciplinary knowledge. Paradoxically, the expert is in some ways closer to the 5-year-old than to the student because both experts and 5-year-olds use their knowledge naturally and generatively. In contrast, the student is able to apply knowledge only very rigidly. The problem with the 5-year-old mind is that many of its ideas are simply wrong. And that is why we need to have disciplines and we need to go to schools that teach for understanding.

DEF: Let's focus a bit more on the education and development of the young child, the "intuitive learner" with her "curious blend of strengths and weaknesses, powers and limitations." What is the nature of this powerful "unschooled mind"? What natural abilities and proclivities should educators know about and respond to if we want to help young children achieve deeper understanding?

HG: In the first years of life, as a result of living in our world, the youngster develops theories of the physical world—for example, that the world is flat, that heavier objects fall more rapidly than lighter objects, that human beings have forces which they magically transfer to inanimate objects, and the like. By the same time, he evolves theories of the social world—that there are good people and bad people, that the good people usually win, that good people always tell the truth, that boys are smart and girls are dumb (or vice versa). These conceptions and stereotypes are often serviceable enough—but they happen to be wrong or at least seriously deficient.

> **Most of us do not replace our earlier misconceptions…they remain entrenched in our minds, ready to spring out when given the slightest opening.**

Educators must acknowledge the existence and power of these ideas. They simply cannot afford to be ignorant of them or to ignore them. Only if one appreciates the points of departure of the student and attempts to deal with them, build upon them, engage them directly, and show their purview and their limitations, is it possible to replace them with more adequate conceptions and ideas.

In the last part of the book, I describe an education which deals with these problems: an education which involves Christopherian encounters, adoption of multiple perspectives, and the rich exploration of relevant semantic domains. *(Editor's Note: Christopherian encounters engage children with unique situations and representations which may challenge them to revise scientific misconceptions.)* If readers want to know more about these ideas, they should read Part III, "Towards an Education for Understanding," and they should attempt to apply those ideas in their own educational realm. I would love to learn of the results.

DEF: *Let me take the role of "devil's advocate" for a moment. Despite its power, isn't the intuitive learner in each of us merely replaced over time, either by more advanced stages of cognition or by the formal learning we experience in schools? If so, why cater to the mind's planned obsolescence?*

HG: This is what Piaget believed; and, as a good Piagetian, I believed in it for many years as well. But I now believe that this idea is wrong. Most of us do not replace our earlier misconceptions; rather, like a Trojan horse, they remain entrenched in our minds, ready to spring out when given the slightest opening. Only those who work in a domain for many years and become experts actually relinquish these earlier "unschooled" conceptions. And perhaps even experts have a tendency to revert to these early, almost primordial views.

Let me use myself as an example. As you know, I am one of the primary critics of standard views of intelligence. I believe that there is no general intelligence, only a variety of different kinds of intelligence. And yet I "catch" myself involuntarily reverting to the view that some people are smart and some people are dumb, very much the same view that my 6-year-old son, Benjamin, puts forth.

DEF: When children enter schooling, you describe the educator's primary role as the presentation of curriculum that at once matches, extends, and challenges children's ways of thinking. What models or examples of exemplary teaching, curricula, and programs come to mind?

HG: I am most impressed by two institutions—one very old, one very new. In the traditional apprenticeship, the individual learns skills and knowledge in a meaningful context from an individual who embodies the desired capacities and knows how to deploy them. From early on, the student appreciates what he can and cannot do, where he is headed, how he compares to others in the novice-to-master continuum. This educational milieu—so different from the arid and artificial context of school—helps students to appreciate how to make use of the skills they are acquiring—the hallmark of an education with understanding.

Incidentally, while the term "apprenticeship" may seem remote from the world of literacies, in fact the model works very well in the sphere of reading, writing, and numeracy. Students need to be in the company of older individuals who exemplify these behaviors, showing that they can be useful, enjoyable, productive. Students whose teachers read and write, and talk about their pleasures, have an entirely different experience from students whose parents tell them to do their homework and then turn on the television for the rest of the evening. If we know one thing from the last quarter-century of research and development, it is that literacy is a property of communities and that students are much more likely to go beyond decoding if they find themselves in the company of individuals who love to read and who turn naturally to writing as a means of working out their feelings, ideas, and beliefs.

> To be able to understand—to be able to use one's knowledge productively, to solve problems, and to raise new questions—is the greatest "high" that I know of.

In a very different way, the educational opportunities provided by the children's museum are also a welcome ancillary to school. In a children's museum, students have the opportunities to approach interesting phenomena and demonstrations in a way that is comfortable to them. They can learn in a hands-on fashion. They can apply some of the principles and concepts of school and see how they work—for example, in the areas of art and science. They can take these demonstrations and intuitive masteries back to school for more formal instruction. Most important, as Frank Oppenheimer once quipped, "Nobody flunks museums."

DEF: What is gained cognitively by children when they experience good schooling?

HG: To be able to understand—to be able to use one's knowledge productively, to solve problems, and to raise new questions—is the greatest "high" that I know of. Anyone who has partaken of this atmosphere will never relinquish it voluntarily; that is what intellectual freedom is about for individuals who have not had it because they live in totalitarian regimes. Anyone who has not had the opportunity to understand and to share that understanding with others is a stunted human being.

DEF: Some critics and observers of education might argue that it's the motivation to think deeply, more than the ability to think deeply, that's lacking in today's students. In your view, would education for understanding encourage children to be more invested and engaged in the work of schools?

HG: This is a chicken-egg problem. Unless students are motivated to explore, to become engaged, to use their literacies, schooling will simply be a burden. But unless students have had a whiff of what it is like to be intellectually engaged, they are unlikely to be motivated to continue and to slog through what is often challenging material. In this regard, I can do no better than to recommend the important work of my colleague Mihaly Csikszentmihalyi in his book *Flow* (Csikszentmihalyi, 1990). Once youngsters receive "flow" from learning and from understanding, school takes on an entirely different and infinitely more positive meaning for them.

> **When things go badly, we just add another test—as if taking the temperature more often would heal the patient.**

DEF: Along with new goals comes the need to measure their accomplishment. In our educational system, this usually translates into more testing. Is this inevitable?

HG: Assessment, yes; testing, no. Any reasonable professional is involved in assessment all the time—his or her work is being assessed all of the time, and much of the assessment is self-assessment. It simply comes with the territory. American students are the most tested and least examined students in the world. When things go badly, we just add another test—as if taking the temperature more often would heal the patient.

We need an entirely new approach to assessment. Assessment needs to be built directly into the curriculum, into the day-to-day running of the school. Feedback must be provided when it is useful, not at the end of the year. And the assessment needs to occur locally, in the classroom, with face-to-face feedback, and not generated from some remote spot, scored by machine, and returned with a score, bereft of suggestions about what to do.

Nearly all of my work is now involved with what is called authentic, or performance-based assessment—assessment which gets directly at understanding. I write about some of our work in *The Unschooled Mind.* Also, I have a monograph, "Assessment in Context," which readers can get if they write me at Project Zero.

DEF: On both the assessment and apprenticeship issues, much time and effort must be invested by adults. What about the feasibility of such methods in the mass-produced, efficiency-oriented conditions of public education? Are we talking about schools as they are currently configured, financially and institutionally?

HG: It would certainly be easier to educate for understanding if classes were smaller, class periods were longer, and there were more resources around. I agree with Theodore Sizer that we should aim for a situation in which no teacher of a discipline is responsible for more than 80 students. (And I would add that no classroom teacher ought to have more than 25 youngsters in a class.)

If we don't make this transition, our schools will become even more irrelevant than they are today.

On the other hand, I have no doubt that much more could be accomplished even at current funding levels. Our school system is top-heavy with administrators who do not improve the quality of education in the classrooms. In some cities, there is one nonclass employee for every classroom employee.

The more that the new assumptions about assessment, individual differences, and education for understanding could be built into teacher education and teacher practice, the fewer additional resources would be needed. They would simply become part of ordinary practice—as they are in many of our better schools today.

To bring this about on a larger scale would require some transition costs—something like going from an agricultural to an industrial model or from a factory economy to a service economy. But I don't think that we have any choice in the matter. If we don't make this transition, our schools will become even more irrelevant than they are today.

DEF: To paraphrase you, we must take responsibility for the uses to which our ideas are put. Do you have any fears about how the ideas in The Unschooled Mind *might be misused in educational practice or in educational policy, or any cautions to offer here about what you do* not *mean in the book?*

HG: I do hope that the book is read and understood! Some will read it as just another jeremiad about our schools. It is not, in fact, an indictment of American schools; rather it is a treatise on what is the matter with schools all over the world, including ones that are considered to be very good. It is a call for a very different kind of educational goal and very different educational means. I am sure that I have gotten many of the details wrong; what I am concerned with is a discussion of the overall vision. Should we be trying to educate for understanding? And if that is not the goal, what should be? I would like at least some of the discussion to center on this pivotal issue.

One more thing. In the book, and in the discussion above, I make critical remarks about teachers and schools. I do not want to be seen as a school-basher or a teacher-basher, however. I am well aware that the conditions in many of our schools make an education for understanding very difficult, perhaps even impossible. Our society makes it very difficult even for well-intentioned and well-educated teachers to accomplish their goals. The responsibility for turning around our education system, and educational systems elsewhere in the world, is *everyone's* responsibility. To pin the blame primarily on educators is to contribute to the problem, rather than to begin to work toward a communal solution.

REFERENCE

Csikszentmihalyi, M. (1990). *Flow: The psychology of optimal experience.* New York: Harper & Row.

WORKS BY HOWARD GARDNER

Frames of mind: The theory of multiple intelligences. New York: Basic Books, 1983.

To open minds. New York: Basic Books, 1989.

The unschooled mind: How children think and how schools should teach. New York: Basic Books, 1991.

Reflections on "The Unschooled Mind": An Interview with Howard Gardner

by Jacqueline Anglin

Q: *In your most recent book,* The Unschooled Mind, *you have been credited for "untangling the mysteries of learning and the current state of cognitive research." From your point of view, what is the current state of cognitive research?*

A: Of course, cognitive research is a gigantic topic. I'm interested in children's cognition and students' cognition. What I particularly focused on in the book was a surprising discovery made over the past 20 years.

In school students are often considered to have a good understanding of the material if they can perform well on tests. And yet when you actually remove those same students from the testing room context, you can see whether they have truly mastered concepts, skills, and facts and so on. If you can place students in a situation where those concepts, facts, and skills are relevant, students typically fail to draw on their knowledge. Even our best students in the best schools don't get it. For instance, they don't know how to use Newton's laws to explain what happens when you're throwing a frisbee; they just haven't been able to make a connection. So even though you give the

From *Mid-Western Educational Researcher*, vol. 6, no. 1, p. 18–20, Winter 1993. © 1993 by the Mid-Western Educational Research Association. Reprinted with permission.

students degrees and call them educated, the research shows that most people do not think about the physical world, the social world, and their own world very differently from the way that they did when they were five years of age.

My book is called *The Unschooled Mind* because I'm trying to describe what the five-year-old mind is like. Most of us walk around thinking like five-year-olds, except in areas where we're experts. Usually individuals are only experts in one or two areas, areas where they've worked for about 10 years. When you're an expert, you really do think differently about the world. Most of us in education are expert readers, in the sense that we read very quickly. We forget what it was like to sound things out or deduce meanings from illustrations. But most of us are not experts in understanding the physical world, the biological world or the psychological world. Yet if we go to school, we may think we are experts until somebody comes around and shows that we can't really use that knowledge.

> Most of us walk around thinking like five-year-olds, except in areas where we're experts.

Q: The research teams that you direct at Project Zero are interdisciplinary and focus on alternative assessments. What research methodologies have served Project Zero particularly well?

A: Project Zero has been in existence for about 25 years. Over the course of that time we have used most of the traditional research methodologies. There have been hundreds of experiments with control groups, statistical analyses, and that kind of thing. We've done many case studies of individuals, classes, teachers, and curricula. We've done a lot of observational and descriptive research where we work with students. For example, we observe what it's like when they're learning a new kind of curriculum. We try to figure out what's going on and create appropriate scoring systems, and the like.

So I would say that we're committed to being eclectic. There is a perennial tension in the educational research world between quantitative and qualitative research. We take the position that the problems should dictate what sorts of methods you use rather than simply embracing one kind of method or another.

Quality research can use a variety of methods. If you're trying to test a hypothesis, usually descriptive or qualitative methods are not very successful. On the other hand, if you are trying to understand what it's like to learn about something new, the experimental method is usually pretty impoverished. At present, a lot of the work that we're doing really involves action research. We go in as researchers with our own conceptions and expectations, but we're not simply observing teachers and students, we're actually involved in formulating the lessons and bringing out the criteria that will be used for assessment. Sometimes, even in co-teaching, we are coaching the teachers.

When you get involved in action research, you realize there are certain limitations on the kind of conclusions you can draw because, in a sense, you are part of the treatment. But if you are trying to conduct educational innovation, it's just impossible to give somebody a book and say "do it"; it doesn't work that way. You have to roll up your sleeves, help and coach, learn from mistakes, discuss, use feedback and so on. So you're a little bit more like an anthropologist, actually living in the bush along with other people; you have to tolerate that degree of ambiguity or messiness in order to be able to do the studies at all.

Q: Could you elaborate on one of the projects in process at Project Zero? Perhaps Spectrum. Could you describe a trail the research has taken?

A: Spectrum is actually an interesting example in that regard. The ideas for Spectrum were developed by David Feldman and myself right after *Frames of Mind* was published in 1983. In *Frames of Mind* I argued that people have different kinds of intelligences, and that different people don't have the same profile of intelligences. So the question arose—even when kids are as young as at three, four, or five years of age, do they already have different profiles of strengths and weaknesses? If you'd asked me 10 years ago what I was going to do, I probably would have said "Develop seven tests, one for each intelligence." I was still a victim of the notion that tests are something that people take at a certain historical moment. You examine them for an hour or so and then you give them a score. But I've had increasing misgivings about that whole psychometric approach.

What ultimately happened with Spectrum was this: we created an environment, the Spectrum classroom, which is sort of like a children's museum. It's very richly endowed with all sorts of materials that kids find interesting: we don't include any materials unless we know that kids like them. We watch the kids over the course of the year, both in free play and in more structured tasks that we devised. At the end of the year, we write a so-called Spectrum report. That report is a prose account of a child's particular intellectual profile at that moment in his or her life, along with some suggestions or recommendations of what ought to be done with that child if you want to build on strength as opposed to areas of weakness.

Now that's how Spectrum ought to be used in a regular classroom where the school has some interest in children but isn't really primarily oriented toward research. Any teacher who has had some exposure to thinking in terms of multiple intelligences categories, some exposure to the kids interacting with the materials that we've devised, ought to be able to get at least a rough-and-ready description. For example, one might conclude that a given child is very strong in music, and strong in certain aspects of spatial but is insensitive to interpersonal issues. I don't think any teacher should want to do more than that with a four- or five-year-old; it would not be an optimal use of time.

> ...a so-called Spectrum report...is a prose account of a child's particular intellectual profile at that moment in his or her life.

On the other hand, we have some quite specific research questions we're interested in. For example, how stable are children's intelligences over time? How does performance in a Spectrum environment compare to performance on an I.Q. test? For such purposes, it's important that we adopt a more structured approach. So we familiarize kids with the materials in a Spectrum classroom and then we introduce some tasks which the kids haven't seen before. That way, we can get a score which reflects the child's developmental level: Is this child a novice or journeyman or beginning to master this particular Spectrum domain? That kind of approach is necessary if you want to answer questions of a scientific nature, but it's not something that is necessary for most teachers. I think it would be burdening to have teachers administer every task with every kid and it wouldn't be necessary. On the other hand, if you want to test hypotheses, then you need to have more control over what is happening. Spectrum is now used in several other sites around the country. Sometimes it's used for research purposes. Sometimes it's used as an effective classroom approach, which nourishes a lot of students' intelligences, and helps them to become engaged in a subject, and provides new challenges as kids master the material that they have been given.

> **Curricula ought to offer some choice, and even when there is a mandated curriculum, lessons don't have to be presented in the same way to each child.**

Q: One term that you continue to use is "teacher as curriculum broker." Could you elaborate on that concept?

A: You could take the position that every person ought to be taught the same thing in the same way, and indeed school would be very easy to do if we could assume that one curriculum taught in one way is the best for everybody. But we have a few thousand years of experience that suggests that that's not true. The conclusion you could draw is that, well, some kids are so stupid that they're not going to learn and so we'll focus on those who do learn and understand the curriculum in the same way. However, you can take the position that curricula ought to offer some choice, and even when there is a mandated curriculum, lessons don't have to be presented in the same way to each child. Everybody should learn geometry or history, I have no objection to that, but it's hardly necessary for everybody to learn geometry and history in exactly the same way.

When I talk about teachers as being curriculum brokers, I mean two things. First, that to the extent you have electives, the teacher's job ought to be to help the students locate the kinds of things that they might find interesting and be good. But even in those areas where the curriculum is mandated, the teacher's job is to be very sensitive to the learning styles, and intellectual strengths of the kids in the class. To the extent possible, the teacher should provide the materials—hardware, software, and peer interactions and the like—which would help that particular child do the best that he or she can.

Often we talk about treating kids equally by giving them all the same treatment. I think that's actually a way of treating kids very unequally. If that case you're consciously biased toward the kids who happen to find that particular treatment congenial. So we might say that kids are really treated equal, when each kid is getting the optimal chance to learn; and if the teacher isn't going to be the broker, I don't know who could be.

Q: You often speak about the reform movements as trying to make schools uniform, using one-dimensional metrics in assessment. Could you discuss current reform efforts?

A: As I said, it is actually easier to run a school if it's uniform. People teach the same stuff, in the same way, people wear uniforms and so on. Kids are pretty resourceful, so some of them do manage to survive in such an environment even though it's not tailor made for them. But, the notion that we can place a child with reference to every other child as if there was a single scholastic hierarchy, is a tremendous arrogance. The I.Q. test, which was developed for one purpose, ended up being the major way in which we think about school in general—the smart kids and the dummies. The smart kids are born smart; we know they should be pushed ahead as far as possible and too bad for the rest. And so you needed to have a more fine-grained analysis of intelligence. There is something like scholastic smarts and maybe it's helpful if you have that kind of smarts to do well in school. But life is a lot more complicated than school, and there's a lot of ways "to do" school.

> **Most of us have a notion that school has to be the way we remember it…. The school can be thousands of different ways.**

Most of us have a notion that school has to be the way we remember it, and that's just rubbish. The school can be thousands of different ways. Since we have thousands of different kinds of kids, probably school should be done a thousand different kinds of ways.

Q: You mention that successful school reform will depend equally on assessment, curriculum, teacher education, and community support. You refer to these as the "four nodes" of school reform.

Can you talk about how your work is addressing any or all of these contexts?

A: In truth, that formula is more of a sign of my own learning than it is an original discovery. Ten years ago when I got into the business of school reform, I figured that if we would just change assessment, everything else would take care of itself. But the truth is that you can have very good assessments but they're worthless if teachers don't have the curricula which demonstrates student learning. Many people say, "Oh, send us the alternative assessment kit or send us the portfolio kit" but they don't change their practices and so you end up with demonstrating no student learning at all. So assessment needs a curriculum that's good enough for it; to put it another way, if you have a good curriculum, you need to have an assessment which shows that the curriculum is working. Alas, a lot of people now embrace interesting curricula but use the same stupid old tests that don't even begin to show the kinds of things that they're supposed to show.

> You can have very good assessments but they're worthless if teachers don't have the curricula which demonstrates student learning.

Even if you have good curriculum and assessment, if teachers don't like them, believe in them, buy them, embody them, or don't want to use them, again they're worth very little. There are many interesting curricula and assessment materials developed in the sixties which are not used today because teachers never bought into them. I think that's partly the teachers' fault, but it's also partly the fault of the makers of these materials who didn't think enough about where the teachers buy into the stuff and want to use it, the community may not want it. The community may want everything done with the Abracadabra Test of Basic Skills or the SAT or with a monotone curriculum, based on a monotone textbook. In such a case, the best motives on the part of the school folks aren't going to amount to anything. I don't spend my time trying to educate the community, but somebody needs to do this. Alas, the tone of political rhetoric about education in this country is an embarrassment.

Q: What questions would you have liked me to ask?

A: As researchers, we're developing lots of new ideas about curriculum, assessment, and about research methodology. People who are involved in teacher education and educational research, I believe, have an obligation to apply these ideas to ourselves. We shouldn't just think of *other* folks as the problem or as the enemy. We have to look at our own teaching. Are we teaching effectively? Can we demonstrate what our students are learning? Are we making use of research findings? Are our curricula as good as they can be? Are they as up-to-date as they can be? Are our assessments worthy of what we're telling other people to do? I'm sure I'm not alone in saying that many of us have not been physicians healing ourselves. We instead assume everything is fine with us, that problems lie elsewhere. And so, I would encourage people interested seriously in reform to look at their own practice, at the findings of their own research, and at their own training of future teachers. Those of us who train teachers are in a very powerful position because we model what we think good teaching is. If we do nothing but lecture and give short answer tests, we can hardly expect our students to go out and to become innovative teachers. That's a big job, it reminds us that it's not easy to change the rest of American education either.

REFERENCE

Gardner, H. (1991). *The Unschooled Mind.* New York: Basic Books.

Section 2

From Theory . . .

Three pieces, all including Gardner as author or coauthor, give voice to the theory of multiple intelligences.

In "The Development and Education of the Intelligences," Joseph Walters and Howard Gardner give a synopsis of Gardner's book *Frames of Mind: The Theory of Multiple Intelligences,* sketch the seven intelligences, and trace a developmental trajectory of the intelligences. The authors discuss the implications of the trajectory for education, targeting explicit instruction and assessments.

A 1987 article, "The Theory of Multiple Intelligences," transcribed from Gardner's oral address to the 37th Annual Conference of the Orton Dyslexia Society, is the cornerstone of this section. In this poignant piece, Gardner converses with his audience as though they were sitting with him in his living room. He discusses the theories of Alfred Binet, Charles Spearman, and Piaget; he tells of an early, unpublished book he sketched out called *Kinds of Minds;* and he shares stories of a sailor in the Puluwat Islands, a student of the Koran, and a Parisian composer as he defines intelligence. In this compelling article, Gardner delineates the seven intelligences, compares his work to others, and concludes with real-life applications of his theory in Project Spectrum and Arts Propel and his novel idea of student curriculum brokers in our "Westist, Testist, Bestist" society.

This section ends with a 1993 article on identifying and assessing children's talents. In "Varieties of Excellence: Identifying and Assessing Children's Talents," Howard Gardner and Mindy Kornhaber define "excellence" and develop an essential element of Gardner's theory—intelligence must be valued in or relevant to an individual's culture. The authors offer recommendations for fostering excellence and cite specific school examples. Discussions of the "Performance of Understanding," the myth of "the Natural," and the "Horatio Alger" myth solidify the authors' arguments for the theory of multiple intelligences.

The Development and Education of Intelligences

by Joseph Walters and Howard Gardner

PART I. THE THEORY OF MULTIPLE INTELLIGENCES

A. Contrasting Points of View

Two eleven-year-old children are taking a test of "intelligence." They sit at their desks laboring over the meanings of different words, the interpretation of graphs, and the solutions to arithmetic problems. They record their answers by filling in small circles on a single piece of paper. Later these completed answer sheets are scored objectively: the number of right answers is converted into a standardized score which compares the individual child with a population of children of similar age.

> The test taken by the eleven-year-olds serves as a reliable predictor of later performance in school.

The teachers of these children review the different scores. They notice that one of the children has performed at a superior level; on all sections of the test, she answered more questions correctly than did her peers; in fact, her score is similar to that of children three to four years older. The other child's performance is "average"—his scores reflect those of other children his age.

A subtle change in expectations surrounds the review of these test scores. Teachers begin to expect the first child to do quite well during her formal schooling, whereas the second should have only moderate success. Indeed these predictions come true. In other words, the test taken by the eleven-year-olds serves as a reliable predictor of later performance in school.

A position paper from Harvard University, September 1984. © 1984 by Harvard Project Zero. Reprinted with permission.

How is it that tests such as these predict the future success of students in school? A familiar explanation speaks freely of "intelligence": the child with the greater "intelligence" has the ability to solve problems, to find the answers to specific questions, and to learn new material quickly and efficiently. These skills in turn play a central role in school success. In this view, "intelligence" is a singular faculty that is brought to bear in any problem-solving situation. Since schooling deals largely with solving problems of various sorts, predicting this capacity in young children predicts their future success in school.

"Intelligence," from this point of view, is a general ability that is found in varying degrees in all individuals. It is the key to success in solving problems. This ability can be measured reliably with standardized pencil-and-paper tests which in turn predict future success in school.

> IQ tests predict school performance with considerable accuracy but they are only an indifferent predictor of performance in a profession after formal schooling.

What happens after school is completed? Consider the two individuals in the example. Looking further down the road we find that the "average" student has become a highly successful mechanical engineer who has risen to a position of prominence in both the professional community of engineers as well as in civic groups in his community. His success is no fluke—he is considered by all to be a talented individual. The "superior" student, on the other hand, has had little success in her chosen career as a writer; after repeated rejections by publishers, she has taken up a middle management position in a bank. While certainly not a "failure," she is considered by her peers to be quite "ordinary" in her adult accomplishments. So what happened?

This fabricated example is based on the facts of intelligence testing. IQ tests predict school performance with considerable accuracy but they are only an indifferent predictor of performance in a profession after formal schooling (Jencks, 1972). Furthermore, even as the IQ tests measure only logical or logical-linguistic capacities, in this society we are nearly "brainwashed" to restrict the notion of intelligence to the capacities used in solving logical and linguistic problems.

To introduce an alternative point of view, undertake the following *Gedanken* experiment. Suspend the usual judgment of what constitutes intelligence and let your thoughts run freely over the capabilities of humans—perhaps those that would be picked out by the proverbial Martian visitor. In this exercise, you are drawn to the brilliant chess player, the world class violinist, and the champion athlete; such outstanding performers deserve special consideration. Under this experiment, a quite different view of *intelligence* emerges. Are the chess player, violinist, and athlete "intelligent" in these pursuits? If they are, then why do our tests of "intelligence" fail to identify them? If they are not "intelligent," what allows them to achieve such astounding feats? In general, why does the contemporary construct "intelligence" fail to explain large areas of human endeavor?

> ...human cognitive competence is better described in terms of a set of abilities, talents, or mental skills, which we call "Intelligences."

In this paper we approach these problems through the theory of Multiple Intelligences (MI). As the name indicates, we believe that human cognitive competence is better described in terms of a set of abilities, talents, or mental skills, which we call "Intelligences." All normal individuals possess each of these skills to some extent; individuals differ in the degree of skill and in the nature of their combination. We believe this theory of intelligence may be more humane and more veridical than alternative views of intelligence and that it more adequately reflects the data of human "intelligent" behavior. Such a theory has important educational implications including ones for curriculum development. Laying out the theory and analyzing its potential impact on education constitute our task for the remainder of the paper.

B. What Constitutes an Intelligence?

The question of the optimal definition of "intelligence" looms large in our inquiry. Indeed, it is at the level of this definition that the theory of Multiple Intelligences diverges from more traditional points of view. In a more traditional view, *intelli-*

gence is defined operationally as the ability to answer items on tests of intelligence. The inference from the test scores to some underlying ability is supported by statistical techniques that compare responses of subjects at different ages; the apparent correlation of these test scores across ages and across different tests corroborates the notion that the general faculty of intelligence, "g," does not change much with age nor with training or experience. It is an in-born attribute or faculty of the individual.

Multiple Intelligences theory, on the other hand, pluralizes the traditional concept. An Intelligence entails the ability to solve problems or fashion products that are of consequence in a particular cultural setting. The problem-solving skill allows one to approach a situation in which a goal is to be obtained and to locate the appropriate route to that goal. The creation of a *cultural* product is crucial to such functions as capturing and transmitting knowledge or expressing one's views or feelings. The problems to be solved range from creating an end to a story to anticipating a mating move in chess to repairing a quilt. Products range from scientific theories to musical compositions to successful political campaigns.

> **An Intelligence entails the ability to solve problems or fashion products that are of consequence in a particular cultural setting.**

MI theory is framed in light of the biological origins of each problem-solving skill. Only those skills that are universal to the human species are treated. Even so, the biological proclivity to participate in a particular form of problem solving must also be coupled with the cultural nurturing of that domain. For example, language, a universal skill, may manifest itself particularly as writing in one culture, as oratory in another culture, and as the secret language of anagrams in a third.

Given the desire of selecting Intelligences which are rooted in biology, and which are valued in one or more cultural settings, how does one actually identify an "Intelligence?" In coming up with our list, we consulted evidence from several different sources: knowledge about normal development and development in gifted individuals; information about the breakdown of cognitive skills under conditions of brain damage; studies of exceptional populations, including prodigies, *idiots savants*, and autistic children; data about the evolution of cognition over the millennia; cross cultural accounts of cognition; psychometric studies, including examinations of correlations among tests; and psychological training studies, particularly measures of transfer and generalization across tasks. Only those candidate Intelligences which satisfied all or a majority of the criteria were selected as *bona fide* Intelligences. A more complete discussion of each of these criteria for "an Intelligence" and the seven Intelligences which have been proposed so far, is found in Gardner's recent book, *Frames of Mind* (1983). This book also considers how the theory might be disproven and compares it to competing theories of intelligence.

In addition to satisfying the aforementioned criteria, each Intelligence must have an identifiable core operation or set of operations. As a neurally-based computational system, each Intelligence is activated or "triggered" by certain kinds of internally or externally presented information. For example, one core of musical Intelligence is the sensitivity to pitch relations, whereas one core of linguistic Intelligence is the sensitivity to phonological features.

> **Each Intelligence must have an identifiable core operation or set of operations.**

An Intelligence must also be susceptible to encoding in a symbol system—a culturally contrived system of meaning, which captures and conveys important forms of information. Language, picturing, and mathematics are but three nearly world-wide symbol systems that are necessary for human survival and productivity. The relationship of a candidate Intelligence to a human symbol system is no accident. In fact, the existence of a core computational capacity anticipates the existence of a symbol system which exploits that capacity. While it may be possible for an Intelligence to proceed without an accompanying symbol system, a primary characteristic of human intelligence may well be its gravitation toward such an embodiment.

C. The Seven Intelligences

Having sketched the characteristics and criteria of an Intelligence, we turn now to a brief consideration of each of the seven

Intelligences. We begin each sketch with a thumbnail biography of a person who demonstrates an unusual facility with that Intelligence. These biographies illustrate some of the abilities which are central to the fluent operation of a given Intelligence. Although each biography illustrates a particular Intelligence, we do not wish to imply that in adulthood Intelligences operate in isolation. Indeed, except for abnormal individuals, Intelligences always work in concert, and any sophisticated adult role will involve a melding of several of them. Following each biography we survey the various sources of data that support each candidate as an "Intelligence."

> **Indeed, except for abnormal individuals, Intelligences always work in concert, and any sophisticated adult role will involve a melding of several of them.**

Musical Intelligence

> When he was three years old, Yehudi Menuhin was smuggled into the San Francisco Orchestra concerts by his parents. The sound of Louis Persinger's violin so entranced the youngster that he insisted on a violin for his birthday and Louis Persinger as his teacher. He got both. By the time he was ten years old, Menuhin was an international performer. (Menuhin, 1977)

Violinist Yehudi Menuhin's Musical Intelligence manifested itself even before he had touched a violin or received any musical training. His powerful reaction to that particular sound and his rapid progress on the instrument suggest that he was biologically prepared in some way for that endeavor. In this way evidence from child prodigies supports our claim that there is a biological link to a particular Intelligence. Other special populations, such as autistic children who can play a musical instrument beautifully but who cannot speak, underscore the independence of Musical Intelligence.

A brief consideration of the evidence suggests that musical skill passes the other tests for an Intelligence. For example, certain parts of the brain play important roles in perception and production of music. These areas are characteristically located in the right hemisphere, although musical skill is not as clearly "localized," or located in a specifiable area, as language. Although the particular susceptibility of musical ability to brain damage depends on the degree of training and other individual differences, there is clear evidence for "amusia" or loss of musical ability.

Music apparently played an important unifying role in Stone Age societies. Birdsong provides a link to other species. Evidence from various cultures supports the notion that music is a universal faculty. Studies of infant development suggest that there is a "raw" computational ability in early childhood. Finally, musical notation provides an accessible and lucid symbol system.

In short, evidence to support the interpretation of musical ability as an "Intelligence" comes from many different sources. Even though musical skill is not typically considered an intellectual skill like mathematics, it qualifies under our criteria. By definition it deserves consideration; and in view of the data, its inclusion is empirically justified.

Bodily-Kinesthetic Intelligence

> Fifteen-year-old Babe Ruth played third base. During one game his team's pitcher was doing very poorly and Babe loudly criticized him from third base. Brother Mathias, the coach, called out, "Ruth, if you know so much about it, YOU pitch!" Babe was surprised and embarrassed because he had never pitched before, but Brother Mathias insisted. Ruth said later that at the very moment he took the pitcher's mound, he KNEW he was supposed to be a pitcher and that it was "natural" for him to strike people out. Indeed, he went on to become a great major league pitcher (and, of course, legendary status as a hitter). (Connor, 1982)

Like Menuhin, Babe Ruth was a child prodigy who recognized his "instrument" immediately upon his first exposure to it. This recognition occurred in advance of formal training.

Control of bodily movements is of course localized in the motor cortex, with each hemisphere dominant or controlling bodily movements on the contra-lateral side. In right handers, the dominance for such movement is ordinarily found in the left hemisphere. The ability to perform movements when directed to do so can be impaired even in individuals who can perform the same movements reflexively or on a non-voluntary basis. The existence of specific *apraxia* constitutes one line of evidence for a Bodily-Kinesthetic Intelligence.

The evolution of specialized body movements is of obvious advantage to the species, and in humans this adaptation is extended through the use of tools. Body movement undergoes a clearly defined developmental schedule in children. And there is little question of its universality across cultures. Thus it appears that bodily-kinesthetic "knowledge" satisfies many of the criteria for an Intelligence.

The ability to use one's body to express an emotion, to play a game or to create a new product are evidence of the cognitive features of body usage.

Perhaps more difficult, however, is the consideration of bodily-kinesthetic knowledge as "problem-solving." Certainly carrying out a mime sequence or hitting a tennis ball is not solving a mathematical equation. And yet, the ability to use one's body to express an emotion (as in a dance), to play a game (as in a sport) or to create a new product (as in devising an invention) are evidence of the cognitive features of body usage. The specific computations required to solve a particular bodily-kinesthetic *problem*, hitting a tennis ball, are summarized by Tim Gallwey:

> At the moment the ball leaves the server's racket, the brain calculates approximately where it will land and where the racket will intercept it. This calculation includes the initial velocity of the ball, combined with an input for the progressive decrease in velocity and the effect of wind and spin and gravity. Each of these factors is recalculated after the bounce of the ball. Simultaneously, muscle orders are given: not just once, but constantly with refined and updated information. The muscles must cooperate. A movement of the feet occurs, the racket is taken back, the face of the racket kept at a constant angle. Contact is made at a precise point that depends on whether the order was given to hit down the line or cross-court, an order not given until after a split-second analysis of the movement and balance of the opponent.

To return an average serve, you have about one second to do this. To hit the ball at all is remarkable and yet not uncommon. The truth is that everyone who inhabits a human body possesses a remarkable creation. (Gallwey, 1976)

Logical-Mathematical Intelligence

In 1983 Barbara McClintock won the *Nobel Prize in Medicine or Physiology* for her work in microbiology. Her intellectual powers of deduction and observation illustrate one form of logical-mathematical Intelligence that is often labeled "scientific thinking." One incident is particularly illuminating. While a researcher at Cornell in the 1920's, McClintock was faced one day with a problem: while *theory* predicted 50% pollen sterility in corn, her research assistant (in the "field") was finding plants that were only 25-30% sterile. Disturbed by this discrepancy, McClintock left the cornfield and returned to her office where she sat for half an hour, thinking:

> Suddenly I jumped up and ran back to the (corn) field. At the top of the field (the others were still at the bottom) I shouted "Eureka, I have it! I know what the 30% sterility is!" . . .They asked me to prove it. I sat down with a paper bag and a pencil and I started from scratch, which I had not done at all in my laboratory. It had all been done so fast; the answer came and I ran. Now I worked it out step by step—it was an intricate series of steps—and I came out with (the same result). (They) looked at the material and it was exactly as I'd said it was; it worked out exactly as I had diagrammed it. Now, why did I know, without have done it on paper? Why was I so sure? (Keller, 1982, p. 104)

This anecdote illustrates two essential facts of the Logical-Mathematical Intelligence. First, in the gifted individual, the process of problem solving is often remarkably rapid—the successful scientist copes with many variables at once and creates numerous hypotheses that are each evaluated and then accepted or rejected in turn.

The anecdote also underscores the *non-verbal* nature of the Intelligence. A solution to a problem can be constructed *before* it is articulated. In fact, the solution process may be totally invisible, even to the problem solver. This need not imply, however, that discoveries of this sort—the familiar "aha" phenomenon—are mysterious, intuitive, or unpredictable. The fact that it happens more frequently to some people (perhaps Nobel Prize winners) suggests the opposite. We interpret this as the work of the Logical-Mathematical Intelligence.

Along with the companion skill of language, logical-mathematical reasoning provides the basis for IQ tests. This form of Intelligence has been heavily investigated by traditional psychologists and it is the archetype of "raw intelligence" or the problem-solving faculty that purportedly cuts across domains. It is perhaps ironic, then, that the actual mechanism by which one arrives at a solution to a logical-mathematical problem is not as yet properly understood.

> Along with the companion skill of language, logical-mathematical reasoning provides the basis for IQ tests.

This Intelligence is supported by our empirical criteria as well. Certain areas of the brain are more prominent in mathematical calculation than others. There are *idiots savants* that perform great feats of calculation even though they remain tragically deficient in most other areas. Child prodigies in mathematics abound. The development of this Intelligence in children has been carefully documented by Piaget and other psychologists.

Linguistic Intelligence

> At the age of ten, T.S. Eliot created a magazine called "Fireside" to which he was the sole contributor. In a three day period during his winter vacation, he created eight complete issues. Each one included poems, adventure stories, a gossip column, and humor. Some of this material survives and it displays the talent of the poet. (see Soldo, 1982)

As with the Logical Intelligence, calling linguistic skill an "Intelligence" is consistent with the stance of traditional psychology. Linguistic Intelligence also passes our empirical tests. For instance, a specific area of the brain, called "Broca's Area," is responsible for the production of grammatical sentences. A person with damage to this area can understand words and sentences quite well but has difficulty putting them together in anything other than the simplest of sentences. At the same time other thought processes may be entirely unaffected.

The gift of language is universal and its development in children is strikingly constant across cultures. Even in deaf populations where a manual sign language is not explicitly taught, children will often "invent" their own manual language and use it surreptitiously! We thus see how an Intelligence may operate independently of a specific input modality or output channel.

Spatial Intelligence

> Navigation around the Caroline Islands in the South Seas is accomplished without instruments. The position of the stars, as viewed from various islands, the weather patterns, and water color are the only sign posts. Each journey is broken into a series of segments; and the navigator learns the position of the stars within each of these segments. During the actual trip the navigator must envision mentally a reference island as it passes under a particular star and from that he computes the number of segments completed, the proportion of the trip remaining, and any corrections in heading that are required. The navigator cannot *see* the islands as he sails along; instead he maps their locations in his mental "picture" of the journey. (Gardner, 1983)

Spatial problem solving is required for navigation and in the use of the notational system of maps. Other kinds of spatial problem solving are brought to bear in visualizing an object seen from a different angle and in playing chess. The visual arts also employ this Intelligence in the use of space.

Evidence from brain research is clear and persuasive. Just as the left hemisphere has, over the course of evolution, been selected as the site of linguistic processing, the right hemisphere proves to be the site most crucial for spatial processing. Damage to the right posterior regions causes impairment of the ability to find one's way around a site, to recognize faces or scenes, or to notice fine details.

Patients with damage specific to regions of the right hemisphere will attempt to compensate for their spatial deficits with linguistic strategies. They will try to reason aloud, to challenge the task, or even make up answers. But such non-spatial strategies are rarely successful.

Blind populations provide an illustration of the distinction between the Spatial Intelligence and visual perception. A blind person can recognize shapes by an indirect method: running a hand along the object translates into length of time of movement, which in turn is translated into the size of the object. For the blind person, the perceptual system of the tactile modality parallels the visual modality in the seeing person. The analogy between the spatial reasoning of the blind and the linguistic reasoning of the deaf is notable.

> For the blind person, the perceptual system of the tactile modality parallels the visual modality in the seeing person.

There are few child prodigies among visual artists, but there are *idiots savants* such as Nadia (Selfe, 1977). Despite a condition of severe autism, this preschool child made drawings of the most remarkable representational accuracy and finesse.

Interpersonal Intelligence

With little formal training in special education and nearly blind herself, Anne Sullivan began the intimidating task of instructing a blind and deaf seven-year-old. Sullivan's efforts at communication were complicated by the child's emotional struggle with the world around her. At their first meal together, this scene occurred:

> Annie did not allow Helen to put her hand into Annie's plate and take what she wanted, as she had been accustomed to do with her family. It became a test of wills—hand thrust into plate, hand firmly put aside. The family, much upset, left the dining room. Annie locked the door and proceeded to eat her breakfast while Helen lay on the floor kicking and screaming, pushing and pulling at Annie's chair. (After half an hour) Helen went around the table looking for her family. She discovered no one else was there and that bewildered her. Finally, she sat down and began to eat her breakfast, but with her hands. Annie gave her a spoon. Down on the floor it clattered, and the contest of wills began anew. (Lash, 1980, p. 52)

Anne Sullivan sensitively responded to the child's behaviors. She wrote home: "The greatest problem I shall have to solve is how to discipline and control her without breaking her spirit. I shall go rather slowly at first and try to win her love."

In fact, the first "miracle" occurred two weeks later, well before the famous incident at the pumphouse. Annie had taken Helen to a small cottage near the family's house where they could live alone. After seven days together, Helen's personality suddenly underwent a profound change—the therapy had worked:

> My heart is singing with joy this morning. A miracle has happened! The wild little creature of two weeks ago has been transformed into a gentle child. (p. 54)

It was just two weeks after this that the first breakthrough in Helen's grasp of language occurred; and from that point on, she progressed with incredible speed. The key to the miracle of language was Anne Sullivan's insight into the *person* of Helen Keller.

Interpersonal Intelligence builds upon a core capacity to notice distinctions among others, in particular contrasts in their moods, temperaments, motivations and intentions. In more advanced forms, this Intelligence permits a skilled adult to read the intentions and desires of others, even when these have been hidden. This skill appears in a highly sophisticated form in religious or political leaders, teachers, therapists, and parents. The Helen Keller–Anne Sullivan story suggests that this Interpersonal Intelligence does not depend on language.

All indices in brain research suggest that the frontal lobes play a prominent role in interpersonal knowledge. Damage in this area can cause profound personality changes while leaving other forms of problem solving unharmed—a person is often "not the same person" after such an injury.

Alzheimer's disease, a form of presenile dementia, appears to attack posterior brain zones with a special ferocity, leaving spatial, logical and linguistic computations severely impaired.

> **The key to the miracle of language was Anne Sullivan's insight into the *person* of Helen Keller.**

Yet, these patients will often remain well groomed, socially appropriate, and continually apologetic for their errors. In contrast, Pick's disease, another variety of presenile dementia that is more frontally oriented, creates a rapid loss of social appropriateness.

Biological evidence for Interpersonal Intelligence encompasses two additional factors often cited as unique to humans. One factor is the prolonged childhood of primates including the close attachment to the mother. In those cases where the mother is removed from early development, normal interpersonal development is in serious jeopardy. The second factor is the relative importance in humans of social interaction. Skills such as hunting, tracking, and killing in prehistoric societies required participation and cooperation of large numbers of people. The need for group cohesion, leadership, organization, and solidarity follow naturally from this.

Intrapersonal Intelligence

In an essay called "A Sketch of the Past," written almost as a diary entry, Virginia Woolf discusses the "cotton wool of existence"—the various mundane events of life. She contrasts this "cotton wool" with three specific and poignant memories from her childhood: a fight with her brother, seeing a particular flower in the garden, and hearing of the suicide of a past visitor:

> These are three instances of exceptional moments. I often tell them over, or rather they come to the surface unexpectedly. But now for the first time I have written them down, and I realize something that I have never realized before. Two of these moments ended in a state of despair. The other ended, on the contrary, in a state of satisfaction.
>
> The sense of horror (in hearing of the suicide) held me powerless. But in the case of the flower, I found a reason; and was thus able to deal with the sensation. I was not powerless.
>
> Though I still have the peculiarity that I receive these sudden shocks, they are now always welcome; after the first surprise, I always feel instantly that they are particularly valuable. And so I go on to suppose that the shock-receiving capacity is what makes me a writer. I hazard the explanation that a shock is at once in my case followed by the desire to explain it. I feel that I have had a blow; but it is not, as I thought as a child, simply a blow from

an enemy hidden behind the cotton wool of daily life; it is or will become a revelation of some order; it is a token of some real thing behind appearances; and I make it real by putting it into words. (Woolf, 1976, pp. 69–70)

This quotation vividly illustrates the Intrapersonal Intelligence—knowledge of the internal aspects of a person: access to one's own feeling life, one's range of emotions, the capacity to affect discriminations among these emotions and eventually to label them and to draw upon them as a means of understanding and guiding one's own behavior. Since this Intelligence is the most private, it requires evidence from language, music, or some other more expressive form of Intelligence if the observer is to detect it at work. In the above quotation, for example, Linguistic Intelligence is drawn upon to convey intrapersonal knowledge; it embodies the interaction of Intelligences, a common phenomenon to which we will return later.

> Linguistic Intelligence is drawn upon to convey intrapersonal knowledge.

We see the familiar criteria at work in the Intrapersonal Intelligence. As with the Interpersonal Intelligence, the frontal lobes play a central role in personality change. Injury to the lower area of the frontal lobes is likely to produce irritability or euphoria; while injury to the higher regions is more likely to produce indifference, listlessness, slowness, and apathy—a kind of depressive personality. In such "frontal-lobe" individuals, the other cognitive functions often remain preserved. In contrast, among aphasics who have recovered sufficiently to describe their experiences, we find consistent testimony: while there may have been a diminution of general alertness and considerable depression about the condition, the individual in no way felt himself to be a different person. He recognized his own needs, wants and desires and tried as best he could to achieve them.

The autistic child is a prototypical example of an individual with impaired Intrapersonal Intelligence; indeed, the child may not even be able to refer to himself. At the same time, such children often exhibit remarkable abilities in the musical, computational, spatial, or mechanical realms.

Evolutionary evidence for an Intrapersonal faculty is more difficult to come by, but we might speculate that the capacity to transcend the satisfaction of instinctual drives is relevant. This becomes increasingly important in a species not perennially involved in the struggle for survival.

In sum, then, both Interpersonal and Intrapersonal faculties pass the tests of an Intelligence. They both feature problem-solving endeavors with significance for the individual and the species. In the individual's sense of self, one encounters a melding of inter- and intra-personal components. Indeed, the sense of self emerges as one of the most marvelous of human inventions—a symbol which represents all kinds of information about a person, and which is at the same time an invention that every individual constructs for himself.

D. Summary: The Unique Contributions of the Theory

As human beings, we all have a repertoire of skills for solving different kinds of problems. Our investigation has begun, therefore, with a consideration of these problems, the contexts they are found in, and the culturally significant products that are the outcome. We have not approached "intelligence" as a reified human faculty that is brought to bear in literally any problem setting; rather, we have begun with the problems that humans *solve* and worked back to the "Intelligences" that must be responsible.

> ...these multiple human faculties, the Intelligences, are to a significant extent *independent.*

Evidence from brain research, human development, evolution, and cross cultural comparisons were all brought to bear in our search for the relevant human Intelligences: a candidate was included only if reasonable evidence to support its membership was found across these diverse fields. Again, this tack differs from the traditional one: since no candidate faculty is *necessarily* an Intelligence, we could choose on a motivated basis. In the traditional approach to "intelligence," there is no opportunity for this type of empirical decision.

We have also determined that these multiple human faculties, the Intelligences, are to a significant extent *independent.* For example, research with brain damaged adults repeatedly demonstrates that particular faculties can be lost while others are spared. This independence of Intelligences implies that a particularly high level of ability in one Intelligence, say mathematics, does not require a similarly high level in another Intelligence, like language or music. This independence of Intelligences contrasts sharply with traditional measures of IQ which find high correlations among test scores. We speculate that the usual correlations among sub-tests of IQ tests come about because all of these tasks in fact measure the ability to respond rapidly to items of a logical-mathematical or linguistic sort; we believe that these correlations would be substantially reduced if one were to survey in a contextually appropriate way the full range of human problem-solving skills.

> Even given a relatively small number of such Intelligences, the diversity of human ability is created through the differences in these profiles.

Until now, we have supported the fiction that adult roles depend largely on the flowering of a single Intelligence. In fact, however, nearly every cultural role of any degree of sophistication requires a combination of Intelligences. Thus, even an apparently straightforward role like playing the violin transcends a reliance on simple Musical Intelligence. To become a successful violinist requires bodily-kinesthetic dexterity and the interpersonal skills of relating to an audience and, in a different way, choosing a manager; quite possibly it involves an Intrapersonal Intelligence as well. Dance requires skills in Bodily-Kinesthetic, Musical, Interpersonal, and Spatial Intelligences in varying degrees. Politics requires an interpersonal skill, a linguistic facility and perhaps some logical aptitude. Inasmuch as nearly every cultural role requires several Intelligences, it becomes important to consider individuals as a collection of aptitudes rather than as having a singular problem-solving faculty that can be measured directly through pencil-and-paper tests. Even given a relatively small number of such Intelligences, the diversity of human ability is created through the differences in these profiles. In fact, it may well be that the "total is greater than the sum of the parts." An individual may not be particularly gifted in any Intelligence; and yet, because of his particular combination or blend of skills, he may be able to fill some niche uniquely well.

Thus it is of paramount importance to assess the particular combination of skills which may earmark an individual for a certain vocational or avocational niche.

PART II. IMPLICATIONS FOR EDUCATION

The theory of Multiple Intelligences was developed as an account of human cognition that can be subjected to empirical tests. The evidence for its educational utility has yet to be assembled. Nonetheless, the theory seems to harbor a number of educational implications which are worth consideration. In the following discussion we will begin by outlining what appears to us to be the natural developmental trajectory of an Intelligence. Turning then to aspects of education, we will comment on the role of nurturing and explicit instruction in this development. From this analysis we find that assessment of Intelligences can play a crucial role in curriculum development.

> Exceptional populations aside...*all* humans possess certain core abilites in each of the Intelligences.

A. The Natural Growth of an Intelligence:
A Developmental Trajectory

We begin by noting that all Intelligences are part of the human genetic heritage; at some basic level each Intelligence will be manifested universally, independent of education and cultural support. Exceptional populations aside for the moment, *all* humans possess certain core abilities in each of the Intelligences.

The natural trajectory of development in each Intelligence begins with *raw patterning ability*. For example, the ability to make tonal differentiations in Musical Intelligence or to appreciate three-dimensional arrangements in Spatial Intelligence represent two forms of raw computational ability. These appear universally; they may also appear at a heightened level in that part of the population that is "at promise" in that domain. The "raw" Intelligence predominates during the first year.

Intelligences are glimpsed through different lenses at subsequent points in development. In the subsequent stage, the Intelligence is encountered through a *symbol system*: language is encountered through sentences and stories, music through songs, Spatial Intelligence through drawings, bodily-kinesthetic through gesture or dance, and so on. At this point children demonstrate their abilities in the various Intelligences through their grasp of various symbol systems. Yehudi Menuhin's response to the sound of the violin illustrates the Musical Intelligence of a gifted individual coming in contact with a particular aspect of the symbol system.

As development progresses, each Intelligence together with its accompanying symbol system is represented in a *notational system*. Mathematics, mapping, reading, music notation, and so on, are second-order symbol systems in which the marks on paper come to stand for symbols. In our culture, these notational systems are typically mastered in a formal educational setting.

> **Although all humans partake of each Intelligence to some degree, certain individuals are said to be "at promise."**

Finally, during adolescence and adulthood, the Intelligences are expressed through the range of *vocational or avocational pursuits*. For example, the Logical-Mathematical Intelligence, that began as sheer pattern ability in infancy and developed through symbolic mastery of early childhood and the notations of the school years, achieves mature expression in such roles as mathematician, accountant, scientist, cashier. Similarly, the Spatial Intelligence passes from the mental maps of the infant, to the symbolic operations required in drawings and the notational systems of maps, to the adult roles of navigator, chess player or topologist.

Although all humans partake of each Intelligence to some degree, certain individuals are said to be "at promise." They are highly endowed with the core abilities and skills of that Intelligence. This fact becomes important for the culture as a whole, since, in general, these exceptionally gifted individuals will make notable advances in the cultural manifestations of that Intelligence. It is not important that *all* members of the Puluwat tribe demonstrate precocious spatial abilities needed for navigation by the stars, nor is it necessary for all Westerners to master mathematics to the degree necessary to make a significant contribution to theoretical physics. So long as the individuals "at promise" in particular domains are located efficiently, the overall knowledge of the group will be advanced in all domains.

While some individuals are "at promise" in an Intelligence, others are "at risk." In the absence of special aids, those "at risk" in an Intelligence will be most likely to fail tasks involving that Intelligence. Conversely, those "at promise" will be most likely to succeed. It may be that intensive intervention at an early age, such as Suzuki training, can bring a larger number of children to an "at promise" level.

> In the preschool and early elementary years, instruction should emphasize opportunity.

The special developmental trajectory of an individual "at promise" varies with Intelligence. Thus, mathematics and music are characterized by the early appearance of gifted children who perform relatively early at or near an adult level. In contrast, the linguistic and personal Intelligences appear to arise much more gradually; prodigies are rare. Moreover, mature performance in one area does not imply mature performance in another area, just as gifted achievement in one does not imply gifted achievement in another.

B. Implications of the Developmental Trajectory for Education
Because the Intelligences are manifested in different ways at different developmental levels, both assessment and nurturing need to occur in apposite ways. What nurtures in infancy would be inappropriate at later stages, and vice versa. In the preschool and early elementary years, instruction should emphasize opportunity. It is during these years that children can discover something of their own peculiar interests and abilities. In the cases of very talented children, such discoveries often happen by themselves through spontaneous "crystallizing experiences" (Walters and Gardner, [1986]). For others, specifically designed encounters with materials, equipment, or other people, can help to instigate such discovery of one's own metier.

During the school-age years, some mastery of notational systems is essential in our society. The self-discovery environment of early schooling cannot provide the structure needed for the mastery of specific notational systems like the sonata form or algebra. In fact, during this period some tutelage is needed by virtually all children. One problem is to find the right form, since group tutelage can be helpful in some instances and harmful in others. Another problem is to orchestrate the connection between practical knowledge and the knowledge embodied in symbolic systems and notational systems.

Finally, in adolescence, most students must be assisted in their choice of careers. This task is made more complex by the manner in which Intelligences interact in many cultural roles. For instance, being a doctor certainly requires Logical-Mathematical Intelligence; but general practice demands a strong interpersonal skill while surgery requires a bodily-kinesthetic dexterity. Internships, apprenticeships, and involvement with the actual materials of the cultural role become critical at this point in development.

Students benefit from explicit instruction only if the information or training fits into their specific place on the developmental progression.

Several implications for explicit instruction can be drawn from this analysis. First, the role of instruction in relation to the manifestation of an Intelligence changes across the developmental trajectory. The enriched environment appropriate for the younger years is less relevant for adolescents. Conversely, explicit instruction in the notational system, appropriate for older children, is largely inappropriate for younger ones.

Explicit instruction must be evaluated in light of the developmental trajectories of the Intelligences. Students benefit from explicit instruction only if the information or training fits into their specific place on the developmental progression. A particular kind of instruction can be either too early at one point or too late at another. For example, Suzuki training in music pays little attention to the notational system, while providing a great deal of support or scaffolding for learning the fine points of instrumental technique. While this emphasis may be very powerful for training pre-school children, it can produce stunted musical development when imposed at a late point on the developmental trajectory. Such a highly structured instructional environment can accelerate progress and produce a larger number of children "at promise" but in the end it may ultimately limit choices and inhibit self-expression.

An exclusive focus on linguistic and logical skills in formal schooling can short-change individuals with skills in other Intelligences. It is evident from inspection of adult roles, even in language-dominated Western society, that spatial, interpersonal, bodily-kinesthetic skills often play key roles. Yet linguistic and logical skills form the core of most diagnostic tests of "Intelligence" and are placed on a pedagogical pedestal in our schools.

C. The Large Need: Assessment

The general pedagogical program described here presupposes accurate understanding of the profile of Intelligences of the individual learner. Such a careful assessment procedure allows informed choices about careers and avocations. It also permits a more enlightened search for remedies for difficulties. Assessment of deficiencies can predict difficulties the learner will have; moreover, it can suggest alternative routes to an educational goal (learning mathematics via spatial relations; learning music through linguistic techniques).

> Assessment of deficiencies can predict difficulties the learner will have; moreover, it can suggest alternative routes to an educational goal.

Assessment, then, becomes a central feature of an educational system. Until now, we have blithely assumed that such assessment can be made. In truth, however, the assessment of intellectual profiles is a task which remains for the future. We believe that we will need to depart from standardized testing. As already implied, we believe that standard pencil and paper short answer tests sample only a small proportion of intellectual abilities and often reward a certain kind of decontextualized facility. The means of assessment we favor should ultimately search for genuine problem-solving or product-fashioning skills in individuals across a range of materials.

An assessment of a particular Intelligence (or set of Intelligences) should highlight problems which can be solved *in the materials of that Intelligence.* That is, mathematical assessment should present problems in mathematical settings. For younger children, these could consist of Piagetian-style problems, in which talk is kept to a minimum. For older children, derivation of proofs in a novel numerical system might suffice. In music, on the other hand, the problems would be embedded in a musical system. Younger children could be asked to assemble tunes from individual musical segments. Older children could be shown how to compose a rondo or fugue from simple patterns.

An important aspect of assessing Intelligences must include the individual's ability to solve problems or create products using the materials of the intellectual medium. Equally important, however, is the determination of which Intelligence is favored when an individual has a choice. One technique for getting at this proclivity is to expose the individual to a situation which is sufficiently complex that it can stimulate several Intelligences; or to provide a set of materials drawn from different Intelligences and determine toward which one an individual gravitates and how deeply he explores it.

> An important aspect of assessing Intelligences must include the individual's ability to solve problems or create products using the materials of the intellectual medium.

As an example, consider what happens when a child sees a complex film in which several Intelligences figure prominently: music, people interacting, a maze to be solved, or a particular bodily-skill, may all compete for attention. Subsequent "debriefing" with the child should reveal the features to which the child paid attention; these will be related to the profile of Intelligences in that child. Or consider a situation in which a child is taken into a room with several different kinds of equipment and games. Simple measures of the regions in which the child spends time and the kinds of activities in which he is engaged should yield insights into that child's profile of Intelligences.

Tests of this sort differ in two important ways from the traditional measures of "Intelligence." First, they rely on materials, equipment, interviews, and so on, to generate the problems to be solved; this contrasts with the traditional "pencil and paper" measures used in Intelligence testing. Second, results are reported as part of an individual profile of intellectual propensities, rather than as a single index of intelligence or rank within the population. In contrasting strengths and weaknesses, they can suggest options for future learning.

Scores are not enough. This assessment procedure should suggest to parents, teachers, and, eventually to the child herself, the sorts of activities that are available at home, in school, or in the wider community. Drawing on this information, the individual can bolster her own particular set of intellectual weaknesses or combine her profile of intellectual strengths in a way that is satisfying vocationally and avocationally.

D. Coping with the Plurality of Intelligences

Under MI theory, an Intelligence can serve both as the *content* of instruction and the *means* or medium for communicating that content. This state of affairs has important ramifications for instruction. For example, suppose that a child is learning some mathematical principle but that this child is not skilled in Logical-Mathematical Intelligence. That child will probably experience some difficulty during the learning process. The reason for the difficulty is straightforward: the mathematical principle to be learned (the content) exists only in the logical-mathematical world and it ought to be communicated through mathematics (the medium). That is, the mathematical principle cannot be translated *entirely* into words (which is a linguistic medium) or spatial models (a spatial medium). At some point in the learning process, the mathematics of the principle must "speak for itself." In our present case, it is at just this level that the learner experiences difficulty—the learner (who is not especially "mathematical") and the problem (which is very much "mathematical") are not in accord. Mathematics, as a *medium*, has failed.

> An Intelligence can serve both as the *content* of instruction and the *means* or medium for communicating that content.

Although this situation is a necessary conundrum in light of MI theory, one can propose various solutions. In the present example, the teacher must attempt to find an alternative route to the mathematical content—a metaphor in another medium.

Language is perhaps the most obvious alternative, but spatial modeling and even a bodily-kinesthetic metaphor may prove appropriate in some cases. In this way, the student is given a *secondary* route to the solution to the problem, perhaps through the medium of an Intelligence which is relatively strong for that individual.

Two features of this hypothetical scenario must be stressed. First, in such cases, the secondary route—the language, spatial model, or whatever—is at best a metaphor or translation. It is not mathematics itself. And at some point, the learner must translate back into the domain of mathematics. Without this translation, what is learned tends to remain at a relatively superficial level; cookbook-style mathematical performance results from following instructions (linguistic translation) without understanding why (mathematics re-translation).

> ...the secondary route—the language, spatial model, or whatever—is at best a metaphor or translation.

Second, the alternative route is not guaranteed. There is no *necessary* reason why a problem in one domain *must be translatable* into a metaphorical problem in another domain. Successful teachers find these translations with relative frequency; but as learning becomes more complex, the likelihood of a successful translation diminishes.

While MI theory is consistent with much empirical evidence, it has not been subjected to strong experimental tests within psychology. Within the area of education, the applications of MI theory are even more tentative and speculative. Our hunches will have to be revised many times in light of actual classroom experience. Still there are important reasons for considering the theory of MI and its implications for education. First of all, it is clear that many talents, if not Intelligences, are overlooked nowadays; individuals with these talents are the chief casualties of the single-minded, single-funneled approach to the mind. There are many unfilled or poorly filled niches in our society and it would be opportune to guide individuals with the right set of abilities to these billets. Finally, our world is beset with problems: to have any chance of solving them, we must make the very best use of the Intelligences available. Perhaps recognizing the plurality of Intelligences and the manifold ways in which human individuals may exhibit them is an important first step.

REFERENCES

Connor, A., *Voices from Cooperstown*, New York: Collier Books, 1982. Based on a quotation taken from *The Babe Ruth Story*, Babe Ruth (and Bob Considine), New York: E.P. Dutton, 1948).

Gallwey, T., *Inner tennis*, New York: Random House, 1976.

Gardner, H., *Frames of mind*, New York: Basic Books, 1983.

Jencks, C., *Inequality*, New York: Basic Books, 1972.

Keller, E., *A feeling for the organism*, Salt Lake City: W.H. Freeman, 1983.

Lash, J., *Helen and teacher: The story of Helen Keller and Anne Sullivan Macy*, New York: Delacorte Press, 1980.

Menuhin, Y., *Unfinished journey*, New York: Alfred Knopf, 1977.

Selfe, L., *Nadia: A case of extraordinary drawing ability in an autistic child*, New York: Academic Press, 1977.

Soldo, J., "Jovial Juvenilia: T.S. Eliot's first magazine," *Biography*, 1982, 5, 25–37.

Walters, J. and Gardner, H., "Crystallizing experiences: Discovering an intellectual gift." In [*Conceptions of*] *giftedness*, R. Sternberg and J. Davidson (eds.), Cambridge: University Press, [1986].

Woolf, V., *Moments of being*, Sussex: The University Press, 1976.

The Theory of Multiple Intelligences

by Howard Gardner

I am very honored to be here. I have long been an admirer of your organization and the man whom you commemorate in your name and in that of the lecture which I am delivering this morning.

I vividly remember three moments of introduction to Samuel Orton and to his work. I first heard of Samuel Torrey Orton when I was researching *The Shattered Mind* in the early 1970s. There were dozens of Europeans who were important in the early study of different kinds of brain disorders, and Samuel Orton was virtually the lone American on that list. He was really decades before his time. In searching for analogies in this field, one might think of him as the Walt Whitman of neurobehavior, or perhaps the Charles Ives of education.

I also heard about the Society in reading an article which was crucial in my own education, an article by Sheldon White on the five-to-seven-year-old cognitive shift. This article was published in 1970 in the bulletin of what was then called the Orton Society.

And, finally, I remember very fondly many favorable allusions to the work of Orton and the Society by my teacher, mentor, and friend, the late Norman Geschwind, who felt extremely close to the workings of the Society and whose students, Al Galaburda and Martha Denckla, will address you later during these sessions.

Having underscored my sympathy with the work you are doing, I have to admit at the outset that I am in no way an ex-

From *Annals of Dyslexia,* vol. 37, p. 19–35, 1987. © 1987 by The Orton Dyslexia Society. Reprinted with permission.

pert on dyslexia or learning disabilities. I do work with brain-damaged adults and with normally gifted children. This has led some people to assume that I also know about children with various kinds of brain difficulties and deficits, but except for some scattered reading, this is not an area in which I can claim any kind of expertise.

I carry out my own work in neuropsychology by studying the acquired alexias, and I certainly believe that alexia has some relevance to developing dyslexia. And for better or for worse, I have had a chance to observe dyslexia first-hand with some close family members, so I have a feeling of what their problems are like and what can (and can't) be done.

What I want to focus on today are some new ideas about cognition and about development, ideas which my colleagues and I have developed, drawing on basic findings in cognitive science and neuroscience. I will describe the theory which we call the "theory of multiple intelligence," tell you something about how we arrived at this theory, what its basic claims are, what's new and different about it, what some of the problems with the theory are. I will then speak about the educational implications of the theory, including some reference to learning problems, and I shall conclude with a moral to my tale.

Let's leave Philadelphia and go to Paris around the turn of the century. At this time, some eighty years ago, the city fathers in Paris approached a psychologist named Alfred Binet and said to him, "We're having a lot of problems picking out which children may have trouble in school. Can you devise some kind of instrument to help us predict who will succeed, and who will fail, in the early grades of the Parisian public schools?" Binet, who was an ingenious fellow, decided to make up a set of items, to give them to youngsters, and to see which items would predict success or failure. He was successful in his efforts and ended up calling what he did an intelligence test. A measure called the "intelligence quotient" was devised to give, in short, an early indication of how smart someone is.

Now I don't want to diminish Binet's achievement. For its time, it was most remarkable, and many people think it was the greatest achievement psychology has ever realized.

Perhaps it is more important to try to figure out *why* it was considered so important. I think it has to do with the ideals of

our own society, of Western society dating back hundreds, perhaps thousands of years, perhaps dating back to Greece, that
what is truly important is human ratio-
nality. That's how we rate people—how
rational they are, how well they can solve
problems. We have a word called
"smart." We talk about people as being
smart or smarter, and, of course, we talk
about people being dumb or dumber.
Now the West is also very interested in
quantities, and so we invented rulers
which measure how tall somebody is,

> That's how we rate
> people—how rational
> they are, how well
> they can solve prob-
> lems. We have a word
> called "smart."

and we also have charts so that if we know how tall somebody is
at three years of age, we can predict how tall he will be when he
is grown up—just multiply toddler height by two.

Now, having been able to quantify physical growth,
wouldn't it be great if one could quantify mental growth? One
could give adults a set of items to tell everybody in the world
how smart they are—you're 130, you're smart—you're 70,
you're dumb. Wouldn't it be even greater if we could take a
little kid half the size of me and give him something which
would allow us to conclude: you're going to be very smart,
you're not going to make it?

Many fashions from Paris make their way across the ocean.
This was no exception. It made its way to California to Stanford
where a test was devised, the Stanford/Binet, a well recognized
name today. And the intelligence test really came into its own in
the first World War with the so-called Army Alpha, used to assess recruits, and from that time on, it has been placed on a very
high pedestal in American society and in other Western societies as well.

As you no doubt have anticipated, I am not entirely satisfied with this state of affairs. And my dissatisfaction early took
two forms in the sense that there are two particular viewpoints
with which I wanted to argue. One was something called "QT"
for quick test. Basically (I quote from memory), an ad for the
QT says, "Would you like to be able to measure someone's intelligence in three to five minutes?" There are three forms which
you can use. You can use one with the severely physically handicapped, even if they are paralyzed, so long as they can signal yes

or no, presumably by winking or something. Perhaps the most unsettling thing of the advertisement for the QT is that it claims you can test both two-year-olds and superior adults, using the same yes-or-no format. And if you write right away to Psychological Test Specialists in Missoula, Montana, you can get the whole thing complete for sixteen bucks. Well, that's the QT. And I just think the notion that you can measure something as precious as a person's intellectual ability in three to five minutes is fatally flawed.

> I just think the notion that you can measure something as precious as a person's intellectual ability in three to five minutes is fatally flawed.

But there are people who even go the QT one step further. Arthur Jensen in California believes that if you simply look at the reaction time—you put on a series of lights and see how quickly someone reacts—you can tell how smart he is. No need for a signal "yes or no" in three to five minutes. Hans Eysenck looks to brain waves. Just stick some electrodes in the head, monitor the brain waves, and you can tell how smart somebody is. Now, how do people get away with this—reaction time and brain waves? Well, alas, the answer is that those things *do* correlate with intelligence tests like the QT. Now there are two conclusions you can draw from this. I prefer to draw the conclusion that the intelligence test notion is pretty silly and the things that correlate are not very revealing either. You probably know by now (it just turned up in the news this week) that height correlates with intelligence. Does that mean that we just go around measuring height instead of administering IQ tests? I hope not, even though at six feet I would be better off than some of you.

Anyway, my second rhetorical antagonist is someone who I hold otherwise in high regard, but not in this particular area, and that's the psychologist of the eighteenth century, Dr. Samuel Johnson. Dr. Johnson was asked, "What is genius?" And he responded, no doubt very quickly, since I venture that he would have done very well in the QT. Dr. Johnson said, "Well, genius is an individual of large general powers, accidentally deflected in one direction or another." Dr. Johnson lived nearly two hundred years before Charles Spearman, who coined the term "G" for General Intelligence. What this was was an early claim for general intelligence. If you had a lot of it, you could use it for anything. It was sort of polymorphous intellect. You could be a politician, a poet, a philosopher, or a pianist. Everything was open to you. If you haven't got a lot of it, forget it. You can't do anything significant.

Now how did I get to be so cynical about these points of view which, for twenty-five hundred years, have held a very honored place in Western society? Well, in fact, it grew out of my own studies. Initially, I didn't think very much about intelligence or intelligence tests. Like most everybody else, I assumed psychologists knew what they were talking about. Then I was trained by psychologists and I was assured that the current wisdom was correct. My own training was under the influence of Piaget. Now Piaget was not terribly interested in intelligence and intelligence tests himself, but, as you may know, he was actually trained in what had been Binet's laboratory, so Piaget's early training included the use of intelligence tests for children. He came to focus on children's wrong answers, and *why* they gave wrong answers, which was a very shrewd insight.

> **Where Piaget got off base was in believing that all aspects of intellect were connected.**

But even though Piaget didn't talk very much about intelligence tests, I guess we can say he did talk about intelligence because half of his books were called something like *The Development of Intelligence in a Child*. Where Piaget got off base was in believing that all aspects of intellect were connected. Remember, he talks about things like concrete operations. If you believe in concrete operations, you believe the following: if a person has concrete operations with one subject matter, he or she is going to exhibit concrete operations in all subject matters, so if you perform concrete operations with logical materials, you are going to use concrete operations with math, space, morality, language, social development. The theory falls apart if one achieves concrete operations with one content, and formal operations with another content, and sensory operations with a third. So Piaget, like intelligence testers and like Samuel Johnson, did believe it all hangs together.

My own work, as has been alluded to, deals with two different populations. I work with brain-damaged adults at the

Boston Veterans Administration Hospital Aphasia Research Center, and I work with normal and gifted children at a research project, called Project Zero, at Harvard. I have been doing that for the last fifteen years. What I became impressed with over and over again in this work was that individuals have very jagged cognitive profiles. You will find the children are very strong in music or in language, very strong in drawing or in dance. One strength simply does not relate to how they are going to be in other cognitive areas. The same irregularity characterizes the brain-damaged patient, somebody who has had a stroke or a tumor or some other kind of lesion. Now it could be the case that when you have had brain damage, everything drops down a little bit. You are used to performing at 240 volts and now you are performing at 180 volts. But it doesn't happen like that at all. On the contrary, what is typical of focal brain disease is that you lose some ability in part or entirely, but most of your other abilities remain pretty much the same. So, based on left-hemisphere injury, you can have a language disorder, difficulty in reading, difficulty in understanding, difficulty in speaking, but you can still find your way around in space, still sing a song, still remain the same person. On the other hand, if you suffer a stroke in an analogous region in the right hemisphere, your language can be ostensibly fine, but you can no longer carry a tune, can't find your way around, can't dress properly, can't make a drawing, and your personality undergoes breakdown as well. Once again, these kind of things cannot be accounted for by a unitary view of intellect.

If you have learned things as a student and you have written about them, you tend to have a certain attachment to outworn views.

Now it's funny how it is when you're a scholar and you are busy running around. Often your own findings will call earlier views into question, but if you have learned things as a student and you have written about them, you tend to have a certain attachment to outworn views.

For a long time, I was a Piagetian and argued favorably for a unitary view of intellect, even though my own findings were calling that position into question. But then I had a very special opportunity. At the Graduate School of Education of Harvard, with which I am affiliated, a Dutch foundation, called the Van Leer Foundation, gave us a very large sum of money. There was only one string attached to this sum of money. It was an interesting string. The string said we should use it to tell what is known about the nature and realization of human potential. Now that is a big, even a grandiose topic. If I were to send in a grant application saying I wanted to study human potential, I would be surprised if I got back an acknowledgment on a post card. It is just too big a topic. It's more West Coast than East Coast. But even though Harvard can be supercilious, when it comes to taking lots of money, it manages to hold its conscience in abeyance.

So we set up the Project on Human Potential and I got a very interesting assignment. My assignment was to summarize what had been established about human cognition and human cognitive potential, based on what has been found out in the cognitive sciences and neurosciences in the past decades. I then decided to use this challenge as an opportunity to put together my own findings about children and brain-damaged adults and findings from other researchers to see if I could come up with a concept of cognition which I thought would do justice to the data. And I knew intuitively I was going to argue that the mind is capable of different kinds of things. In fact, over ten years ago, I actually sketched out a book called, *Kinds of Minds*, which never got anywhere, but buried in my unconscious was the notion to do this. But I wanted to do it right.

I knew intuitively I was going to argue that the mind is capable of different kinds of things.

I then made a fateful decision. I decided to call the different kinds of minds *intelligences*. This was a feisty thing to do. If I had called them talents, people would have said, "Oh, yes, yes, people have many talents," and then would have just gone on about their business, and particularly psychometricians whose stock-in-trade is to study intelligence. They own it. If I called what I was doing *intelligences*, this would be a direct challenge to people who think they know what it is, they know how to study it, test it, etc. So I decided to call what I was studying *intelligences*, and my prediction was successful. I have a whole sheaf of negative reviews saying I don't know what I'm talking about when I talk about intelligence. And, of course, what this really means is, you're trying a different way and it takes away from what we psychometricians are trying to do, which is to measure reaction time or recall of digits backward.

To give you a feeling of what I mean by intelligence, let me describe to you three different end-states. These are roles that people can occupy in different cultures, roles which, if they had a word for intelligence in those cultures, would capture these abilities, but which I claim cannot be captured by our standard tests of intelligence.

The first one is a sailor in the South Seas, one who finds his way around hundreds and even thousands of islands, looking simply at the configuration of the stars and the sky, feeling the flow of the water, and occasionally locating a landmark on an island. How does a person do this? It is very difficult. If they had a word for smart in the Puluwat Island of the Carolina Chain, that would have to capture this particular ability. There is no reason in the world to think that the person who is a good sailor in the Puluwat Islands can tell you who wrote the Iliad or what the difference between praise and punishment is, two favorite items of the intelligence quiz. That's end-state number one.

Number two was again chosen to be contentious. (You may discover a cognitive style at work here.) This is a student in an Islamic culture, studying to be a religious leader. He has to memorize the Koran. That is a big task, several hundred pages in a language he doesn't know. Then he has to learn how to argue about the Koran, and then he goes to the Holy City, studies the Koran a little more, and if he's successful, he then becomes a religious leader himself. Again, if they had a word for *smart* in a religious literate culture, it would be for somebody who could do this sort of thing because that is valued in a place like Iran.

The third end-state is a more contemporary one. It is a Parisian adolescent who composes music on her microcomputer. She programs computers to compose music. Once again, a word like *smart* might capture that particular ability, but there is no reason to think you can pick out a talented composer using standard intelligence tests which never incorporate music.

So I had those three end-states in mind. I thought about

other ones, too, the kinds of roles which are valued across different societies: dancers, choreographers, athletes, politicians, chiefs, psychoanalysts, sorcerers, shamen, hunters, fishermen, and so on. In different societies, these kinds of things are valued, and if you had tests for young kids, you know as well as I do that intelligence tests would not necessarily pick up kids who had these particular talents. So that was the intuition behind my enterprise.

I next needed a definition of an intelligence. I was not going to presuppose whether there was just one or more than one. *An intelligence is an ability to solve a problem or to fashion a product which is valued in one or more cultural settings.* Now how does that resemble other definitions and how does it differ? It says nothing about whether it is inborn or acquired. It says nothing about whether you can test it in a minute or an hour, using a no-or-yes format or brain waves. It talks about solving problems which intelligence tests also do,

> **Psychologists want to study intelligence as if it is a pristine quality which somehow exists, can be pinned down, and perhaps localized.**

and it also talks about fashioning products, doing things like writing a symphony or a poem or making a painting or creating scientific theories. Creating a scientific theory is not problem-solving. It is really problem-finding. It is doing something new and there is nothing in the intelligence test which relates to this. How can you in an hour tell if somebody is going to develop something into a scientific theory. It just wouldn't work.

Finally, I talk about abilities which are valued in a cultural setting. My definition is culturally relative. This bothers psychologists. Psychologists want to study intelligence as if it is a pristine quality which somehow exists, can be pinned down, and perhaps localized. I think that's a forlorn endeavor. I think intelligence needs to be viewed in a cultural context. Probably everybody in this room can do something better than anybody else in the world. Maybe it's counting the crumbs on this rug. Do you want to call that intelligence? Unless it is valuable, in whatever cultural setting, I find it foolish to consider it intelligence. This is obviously the controversial part of my theory, but I will be happy to defend it on your time, though not on mine.

That's my definition. I didn't even have a criterion or a set of criteria. What counts as intelligence? What doesn't? Here lies the science in my enterprise, such as it is. What I did with my colleagues was to survey several literatures to look for evidence of intelligences, and when the several literatures all pointed to something as a candidate intelligence, it made my final list. If, on the other hand, as was often the case, a candidate showed up on one list but not on another, would be counterindicated by a third, or reorganized by a fourth, then it lost credibility as intelligence.

Let me tell you what those criteria are. I have already mentioned the first few. I looked at the development of different abilities in children. How do things like moral development, social development, and so on take place? What is the correlation between one form of development and another? Second, I looked at the breakdown of abilities under conditions of brain damage. What sort of things break down, what they break down with, and what sort of things are separate from one another? As probably everyone in this room knows (partly because I said it just a minute ago), things don't operate all together, and when you look at the decoupling of different cognitive abilities, there's very powerful evidence that they are different intelligences.

> ...when you look at the decoupling of different cognitive abilities, there's very powerful evidence that they are different intelligences.

It is also very convincing. We're all kind of materialists in a philosophical sense, and we like to think we can tie things to particular structures of the brain. And if I can say *this* structure seems to subserve *this* function, and *that* structure seems to subserve *that* function, it is convincing. It is convincing to people who read the Sunday supplements. It is also convincing to scientists. So evidence from brain damage was an important source.

I then looked at what I call *exceptional populations*, which is getting very close to home of The Orton Society. There are the prodigies, children who are extremely gifted in one area but who are ordinary in other areas. Most prodigies are very smart in math or music or chess and perfectly ordinary in other areas. You can read about this in an excellent study of prodigies, *Nature's Gambit*, by my colleague, David Feldman.

I looked at autistic kids who had exhibited a very jagged cognitive profile, children with learning disabilities, who again showed very jagged cognitive profiles, and this evidence from exceptional populations provided a third line of thinking about different intelligences.

Let me mention other sources very briefly. What do we know about the evolution of cognition over the millennia? What do we know about cognition of different species? What do we know about cognition of different cultures, like the Puluwat Islanders? And finally, two sources of evidence from psychology. One is correlations among different tests, performing factor analysis: which tests correlate, which tests don't? And finally, we looked at the results of tests of generalization and transfer. To train somebody in area A does not necessarily improve his performance in area B. Now one of the big findings in psychology over the past years is that transfer is very, very difficult to get. It is hard to train somebody in area A and get payoff in area B. We have known this since Edward Thorndike looked to see if he taught somebody Latin, it would make him better in geometry. It wouldn't make him better in Greek. In fact, it was a happy day if it made him better in Latin! Transfer is very difficult to get.

This suggests that intellect is modular. Our minds and our brains are composed of different modules, and it is difficult to get transfer from one module to another. This flies very much in the face of most concepts of intelligence, from which psychologists have not drawn the proper conclusions. Anyway, to follow up this information, I performed what I call a *subjective factor analysis*. An objective factor analysis, as I have said, is a mathematical operation performed on the scores. We couldn't do this with my data. The data didn't exist in that form. So subjective factor analysis was done by a more personal computer. The only thing that kept it from being *completely* subjective is that in my book, *Frames of Mind*, I do review the evidence on each of the intelligences. So you can really see what I say about musical intelligence, linguistic intelligence, and the others, and you can differ if you like.

So I had my definition. I had my criteria. I had my personal computer and my interpersonal computer. And I then came up with a list of seven intelligences. Now there's nothing sacred about the number seven, despite George Miller, and I do not claim that I have necessarily identified the right seven intelligences. Of course, I think that I have. What I am trying to argue is that intelligence is basically a pluralistic concept. Humans have evolved over thousands or millions of years into different kinds of problem solvers and problem finders as well, and you have to understand that process if you want to figure out how people learn and how they develop and what they can and can't do. So the seven intelligences are really for illustrative purposes, and I will illustrate each by giving one or two examples of individuals who have high development in those particular intelligences.

> I don't think *any* intelligence is inherently more or less important than others.

Linguistic intelligence. Poets have lots of linguistic intelligence. I once took a course with Robert Lowell, and he would read a student's poem and he would comment very penetratingly about the poem. He would pick out a particular word in the poem and he would do something that absolutely astounded me. He would take that word and tell you how every major poet in the English language had used that word over the centuries. His mind was organized in that way. I venture to say that if everyone in this room, for the rest of his life, tried to organize his mind in this way, he would not be able to succeed. It would be very hard anyway.

Logical mathematical intelligence. Logicians, mathematicians, and scientists obviously have this form. Piaget thought he was studying all intelligence, but I believe he was basically studying logical mathematical intelligence, one kind of intelligence.

I mentioned linguistic and logical mathematical intelligence first, not because I think they are the most important—I don't think *any* intelligence is inherently more or less important than others. In fact, which ones are important changes over time. But in our society, the linguistic and logical mathematical are considered to be the most important, and the intelligences you ought to have if you just have one or two intelligences.

If you look at standardized testing, IQ testing, SATs, they test the linguistic and logical mathematical intelligences. If you are lucky enough to be good in both of those intelligences, you'll do well in tests, you'll do well in school, you'll probably get well-placed professionally. It doesn't necessarily predict that you will do well once you get out of school. The correlations are not impressive. But if you stay in school forever, as professors do, you'll probably continue to do well. Professors, like everybody else, like to create tests in their own image.

> **Having a certain kind of intelligence doesn't predict whether you're going to be an artist or a scientist.**

I mentioned five other intelligences. *Musical intelligence*— Leonard Bernstein has lots, Mozart had even more. *Spatial intelligence*—the ability to form a representation of the world. In your mind you operate on that representation of the spatial world. Painters, sculptors, architects, engineers, geometers, surgeons, sailors in the South Seas exhibit lots of spatial intelligence.

You will notice that I mentioned artists. I also mentioned engineers. That is important because having a certain kind of intelligence doesn't predict whether you're going to be an artist or a scientist. But it *does* predict the *kind* of art you are likely to do or the *kind* of science you are likely to do.

I see some heads nodding. Those of you who work with dyslexic children know that they often have language problems, but they are very good at spatial tasks. And that's why you can look at artists and architects, and certain kinds of physicians and engineers, and find individuals who are dyslexic but are using their spatial intelligence to great effect.

The same case obtains to *bodily kinesthetic intelligence*, the ability to use your whole body, or part of your body like your hand or your mouth, to solve a problem or fashion a product. Bodily intelligence is used by dancers, choreographers, athletes, mimes, surgeons again, crafts people, people who use their hands and bodies in a problem-solving kind of way.

I also distinguish two personal intelligences. It is difficult to understand and to measure these forms but they are tremendously important. I think, at least nowadays, a personal intelligence is probably as or more important than the others, but we don't really know how to study it properly.

> **Being strong in one intelligence has no particular implication about strength in other intelligences.**

Interpersonal intelligence is the ability to understand other people, what motivates them, how they work, how to work practically with them. Salesmen, politicians, teachers, religious leaders, are individuals who have, or should have, high degrees of interpersonal intelligence. Ronald Reagan may fail in some of the other intelligences, but he has lots of personal intelligence and it is very useful. (Note: These words were uttered in November 1986, before the Iran-Contra scandal broke.) Jimmy Carter probably has thirty more IQ points than Ronald Reagan, but is not thought of as equally successful. *Intrapersonal intelligence* is the correlative ability turned inward: an effective working model of oneself and the ability to use that model effectively in light of your desires, needs, wishes, fears, and skills. Intrapersonal intelligence includes knowledge of our other intelligences and that is tremendously important.

Now, it is a little difficult to say who has a high degree of intrapersonal intelligence. Secretly, we all think we do, but we couldn't all be right—just ask our spouses! However, I think psychotherapy is relevant here: A person who is a successful product of psychotherapy usually has an enhanced and more accurate notion of his or her own self.

So those are the seven intelligences. I think of them as seven computational devices in the head which we possess as a species and are able to use when certain kinds of information or contents come in. Being strong in one intelligence has no particular implication about strength in other intelligences.

In any ordinary form of human activity you have numbers of intelligences working together, but they work together in unpredictable ways. Only in a freak do you see a single intelligence operating alone. It is messier in the rest of us. However, if you look at us all carefully, you will find very few of us have exactly the same level or configuration of intelligences.

So I have given you a definition, a set of criteria, and a list of candidate intelligences. What can I say about my theory with reference to other theories? Most of you know that I by no means am the first person to promote a pluralistic view of intellect. Thurstone talked about the seven factors of the mind, which have some resemblance to mine. Guilford talks about 150 different types of components, so he has 143 more than I do.

Why, then, is Gardner's theory any different from the others'? I think it is important for me to say something about that. First of all, the theory is biologically based. I am making a claim about how the brain has evolved and how it is organized. I am making a claim, so to speak, about the "natural kinds" of minds. If you could open up the skull and figure out what it is organized to do, it turns out to be organized to do basically seven things well. All other intelligence theories, to my knowledge, draw on the results of tests. My theory is not based upon a mere empirical correlation among tests, but rather upon a biological analysis.

> I am making a claim about how the brain has evolved and how it is organized. I am making a claim… about the "natural kinds" of minds.

There is also a developmental facet to my theory. Each intelligence has its own developmental trajectory. It begins at a certain point. It has crystallizing moments where it flourishes and sensitive periods where small factors exert major effects. It achieves a peak and a decline which can be rather precipitous or much more gradual. A whole science remains to be invented on the developmental trajectories of each of the intelligences and the subintelligences. I have no doubt that capacities like logical thinking develop in a very different way than capacities like personal intelligence. That is why it is ridiculous to claim that one can test two-year-olds and superior adults using the same short yes-or-no test. Such a claim shows developmental insensitivity. I must say that every intelligence test that I know of is developmentally blind. That does not mean that testers use exactly the same items for two-year-olds as they do for adults. Basically, they use the same *kinds* of elements all the way through, which shows as nondevelopmental bias.

How else is my theory different from all other theories? Consider my focus on cultural roles. I care about how intelligences are realized in different types of cultures and settings. So, for example, if you take my three different end-states, they each call for a different kind of intelligence. If I couldn't find an intellectual capability that was of value in a cultural setting, it would cease to be of interest to me. It is quite possible somebody could break the books on an IQ test, and score 287, but wouldn't have any ability that is useful in the culture. And that's why I often think IQ tests are useless. In fact, Norman Geschwind used to point out that you could remove somebody's frontal lobes, and that individual would still have an IQ of 140. But, alas, such people sit around like vegetables and never initiate any activity. What sense does it make to call someone like that a genius?

> If you take away one point from this lecture, let it be that *the mind is organized in terms of content.*

Another way in which my theory is different is that I speak in terms of vertical rather than horizontal organizations of mental faculties. If you look at any psychology textbook, you will find chapters on perception and learning, on memory and attention. The assumption is that there are basic "horizontal" laws of learning and they cut across all kinds of content. So, too, for perception, memory, and the like.

A vertical theory of faculties holds that the best way to cut the cognitive pie is vertically, in terms of content. If you take away one point from this lecture, let it be that *the mind is organized in terms of content.* It matters whether you are dealing with language, music, space, other people or yourself, or your body. Moreover, laws of learning, memory, perception, and the like are organized around those contents. There are laws for learning language which are not necessarily the same as those for learning about other people or about bodily space. Each content, each vertical faculty, has its own principles of learning, memory, perception. This is very radical and it hasn't been proved yet, but there are some interesting lines of evidence that point that way, particularly in neurological studies.

Also, your own intuition supports this. Think about somebody you know who has a good memory. Now ask yourself the following questions about that person. How does that person remember a song he heard on the radio yesterday? How does he remember a dance step that he was taught some months ago? How does he remember a group of people who came to a dinner party last year? The answer is you don't know. That is because, when you talk about good memory, you are really talking about good verbal memory, somebody who can remember all those date of major battles in the 18th century. We use the word good memory in this way, and we don't pay attention to other kinds of memory. But clearly, memory is a faculty which may not work the same way with different kinds of material. We know that someone's verbal memory has zero predictive powers about his visual-spatial or musical capabilities.

The final way in which my theory differs from other theories is that it makes some clear-cut claims about gifts and about creativity. Let me say a word about this, since I know you are interested in unusual talents. Gifts are domain-specific. People may be highly gifted in one area and it doesn't give any clue about how gifted they are in other areas. Talk about people being gifted means that, exposed to the same amount of material as other people, these individuals develop much more quickly. The opposite side of the coin, the deficit, means you're "at risk." If a person at risk is given the same kind of information, the same kind of material, he will not progress as quickly as other people. Gifted programs in schools which admit people with an IQ over 130 but don't admit people with an IQ of 129 are predicated on the notion that gifts are general, or that there is a simple academic gift, which is a more modest claim, but I don't think either of those are true. Gifts are much more domain-specific and so is creativity. I don't believe for a second that if Mozart had been born in Einstein's home and Einstein had been raised in Mozart's home, Mozart would have been the greatest physicist of the eighteenth century, and that Einstein would have been the greatest musician of the past century or vice versa. They

> **People may be highly gifted in one area and it doesn't give any clue about how gifted they are in other areas.**

would not have been able to deal with the radically different situations.

Creativity, doing something new in a field, is also domain-specific. The notion of creativity tests, which can tell you in half an hour how creative you will be, is as insipid as the idea of intelligence tests which, in a half hour or an hour, can tell you how smart you are.

I want to turn now to some educational implications of the theory. I think we can use multiple intelligence theory as a way of analyzing educational encounters. An educational encounter is any situation in which a person is learning something, or is trying to, in school, watching television, reading a book, walking around Constitution Hall. We can analyze this encounter in terms of intelligences. What's the content? Are you learning a language? Are you learning logic? What's the means? Does it involve using language, using logic, using space?

> In the modern secular school, the school of today, language is still important, logic is more important, interpersonal is not particularly valued.

Different educational powers call for different intelligences. The Puluwat sailor was using spatial intelligence. The Koran student was using linguistic intelligence largely, logical intelligence to some extent. Also crucial for the Koranic student are personal intelligences. If you can't form a relationship with a religious leader, you're not going to make it. Interpersonal intelligence is not as important to our society as it is in the traditional society until you get to graduate school. There, if you can't form a relationship with your mentor, forget it.

In traditional schools, educators put language on a pedestal. Logic and interpersonal skills are also important. In the modern secular school, the school of today, language is still important, logic is more important, interpersonal is not particularly valued. But intrapersonal intelligence becomes crucial. You really have to know your own skills, particularly if you live in a pluralistic society. I also think that in the society of the future, logic will become even more important.

The configuration of valued intelligences changes over the millennia. In preliterate cultures, people who today have reading problems had no trouble at all. If, in a hundred years, we move away from literacy, The Orton Society may have to disband! Speaking more generally, if one takes into account the existence of different intelligences, one can analyze why learning occurs in one situation, and not in another, on the basis of the intelligences which are needed, and the ones which are actually used.

So far, I have been speaking mostly on a theoretical level. I want, in conclusion, to talk about some of the work that we have been doing in the schools. We have two applied projects in the community, one working with preschoolers and one with adolescents. In Project Spectrum, we are devising new means of assessing the intelligences of young children. We do this by setting up a very richly-equipped classroom, and by observing the activities in which children participate spontaneously. We observe interest, depth of exploration, change over the course of a year. At the end of the year, we produce a Spectrum report, a portrait of the child, delineating his major intelligences and his areas of weakness, and we wed this to concrete suggestions about what the child (and his family) might do in the future. This practice is consistent with my notion that we psychologists should spend less time ranking people and more time making concrete suggestions which may be of help.

> **We psychologists should spend less time ranking people and more time making concrete suggestions which may be of help.**

In Arts Propel, a project being carried out at the junior and high school level, we are attempting to assess students' strength in the arts and humanities. We favor here a portfolio method, where students assemble not only their finished products, but their notes, sketches, goals, self-criticisms, and comments. The portfolio is designed to function as a kind of cognitive record of the student's intellectual growth over a period of time. We hope that, if successful, such portfolio methods might be used as well in other areas of the curriculum which sample the full range of human intelligences. And, perhaps some day, student portfolios, properly evaluated, will serve as an adjunct to, or perhaps even a replacement for, standardized test scores in a college admissions packet.

I think the school of the future could be organized around these ideas. There could be *assessment specialists* whose job it is to figure out the multiple combinations of intelligences (or subintelligences) which each child has. We could then have *student-curriculum brokers* who connect students not only with the kind of curricula they should be pursuing, but also with the *ways* in which those curricula should be presented. One of the positive features of modern technology is that we make available a much larger set of ways of teaching. We may as well try to match children and their learning style with a curriculum that they are going to take, either electively or to fulfill requirements.

> I am worried chiefly about those students who don't shine in language or logic, but who possess other kinds of gifts and talents.

Finally, we talk about *school-community brokers*. These individuals find vocational options and avocational options in the wider community. They then direct youngsters to these community opportunities, which presumably match more closely to the child's own intellectual configuration.

One may ask about the need for integrating students with the wider community. Now I am not concerned about those students who excel in language or in logic. They will do well in traditional school, will get into good undergraduate and graduate programs, and may well shine later "in the real world." I am worried chiefly about those students who don't shine in language or logic, but who possess other kinds of gifts and talents. These students will be well served by an educational system which brings to their attention those opportunities in the wider community which make particular use of their combination of intelligence.

You may feel my list of different experts sounds utopian. Can we really have all of these specialists? I feel that the problem is not a lack of resources, either human or technological, but rather a lack of will. Nowadays, there is tremendous pressure to treat everyone in the same way, to give them the same curricula and to subject them all to the same quick tests. It is this way of thinking and evaluating, and not the resources themselves, which needs to be changed by a universal act of will if we are to have a more humane and individual-centered school of the future.

Let me now say something about how all this relates to the education of students with learning problems. Special education has often been disparaged by the wider society, but this is one area where I think that the special educators will be the revolutionaries. That is because special educators and learning-disability experts have long known that individuals learn in different ways and that education is most effective when these individual differences are taken into account or even placed at the fore.

...special educators and learning-disability experts have long known that individuals learn in different ways...

A second and related implication has to do with the ways in which we actually teach individual children. We need to ask much finer grained questions about the nature of the subject matter and the kinds of particular abilities and deficits possessed by each child—normal, supernormal, disabled, or impaired in one or another respect. Once again, I think that special educators have the edge here because they have long been looking for the extra leverage, personal, curricular, or technological, which can support an individual child and can convert an unsatisfactory performance into an adequate or even a superior one.

We must confront the possibility that there may be certain subjects or concepts which will prove very difficult for students with certain kinds of deficits. We must have a strong effort to teach these materials, but there may come a point where it is simply a poor use of time to continue to knock one's head (and the student's head) against the same stone wall. Part of the burden of the theory of multiple intelligences is to spell out alternative ways of communicating a concept but also to indicate when such a concept maybe very difficult to convey using alternative means.

A happier part of this tale is that often deficits go hand in hand with strengths. This unexpected coupling occurs for at least two reasons. First of all, it seems to be the case that disabilities of certain sorts correlate with strengths of other sorts, at least in certain cases. Thus children who are dyslexic often show enhanced facility at visual and/or spatial tasks. The second reason stems from dealing with adversity. No one needs to recommend adversity and there is all too much of it in the world. It turns out, however, that the experience of dealing with, and conquering a disability, is often a great ally in dealing with subsequent challenges.

> There should be recognition of, and serious attempts to make full use of, all combinations of human intelligences.

I am waxing fairly moralistically at this point and so it is time for me to turn officially to the morals which I promised you. I have accused our society of being "Westist, Testist, and Bestist."

Westist—in the sense of valuing too highly a certain combination of language and logic which has been advantageous in our history but which may not be all things to all people.

Testist—in the sense that we try to make a test for everything and that we lose interest in those abilities which we cannot quantify. We too often let the testing tail wag the educational dog.

Bestist—in the sense used by David Halberstam in his book, *The Best and the Brightest.* You will recall that Halberstam spoke ironically of the college professors and "bright" individuals who got our country into the Vietnam mess and could not then extricate us.

We need to be able to draw on a much wider set of talents. There should be recognition of, and serious attempts to make full use of, all combinations of human intelligences. If we succeed in doing this, individuals will feel better about themselves. With enhanced self-esteem, they may be more inclined to contribute to the general welfare of the community. And they may also be able to help us solve some of the intractable problems which have certainly eluded the best and the brightest. Recognition of the range of human intelligences may not guarantee our survival, but I think that it enhances the probability that we will be able to live together in some semblance of harmony in a world which is less troubled than ours today.

The Samuel Torrey and June Lyday Orton Memorial Lecture, delivered at the 37th Annual Conference of The Orton Dyslexia Society, Philadelphia, Pennsylvania, November 13, 1986. This present version is a transcript of the oral address, corrected only for comprehensibility.

The research reported here was supported by the Veterans Administration, the Van Leer Foundation, the Spencer Foundation, the Rockefeller Foundation, and the National Institute of Neurological Diseases, Communication Disorders, and Stroke (NS 11408).

Varieties of Excellence: Identifying and Assessing Children's Talents

by Mindy Kornhaber and Howard Gardner

LOOKING AT VARIETIES OF POTENTIAL EXCELLENCE
Since early 1989, members of a research group at Harvard
Project Zero have been spending several hours each week
watching videotapes. The tapes are not produced by major motion picture studios; yet in their own way, they are quite compelling. The tapes show urban public school students giving
presentations about projects they were to have worked on over
a period of several weeks.

Among the projects we are examining are ones done by
youngsters at the Key School, a public elementary school in Indianapolis. The school was inspired in part by Gardner's theory
of multiple intelligences (1983), which asserts that all individuals possess several, different intellectual competences. The Key
School provides opportunities for children to use the full array
of these competences each school day. Teachers at the school
encourage children to employ their unique combinations of
competences in realizing the school projects as well as other
work (Olson, 1988).

Key School projects are based on broad, schoolwide
themes, such as "Heritage," "Connections," or "The Renaissance: Then and Now." The themes provide a focus for the entire curriculum. Thus, during "The Renaissance," the art

A position paper from Columbia University, Teachers' College, New York,
March 1993. © 1993 by the National Center for Restructuring Education,
Schools, and Teaching. Reprinted with permission.

teacher helped students to construct life-size paintings of Renaissance-era people. The music teacher encouraged students to learn Renaissance music on the recorder or the violin. Classroom teachers discussed the theme both in historical terms and in terms of the current rebuilding of the children's own city.

At the Key School, youngsters work alone or in small groups to create their projects. Much of the actual work is carried on outside of school, often at home. Toward the end of the theme period, the children present their projects to their classmates. Their presentations are videotaped for the children's individual "video portfolios." These video recordings represent an attempt by the Key School to document interests, strengths, and achievements that are not readily captured by standardized tests or other written assessments.

Our research group's charge is to devise an assessment scheme for student projects at the Key School and elsewhere. The assignment is more complicated than it sounds. Like adult efforts, the student projects and presentations vary widely in quality. In addition, the projects do not all explore the same domains of knowledge, such as science or history or music. Not all the projects have a similar format. Even when keeping a topic constant, such as "The Renaissance," we find efforts that range from the familiar book report, to scale-model buildings, to musical performances.

Noting this difficulty, and having looked at many students' efforts, both on videotape and in classrooms, we believe that some of the most notable projects have been done by an African-American elementary school girl we will call Kimberly. Kimberly's projects usually entail a drama or dance performance. One was an extended and well-rehearsed balletic dance to contemporary, popular music. In another she researched and rehearsed a variety of dances that were in vogue during this century. She then performed the dances to music appropriate to their respective eras. Alongside this, she created a poster of drawings showing fashions that were worn during each decade of the century. For the "Heritage" theme, we watched her deliver from memory an expressive dramatic monologue based on the experiences of a slave girl.

In nearly all of her projects, Kimberly demonstrates excellence by giving skillful performances on challenging assignments in disciplines that are widely appreciated in the larger society. Her achievement is not surprising given her talent and her delight in and dedication to dance and drama, as well as the support she receives both at home and in school for her efforts. Nor is it surprising that Kimberly was subsequently admitted to a magnet school for the arts based on her dance and drama auditions. What may be more surprising is that this school success comes in the face of marginal results on IQ tests and a failing grade on the state's standardized test of math and English.

> This school success comes in the face of marginal results on IQ tests and a failing grade on the state's standardized test of math and English.

Project Spectrum, a research group launched six years ago by David Feldman at Tufts University and Howard Gardner at Harvard Project Zero, is another effort aimed at exploring the range of human competences. Investigators in this group focus on preschoolers and early elementary school children. Project Spectrum researchers have devised an inviting collection of classroom materials that help them, as well as teachers, assess and build on a given child's intellectual strengths. Among these materials are games that call on children to use their linguistic and mathematical abilities. There is a scale model of the classroom and its inhabitants through which social and spatial abilities can be plumbed and developed. In addition, Spectrum uses musical instruments, dance and movement exercises, and machinery of various complexity, which children are free to take apart and reassemble (Krechevsky, 1991; Krechevsky and Gardner, 1990; Malkus, Feldman, and Gardner, 1988).

This assembly activity helped to reveal an extraordinary strength in an at-risk boy. "Jay" did poorly on standardized tests, and evinced little skill, interest, or persistence in traditional classroom activities that focused on language and numbers. Nor was this youngster adept at socializing with his classmates or teacher. In fact, his teacher later admitted she had already given up on him. What kept her awake for several nights reconsidering this judgment was watching Jay become totally engaged in taking apart a food grinder, intently studying its mechanism, and then putting it back together in a careful way. His performance on this task was not only superior to his work in other activities, but it was also better than that of his peers. It was obvious to all concerned that, at least in this mechanical domain, he was capable of concentrating, proceeding in an orderly fashion, and doing a skillful job in which he took pleasure and pride.

These research projects and the examples of Jay and Kimberly help illustrate two key points on which we will expand in this essay. The first is that human beings possess a varied array of mental competences, strengths, or "intelligences" (Gardner, 1983) that they can combine and call on in different ways to achieve excellence in diverse disciplines. Furthermore, excellence in these disciplines, or domains of knowledge, is developed and exhibited in different ways. Most schools miss opportunities to support the development of excellence because their curriculum, assessment, and pedagogy neglect all but linguistic and logical-mathematical competences.

> Those who are deemed excellent have developed their competences in meaningful contexts over an extended period of time.

Our second key point is this: Those who are deemed excellent have developed their competences in meaningful contexts over an extended period of time (Bloom, 1985; Gardner, 1990; Hayes, 1985). While these individuals may have possessed certain strengths from an early age, none is excellent from the beginning. Instead, they engage in a series of efforts, which include many small victories and defeats, which ultimately enable them to meet high standards in a discipline (See Collins, Brown, and Newman, 1989). To help young people excel, schools need to create conditions that foster sustained engagement and encourage reflection on one's own and others' efforts.

In this paper we begin by detailing the range of intellectual competences that human beings possess and the evidence in support of these competences. We do this because these competences serve as one of the foundations for excellence. However, it is also evident that excellence is not solely skill-based; individuals' minds intersect with the domains of knowledge and system of values maintained by their cultures (Csikszentmihalyi, 1987; Csikszentmihalyi and Robinson, 1986;

J. W. Gardner, 1961; Goodnow, 1990; Keating, 1984; Rogoff, 1990). Therefore, we also discuss socially based foundations of excellence. These include the values and practices of the wider society as well as the schools. Such values and practices help to establish the degree of engagement and the domains of engagement that appear worthwhile to individuals.

BROAD AND NARROW VIEWS OF EXCELLENCE
Excellence depends on the meshing of complex aspects of individuals' minds and of cultures' values and practices. Despite this complexity, it is possible to formulate a reasonably succinct definition of excellence: Excellence consists of regular, high-level performances in domains of knowledge that are relevant to an individual's culture. Our first task in this section is to "unpack" our definition by characterizing domains of knowledge and high-level performances. Following this, we examine varying conceptions of the mental abilities that account for individual perfor-

> **Excellence consists of regular, high-level performances in domains of knowledge that are relevant to an individual's culture.**

mances. We do this in preparation for exploring how values and practices in the wider society affect the development of these mental abilities.

Domains of knowledge consist of bodies of facts, principles, and skills that evolve over time because they play a useful role in sustaining a culture's economic or social needs (Csikszentmihalyi, 1990). Obviously, cultures' needs vary and change. As a result, there are many domains ranging from dance to car repair to shamanism. A domain that is useful in one culture may be less appreciated elsewhere. Shamanism is a vital part of many cultures in the world. In Western Europe, however, it is not. As a result, there are few, if any, European practitioners of shamanism. Despite their great number and variety, "authentic" domains such as shamanism, anthropology, dance, or car repair share several features:

Practitioners. As indicated above, domains of knowledge are *practiced* in their culture (J. S. Brown, Collins, and Duguid, 1989). There is at least a small band of individuals, and probably a sizable number of people, who work in the domain, who communicate with each other in some fashion, and who may contribute to the domain.

Repertoire. A domain's practitioners share certain kinds of skills and knowledge, such as interviewing and observing in cultural anthropology, or conducting rituals in shamanism, or diagnosing and repairing car problems in the domain of auto mechanics. Practitioners of a domain make use of a repertoire of laws, principles, theories, and models of explanation or evidence (Chi, Glaser, and Rees, 1982; Perkins *et al.*, in preparation). These guide them in their work and help them to refine their practice.

Time. Because domains are rich with content and practices, it takes time to become a skilled practitioner (Hayes, 1985; Perkins and Salomon, 1987). As noted earlier, people are not born excellent. Instead, they advance through a domain, usually in a series of steps. These steps may be formally recognized, as they are in a traditional apprenticeship (Feldman, 1980).

Varied Effort. Since domains are rich, the routes into skilled practice may take many forms. In literate communities, broad aspects of many domains are captured in books. Despite this, it is important to recognize that only in extremely few domains can individuals achieve expertise solely by reading about them. Just as in nonliterate communities, individuals must "get their hands dirty" by, for instance, attempts at fixing a car or conducting interviews and by having others respond to these efforts (Polanyi, 1958).

Recognition of Expertise. Finally, because those in a domain draw on a pool of shared principles, skills, and facts, other practitioners and informed appreciators (e.g., a dance critic) can usually recognize individuals who excel in the domain. These two groups help constitute the "field" that can bestow official awards or recognition of excellence (Csikszentmihalyi, 1987; Gardner, 1988). The field's judgment is based on an individual's ability to make flexible use of the domain's facts, skills, and principles to tackle some of the domain's most complex matters with success.

We consider an instance of such flexible use to be a *performance of understanding* (Gardner, 1991a). A performance of understanding may be seen when a student solves a math problem that is new to her; or when a student like Kimberly performs a monologue that moves her audience; or when Jay handles a new machine and through this reveals how all the parts work together. We believe that, in Western culture, excellence consists of strings of such performances on genuinely challenging matters in the domain. (In other cultures, which may value faithful demonstrations of traditional skills on traditional problems, a different definition of excellence may hold; see Gardner, 1989.)

Given that excellence takes place in many domains, and that it is determined on the basis of diverse kinds of high-level performances of understanding, it seems counterintuitive to maintain that excellence relies on just one or two underlying mental abilities. Nevertheless, a widely held but narrow view of excellence is based on just this premise. We need to contend with the narrow view because it has a long and influential history in Western culture generally and in our schools in particular.

> ...it seems counterintuitive to maintain that excellence relies on just one or two underlying mental abilities.

The narrow view of excellence regards the linear, abstract reasoning characteristic of the domains of mathematics and logic as the basis for accomplishment in all disciplines. This belief extends from Plato, through Descartes and Bertrand Russell, to many contemporary psychologists, from psychometricians to Piaget. Typically, schools have focused their efforts around a slightly expanded version of the narrow view. This scholastic version allows language to spread beyond the linear, prepositional argumentation of essayist literacy (Goody and Watt, 1963; Olson, 1977) to encompass creative literature.

The narrow view often prevails in schooling for a number of reasons. First, schools came along specifically to transmit the abstract notations that people invented to capture regulations, knowledge, and accounting techniques prized by the leadership of early civilizations (Csikszentmihalyi, 1990; LeVine and White 1986). Thus, schools were places in which the capacity to manipulate abstract symbols, as is characteristic of logic and math, were highly valued (Gardner, 1990).

Second, early schools were largely training grounds for the next generation of leaders. Their charges were usually the sons of the elite or other boys who were deemed particularly apt at learning symbol systems, manipulating them, and memorizing long passages comprised of them. It is easy to imagine that a confounding of social status with particular kinds of symbol manipulation would support a narrow view of excellence.

> It is easy to imagine that a confounding of social status with particular kinds of symbol manipulation would support a narrow view of excellence.

Yet a third reason for the narrow view of excellence, both in schools and throughout Western society, was the widespread adoption of intelligence testing. Modern forms of intelligence testing were developed when schools became mass institutions. The initial purpose of this testing was to identify those children who were not able or willing to learn what was taught in school and provide them with remediation. The first test, published in 1905 by Alfred Binet and Theodore Simon at the request of the French government, consisted of a variety of short practical tasks. These were not based in the practices of a domain as they were learned over time. Instead, children were asked to do such things as follow simple instructions (e.g., to be seated or pick something up from the floor), to count backward, to repeat sentences of different lengths, to name familiar objects from pictures of them, and to copy geometric forms (Binet and Simon, 1905). A single score, known as a "mental age," was assigned to the child's effort.

Despite this numerical label, Binet himself did not hold a narrow view of intellectual competences. Instead, he asserted that intelligence was a complex characteristic of diverse qualities. Furthermore, Binet made no claims about the origins of intelligence and asserted that intelligence was remediable. He argued against using test scores to consign children to a basically custodial classroom (Binet and Simon, 1905; Gould, 1981).

Unfortunately, Binet's ideas about human abilities were subverted when his tests were adapted for mass administration by Lewis Terman and others in the United States. In books that explained and advocated these adapted tests as a means to solve the organizational dilemmas of expanding schools systems, Terman (1916, 1919, 1923) offered his own ideas about intelligence: It was genetically determined, irremediable, and readily ascertained, like the amount of gold in ore, "by sinking shafts, as it were, at a few critical points" (Terman, 1919, p. 1).

Thus, Terman's work, as well as that of many others involved in the development of intelligence tests (see Gould, 1981), promoted narrow views about the bases for excellence. Equally important, the acceptance of testing fostered the belief that valid assessments about individuals could be divorced from practices within authentic domains. "Science" could efficiently discern whether individuals had the capacity for excellence largely by the way they responded to short-answer paper-and-pencil tests. Edwin G. Boring, a prominent psychologist and a historian of this domain, captured the involuted nature of the testing movement: "Intelligence is what intelligence tests measure" (Boring, 1923). And what the tests tended to measure was a very limited range of language and logical-mathematical problem solving.

> The acceptance of testing fostered the belief that valid assessments about individuals could be divorced from practices within authentic domains.

While some theorists nominate language and mathematical logic as the bases for excellence in all domains (Eysenck, 1981; Jensen, 1969; Spearman, 1927), others have disputed that claim. Those opposing the narrow view usually base their arguments on an alternative form of the statistical technique called factor analysis (Guilford, 1967; Thurstone, 1938). Such analyses attempt to identify the mental abilities that account for the positive correlation among different intelligence tests. These analyses have determined that anywhere from 2 to an unwieldy 120 underlying factors are responsible for intellectual performance.

There are at least two significant problems in such arguments. One is that the number of factors any reputable factor theorist posits results from the use of different, but defensible, statistical techniques. Second, these analyses are based on outcomes of intelligence tests. They do not look beyond the puzzles these tests employ to ascertain the kinds of cognitive capacities human beings rely on when they encounter genuine problems in an authentic cultural domain. Thus, both claims as well as many counterclaims about the nature of individual competences have focused on results from assessments that look only at limited performances in a small band of human competences (Gardner, 1991b; Sternberg, 1990).

Rather than just attempting to explain the correlations among intelligence tests, Gardner (1983) sought to account for the cognitive bases that enable people to perform in the broad range of domains humankind has developed. To determine these cognitive foundations, he relied on a variety of evidence. He took into account the outcomes of intelligence testing. In addition, he considered evidence from evolutionary biology, cross-cultural studies, and psychology. In particular he looked at the development of different symbol-using capabilities among normal children; the unusual profile of these capabilities in prodigies, autistic individuals, and *idiots savants*; and the selective sparing of injury of symbolic capacities in brain-damaged individuals.

> **Gardner sought to account for the cognitive bases that enable people to perform in the broad range of domains humankind has developed.**

These investigations indicated that several different capacities and skills are present in all cultures. These competences tend to develop at different rates, to reach greater and lesser degrees of finesse in the absence of rigorous instruction, and to be governed by different areas of the brain. For example, use of language develops at a rapid rate in all normal individuals with very little tutoring. The ability to work in mathematics, in contrast, varies among cultures, develops slowly among individuals, and usually requires formal instruction to reach high degrees of skill. Furthermore, illness or injury that renders an individual incapable of speech may have little or no effect on mathematical skills (Gardner, 1983).

Based on this research, Gardner proposed his theory of multiple intelligences (Gardner, 1983). According to this theory, there are at least seven relatively autonomous intelligences: linguistic, logical-mathematical, musical, spatial, bodily-kinesthetic, interpersonal, and intrapersonal. In Gardner's theory, an intelligence is a potential that enables a person to solve genuine problems or to fashion products that are valued in some cultural setting (Gardner, 1983, Chap. 4). Each intelligence gives a person access to forms of thought that prove especially appropriate to handling specific types of content or problems.

Only in rare cases of pathology do intelligences appear in isolation. For normal individuals to function in and across cultural domains, several intelligences or competences must be coordinated. Thus, a dancer relies on bodily-kinesthetic and spatial competences to control her movements through time and space. She also needs inter- and intrapersonal competences to access her own feelings and convey these with expression to an audience. A mechanic needs spatial and bodily-kinesthetic competences as well. He uses the former to figure out how parts relate to each other and the latter to take apart and assemble components. He may also need some logical-mathematical skills to measure how things fit together and to test parts systematically to see which one is failing to operate as it should. An anthropologist requires a great deal of interpersonal intelligence, but logical-mathematical competence may come into play as she tests her theories, and linguistic competence is essential in explaining her findings and writing them up.

> Each intelligence gives a person access to forms of thought that prove especially appropriate to handling specific types of content or problems.

We believe that excellence in dance, mechanics, anthropology, and nearly all other domains tests on a broader array of competences than the traditional narrow view acknowledgments. Excellence depends, however, not only on an individual's underlying competences. It also depends on socially based conditions that enable the development of competences through sustained engagement in meaningful, domain-relevant tasks.

CONDITIONS FOR THE ACHIEVEMENT OF EXCELLENCE

One way to think about the development of excellence is to place it within the context of general human development. Unlike many other species, human young are not born in the morning able to set off running with the herd an hour or so later. As is the case with human development generally, excellence within domains of knowledge requires sustained support from nurturing adults. It rarely if ever materializes solely out of the resources of an individual's mind (Feldman, 1986).

The support needed for the development of excellence is threatened by numerous myths and practices of American society. Rather than intoning a litany of these, we focus first on two prominent myths and some of the beliefs that flow from them.

The Myth of "The Natural"

As the adaptation and popularization of intelligence tests by Lewis Terman indicates, Americans sometimes appear all too willing to believe that excellence depends primarily on innate ability. Parents in America are far more likely than their Asian counterparts to accept the idea of inborn talent as an explanation for their children's achievement (Stevenson, 1990; White, 1987). While Japanese parents insist that their children have lots of homework, American parents do not necessarily want their children to be saddled with the amount of work that may be needed to make significant progress in a domain. Though there are several reasons for this (see, for example, Barrett, 1990), the myth of natural talent—that "you've either got it or you don't"—probably plays a potent role. This myth makes it hard to justify foregoing free time and devoting energy to challenges for which one simply "hasn't got the knack."

> …excellence within domains of knowledge requires sustained support from nurturing adults.

If we love the natural, it makes sense that we are not terribly fond of "the grind." The grind is a student who gets ahead of others by working harder. The grind violates the myth of the natural by forcing others to notice that, with extra work, they too might excel. Thus, rather than gaining support for engaging in challenges over time, hard-working students may be seen as breaching acceptable community norms and beliefs (see Horowitz, 1987).

It is worth noting that violating community standards is rarely appreciated anywhere. Thus, the issue is not that Japanese students are diligent and the Americans are lazy, but rather that both operate to maintain the support of those around them. Generally neither wants to stand too far outside of the behaviors accepted by their parents or peers, since such deviation threatens their social ties (see, for example, Fordham and Ogbu, 1986).

Unfortunately, for a variety of historical reasons (see Bailyn, 1960; Hofstadter, 1963), the predominant U.S. views about grinds, intellect, and scholarship are not terribly conducive to achieving excellence or inculcating it as a goal among students. Hofstadter (1963) noted that we are a pragmatic culture in which displays of intellectual strength are subject to suspicion. The upshot of such views is not surprising. As John. W. Gardner (1961, p. 102) wrote, "We cannot scorn the life of the mind and expect our young people to honor it." At best, even if we do not scorn the mind, the messages from nurturing adults and the larger society may be ambivalent enough to undercut motivation for sustained work toward excellence, especially in intellectual endeavors.

> "We cannot scorn the life of the mind and expect our young people to honor it."

The "Horatio Alger" Myth

The Horatio Alger myth may be seen as both contradictory and complementary to the myth of the natural. Its message is that anyone who works hard enough will succeed. This myth is less contradictory than it appears, because it is usually applied to pragmatic, financial success rather than to more "mental" achievements. At the same time, this myth complements the natural because it too posits that the resources individuals need to excel are largely within their personal sphere. In both myths, success comes from drawing upon one's own strengths, whether innate or self-forged. Thus, both help to explain some of the dearth of dedicated effort among those who might nurture excellence in the young.

While the myth of the natural undoubtedly has some impact on everyone, the Horatio Alger myth may have more definitive effects on groups of people who, historically, have not reached the levels of income or school achievement of white, middle-class men (Lewis, 1979; Sniderman, 1989). Flowing from the Horatio Alger myth is a belief that if parents just worked hard enough, they would solve their own problems, provide for their own families, and deliver eager and charming young learners to the schoolhouse door. The Horatio Alger myth undermines support for excellence at the wider societal levels by allowing Americans to neglect problems in their social structure (Patterson, 1986; Sniderman, 1989). These problems deliver to classrooms children who lack nutrition, housing, medical care, and other basic needs. In the absence of these basics, it is difficult for many children to engage their competences or to find the work of school compelling (Fine, 1986; Quality Education for Minorities Project, 1990).

> The Horatio Alger myth undermines support for excellence at the wider societal levels...

The Horatio Alger myth also makes it possible to blame the poor, minorities, and women for their absence from fields and institutions from which they have been excluded (Lewis, 1979; Ryan, 1976). If those who work hard succeed, and if legal obstacles have been largely lifted, what excuse can there be if such individuals do not get into doctoral programs or enter the sciences? The fallback answer for some is that these people lack "natural" ability.

Both myths ignore the barriers created by historic forms of discrimination, which have an impact on individuals' motivation to develop their competences over time in school (Comer, 1988a, 1988b; J. W. Gardner, 1961; Ogbu, 1978; Wilson, 1987). As a result of exclusionary practices, the "cultures" of certain domains and occupations appear uninviting to some groups, and the routes into and through these domains are obscure. Thus, young women have not entered engineering, mathematics, or the physical sciences in numbers that reflect their abilities to grasp and succeed in these fields (Armstrong, 1980; Chipman, Brush, and Wilson, 1985; Kahle, 1985). Too many young black people do not enter or graduate from four-year colleges. Of those who do, extremely few pursue hard sciences (American Council on Education, 1988; Green, 1987; Thomas and Hirsch, 1989; Wilson and Justiz, 1987/1988). There is little, if any, reason to assert an uneven distribution of competences that would make some groups of people more likely than others to succeed in given domains; yet, our social practices have, in Jacqueline Goodnow's words, made it seem as if "some skills and some areas of knowledge belong to some people more than to others" (Goodnow, 1990, p. 264).

COMMUNITY INVOLVEMENT IN THE CREATION OF MEANINGFUL CONTEXTS

It is unlikely that the myths and values that undermine the creation of contexts for engagement will suddenly evaporate. Certainly, schools by themselves cannot radically alter beliefs created over the course of American experience. Nor do we think schools can bring about equality in the society at large, in the absence of economic and social policies that support families, children, and equitable access to quality education (Birch and Gussow, 1970; Cohen, 1989; Fine, 1988; Orfield, 1988; Orfield and Peskin, 1990). Having looked at these myths and their impacts, however, we do think that schools can help youngsters within their immediate sphere develop their competences in domains of knowledge by creating meaningful contexts for engagement.

> **If less privileged students are to develop their competences in schools, schools may need to forge greater alignments with people in the school community.**

Schooling and its practices look irrelevant to many students (Sarason, 1983), not just to those in difficult circumstances or those who have faced historic discrimination. Yet among more fortunate students there is an alignment between the school and the community that makes schooling seem important, if not often intriguing, to those within it. It is at least this level of meaningfulness that suburban districts have counted on and cultivated to foster student cooperation and effort (Comer, 1988a).

If less privileged students are to develop their competences in schools, schools may need to forge greater alignments with people in the school community. If members of the community are treated with respect and community issues are considered matters worthy of study, students may come to see the school as part of their own value system rather than as something foreign to it (Comer, 1980).

We recognize that relationships between minority communities and teachers have often been fraught with tension due to issues of social status, culture and language, perceptions of power, and limitations on time (Bastian *et al.*, 1986; Comer, 1980, 1984; Heath and McLaughlin, 1987; Lightfoot, 1978, 1980; Trubowitz, 1984). Nevertheless, we see some hope for alignments in the many schools that have established meaningful involvement with their communities, perhaps most notably the Comer schools.

In Comer's model, parental involvement is not seen as a burden, but as a plus. Parents are encouraged to participate through a parents' group and to serve as classroom aides, tutors, and volunteers (Comer, 1980, 1988a, 1988b). Furthermore, the governance of these schools includes parents, teachers, and other school staff as well as the principal. Rather than the usual route to co-opting parents via the "put a parent on a committee" approach (Wilson, 1983, p. 160), Comer schools devote the time, energy, and training necessary for parents to have a real voice in running the school (1980, 1988a). Such long-term relationships between homes and schools reinforce the value of sustained effort in school work and have yielded better levels of achievement in these schools and elsewhere (Ascher, 1988; Henderson, 1987).

> ...schools can create meaningful contexts for engagement by making the life of the community an object of rigorous study.

Dissonances between communities and schools exist not only because of the impediments to communication between them. They also exist because of "silencing" (Fine, 1988). These are attempts to ignore prominent aspects of nonschool life that children carry with them to class. Rather than shutting out community life, its patterns, problems, and strengths, schools can create meaningful contexts for engagement by making the life of the community an object of rigorous study. Like anthropologists, sociologists, or political scientists, teachers and students can attempt systematically to answer questions such as:

What are the important events that happen in the community? Are there regularities or patterns in these events? If so, what are the reasons for their recurrence? How do we know these are the reasons? What might change the conditions in the community? If one of the goals of schooling is to help young people become skillful citizens, harnessing students' concerns to study of these matters is an important and valid task (see Fine, 1988).

> **Ethnographic skills encouraged teachers to look closely at their own habits and their beliefs about students and learning.**

While the above suggestion is redolent of "critical pedagogy" (Freire, 1989; Giroux, 1988), others who are not known for that ideology use similar strategies in building meaningful involvement with the community. Comer's work in New Haven offers one example. In the schools' "social skills curriculum" there is a unit on elections geared toward helping students see themselves as players in the political process. Students prepared to talk with candidates about substantive issues, including those they uncovered in a walking tour of the city, which highlighted disparate conditions in different areas of the city. They wrote to the candidates to invite them to the school to discuss their platforms. Because of their research, the students could do more than listen politely; they questioned the candidates and were ready with follow-up probes to the candidates' answers (Comer, 1980).

The efforts to make the community a source of curriculum can enhance the school context not only for students but for teachers. An example of this comes from the ethnographic work of Shirley Brice Heath (1983). Heath helped to lower the cultural barriers between school and home by building understanding of home communities among teachers through ethnographic projects. Ethnographic skills encouraged teachers to look closely at their own habits and their beliefs about students and learning. Ethnography also led the teachers on a quest to understand why and how the languages and cultures that students brought to school differed from school practice. This understanding made it possible for teachers not to reject the patterns that young children brought with them but to adapt their materials and teaching methods to help children bridge the differences between home and school.

In summary, schools should foster alignments with their community because this helps students engage their competences and thus enhances the possibility that they will excel. To build alignments, schools need to help family and community members to feel comfortable in a two-way conversation with school personnel (Herman and Yeh, 1983; Lightfoot, 1980; S. H. Wilson, 1983). This dialogue can be facilitated in part by training school personnel and community members to work together (Comer, 1980, 1988a, 1988b). It can also be achieved through changes in school governance and structure. Structural changes should be geared to enable counselors and teachers to have more sustained contact with individual students (Fine, 1988; Powell, Farrar, and Cohen, 1985; Sizer, 1984). Without this, the stresses operating on many teachers and many families—urban, minority, and even privileged—will continue to make involvement difficult to secure (Heath and McLaughlin, 1987). Finally, making the community itself a valid topic for rigorous study is a way to lessen the dissonance between school and community and to enhance students' competences (Fine, 1988).

Each of these efforts is a way to renew adult interaction with young learners and to provide the kind of meaningful relationships and contexts that promote excellence. Yet each must still be seen as only one part of a complex endeavor against myths and practices in schools and the larger society that make the development of competences problematic.

PEDAGOGY

Until this point we have underscored that excellence takes place in disparate domains; that individuals have a variety of competences that enable them to perform in these domains; and that excellence requires extensive engagement in domain-relevant practices and in meaningful contexts. Now the question is: How can teachers help nurture these competences over time not only in anthropological or political studies of the community, but in other topics where there may be a less immediate affective lure?

Disengagement can stem from many sources. Silencing is one. Another is the narrow range of intellectual competences that students can regularly use in school. Especially after the early elementary years, youngsters are asked to grasp the workings of subjects ranging from social studies, to math and science, to English and foreign languages primarily through linguistic and logical-mathematical intelligence. Those few who can do this may become "A" students (although as we will see later, they may still not achieve performances of understanding). For students with intellectual strengths outside the traditional two, however, schooling provides too few "hooks" to allow for even this "paper" achievement.

In schools, domains of knowledge seem restricted to, or adequately represented by, notations on paper (or computer screens). Outside of schools, however, domains of knowledge are comprised of facts, principles, and skills that are susceptible to contributions and parsing by many different competences. Different combinations or "profiles" of intelligences can serve as routes into and through the same domain. So, for example, a mechanic can proceed to understand auto engineering by relying heavily on bodily-kinesthetic and spatial intelligences to work with engine parts and figure out how their connections work. Such an approach could be one route for a child like Jay. Others may proceed from their logical-mathematical intelligence, which might look toward physics principles to explain why certain parts have to be present and function in certain ways. This approach could have been an important route for Click and Clack, the MIT-educated car experts that engine tinkerers hear on National Public Radio.

> **Different combinations or "profiles" of intelligences can serve as routes into and through the same domain.**

A teacher who acknowledges other intelligences as legitimate ways of knowing stands a good chance of encouraging sustained engagement among her students. Such a teacher can use a student's strength as springboards into various areas of the curriculum (Walters and Gardner, 1985; Kornhaber and Gardner, 1991). Thus, rather than relying solely on linguistic intelligence to make history comprehensible, Jay's teacher could exploit his spatial and bodily-kinesthetic strengths and his mechanical interests. She could have him explore the differences between older and more modern forms of transportation and farming equipment and ask him to think about the reasons for these changes and the impact they have had. Jay's same gifts might also facilitate learning of mathematical concepts. Given that he readily assembled a series of gears as well as grinders, he might be encouraged to think about proportions and ratios. His talents could also be drawn on in the realm of physical sciences. What are the mechanics of simple machines like planes or levers? By virtue of using the machine as an analogy for the body, it may be possible to lure a child like Jay into thinking about biological sciences. How do different systems in the body enable it "to work"? Tapping into Jay's understanding of the mechanical domain might also be a means to build up his linguistic and interpersonal skills. In the former, it would be worthwhile to ask Jay to keep a notebook of his thoughts about different mechanisms. In the latter, he might be encouraged to serve as a resource person or local expert (see Brown and Palincsar, 1989) to other members of the classroom who have questions about the workings of mechanical things.

Domains of knowledge are rich with possibilities for engagement and therefore excellence.

Similarly, Kimberly's teachers at the Key School could engage her interpersonal, bodily-kinesthetic, and spatial intelligences to grapple with diverse areas of the curriculum. We saw inklings of Kimberly's willingness to exploit her competences in the area of history with her exploration of changes in costume, music, and dance, which drew her into library research. These same intelligences and interests can be used to strengthen her language skills as well. Kimberly's teacher could encourage her to write her own dramatic monologues, or have her conduct interviews with performing artists and write up what she has learned. Given her interests and profile of strengths it is possible to envision ways of making a unit on the body truly intriguing for this child. How do muscles develop? Why does exercise make a difference? What other systems does the body rely on to maintain health and strength? Physical sciences might be broached through topics like acoustics and lighting that coincide with her interest in stagecraft. How does sound carry to the back of the audience? How do so many different colors come out of just the few gels that cover the stage lights?

As these examples indicate, domains of knowledge are rich with possibilities for engagement and therefore excellence. To exploit these possibilities we need to consider children's strengths and interests at the same time that we play on the many elements of the domains themselves. Gardner (1991a) has claimed that one way to do this is through "entry points." These are more or less harmonious with different students' learning styles, and they roughly map onto strengths in different intelligences. Gardner has hypothesized that there are five entry points and that all domains can be broached by applying any of these five to central or generative topics in a domain. The following illustrations may help to make these ideas more concrete:

In attempting to help students develop an understanding of American history, a teacher could focus on the central topic of democracy and employ a *narrational entry point.* Here the focus would be on major figures, their motivations, and conflicts between major figures. This entry point would emphasize the way different people helped to shape events like the American Revolution and craft documents like the Declaration of Independence and the Constitution. The same entry point applied to biology might focus on a central topic of evolution through exploring Charles Darwin's adventures on the Beagle, and the way this voyage influenced his thinking and methods.

It is also possible to build understanding of biology and history through a *quantitative-logical entry point.* In this case, a teacher could explore democracy by looking at voting blocks. She could then have students consider the implications of voting blocks for various kinds of legislation. In the case of evolution, the study of the laws of genetics and principles of variation would be salient.

A *foundational entry point* provides a third approach. This examines the basic philosophical concepts within domains, the origins of these concepts, the reasons they are important, and the ways in which they relate to other concepts within and beyond the domain. With this entry point, democracy could be explored by asking about its central principles and by comparing how the rights and duties of citizenship under democracy compare with those under other forms of government. In evolution, a foundational approach examines the root metaphors of this concept and contrasts it with other ways of thinking about speciation and the course of nature over time. Thus, a teacher could contrast the Darwinian concept of evolution with that of Lamarck and with other biological or philosophical systems that attempt to shed light on the diversity of life.

An *aesthetic entry point* emphasizes artworks and literature as well as patterns and forms deductible through human senses. A teacher who helps students to think about democracy through this entry point might look toward public symbols and literature. A teacher could have students create new artworks that they think express this concept. In the study of evolution, an aesthetic entry point could look at the pattern of variation of features within species. A teacher could also call on students to devise a classification scheme for insects or plants based on the patterns they see.

> An *aesthetic entry point* emphasizes artworks and literature as well as patterns and forms deductible through human senses.

Finally, there is the *experiential entry point*. This seeks to build understanding through hands-on practice. When it is applied to democracy, it is possible to imagine a group of students involved in organizing a "town meeting," working on a local referendum issue, or, as with Comer's students, grilling politicians about their platforms. The experiential entry point to evolution could call on students to breed fruitflies and take note of variations and mutations across generations.

The notion of different entry points is not a new one. Good teachers have always sought ways to make subject matters accessible to diverse students by appealing to their strengths and interests. The means by which teachers accomplish this, however, is not always schematized or conveyed to others. This framework is intended to provide a basis for systematic study, development, and dissemination of the ways teachers help students use their learning styles to engage them in different domains.

In addition to drawing on students' strengths, good teachers are often able to exemplify genuine performances of understanding in a domain. For example, in a history lesson, they make clear that the domain is not just a matter of providing correct names, places, and dates on short-answer quizzes.

Rather, they can show how history works in practice. For example, these teachers can gather evidence from original sources and site visits. They can explain how they interpret evidence and how they weigh the role of human motivation in evaluating conflicting accounts. They can also put what they have learned from the evidence into a coherent and defensible story that is accessible to others (Tuchman, 1982).

In addition to drawing on students' strengths, good teachers are often able to exemplify genuine performances of understanding in a domain.

Teachers who exemplify such performances of understanding, and who "externalize," or reveal, the thought processes used in such performances, are affording their students a cognitive apprenticeship (Collins, Brown, and Newman, 1989). These teachers provide a model for thinking in a domain (Greeno, 1990). It becomes clear that being a practitioner of history or any other domain requires more than isolated facts or "formulaic methods" (Collins, Brown, and Newman, 1989, p. 454). Demonstrating and externalizing domain practices not only model understanding but build needed connections between schools and the outside world.

A further way that teachers provide a cognitive apprenticeship is by connecting their efforts in the classroom to events in the rest of the world. Thus, their efforts are not limited to well-worn problems but offer new and challenging issues in domains. For instance, a social studies teachers might gather evidence and put together a coherent story about why people do not vote or about how democracy is being realized in different Eastern European countries. A science teacher might connect the laws of genetic inheritance to current efforts to map the human genome and the implications of such a mapping. In short, their performances are not just good "school performances" but ones that have meaning in real-world contexts.

There is no doubt that the idea of apprenticeships in education is "trendy." There are books and many articles that deal with this topic (Brown, Collins, and Duguid, 1989; Collins, Brown, and Newman, 1989; Gardner, 1987, 1989, 1990, 1991c; Hamilton, 1990; Lave, 1988; Rogoff, 1990). We do not want to oversell it. Indeed, aspects of certain domains and the learning styles of certain students make traditional "mimetic" forms of instruction useful in some situations (Jackson, 1986). For example, it is unlikely that high schoolers will achieve excellence in a second language without some drill and reiteration of verb forms and pronunciation. It is also true that not all teachers can provide apprenticeships for the many different learners in a class (Palincsar, 1989; Wineburg, 1989).

Nevertheless, the popularity of apprenticeship is based on sound reasoning. Until the advent of mass education, children learned domains in rich and meaningful contexts by observing domain practices and by developing skills by working on tasks the community relied on. This learning afforded regular and informal feedback from those "older and wiser." It also allowed children to draw on diverse strengths and to use tools and other supports provided by the environment and the adults around them (Gardner, 1990; Resnick, 1987). A traditional apprenticeship is a somewhat more formalized system, in which increasing levels of skill are clearly demarcated by the kind of tasks the apprentice is allowed to do. In these highly contextualized circumstances, the great majority of children were able to assume competent roles in their society.

Excellence is unlikely to evolve without engagement in at least one domain.

While outcomes of schooling cannot be divorced from the effects of social values and supports, there are indications that the decontextualized environment of schooling is not engaging (Jackson, 1968; Sarason, 1983). Excellence is unlikely to evolve without engagement in at least one domain. Thus, a growing number of authors have suggested that schools arrange apprenticeships for students with organizations or individuals outside the schools, if the school itself cannot provide them (Fine, 1988; Gardner, 1989, 1991c; Hamilton, 1990; Sarason, 1983).

In addition to using apprenticeships and different entry points, teachers can provide support for diverse learners in other ways. Many researchers and teachers have studied how children working collaboratively help each other to foster understanding (Berger, 1991; Brown and Palincsar, 1989; Brown, 1990; Brown, Collins, and Duguid, 1989; Hatano, 1991). One of the keys to these group efforts is that students attempt to make sense of a complex problem in a domain. Thus, rather than just trying to answer questions on a worksheet, a group of students working together may seek to grasp a concept such as density by experimenting with liquids and objects of different size, shape, and weight.

Another significant element of these collaborative efforts is that they call on interpersonal and intrapersonal intelligences. Brown and Palincsar (1989) have found that an important component in cooperative learning is that children are taught about effective group and metacognitive processes. For example, in the metacognitive realm, these researchers have coached children to ask their classmates to summarize, clarify, and formulate questions in order to help group members consolidate their understanding. Eventually these metacognitive techniques become a natural part of the group's discussions. In the realm of group process, students need to learn that each member of the group can play important but different and complementary roles. Thus, one student could have specific knowledge or expertise to help the group, another might provoke understanding by being critical or a doubter, a third might keep track of unanswered elements or new questions that pop up. This person can remind the group of questions that help its members stretch their knowledge even further (Brown and Palincsar, 1989).

> **Students need to learn that each member of the group can play important but different and complementary roles.**

An important part of group learning experiences is that students not only work together, but that each student is responsible for being able to report on the results of the group's effort (Hatano, 1990). Thus, while members may play different roles, and while some may be more vocal than others, all must work to ensure everyone understands the problem and can give an account of what the group has done. In this group effort, children gain domain-related knowledge, as well as intrapersonal understanding of their own strengths and interpersonal understanding by seeing the needs and contributions of others.

Like apprenticeships, collaborative learning reflects properties of learning outside of school (Brown, Collins, and Duguid, 1989; Resnick, 1987). In the nonschool world, no one is expected to know all the information, play all the roles, and rely solely on himself to work out complex problems. In essence, "intelligence" is distributed among many resources, including other people, books, and equipment like blackboards and calculators (Gardner, 1991b; Pea, 1990; Resnick, 1987). Analogously, in collaborative learning, neither teachers nor students need to know everything. Instead, they need to know how to use a variety of resources and thinking strategies to develop their understanding (Brown, 1990).

> "Intelligence" is distributed among many resources, including other people, books, and equipment like blackboards and calculators.

Cooperative learning has been helpful in many classrooms (Collins, Brown, and Newman, 1989; Brown and Palincsar, 1989). This technique appears especially useful among students whose communities or cultures are not especially enamored of competitive social interaction (Fine, 1988). Collaborative studying, as researched by Uri Triesman, has also been a road to achievement in mathematics among black college students. However, like apprenticeship, cooperative learning is not the only route to excellence for all children in all domains. If there were one such route, no doubt it would have been found by now.

Rather than looking toward a formula, we look for teachers who recognize not only individual strengths, but the potential for these strengths to be exercised in meaningful ways. Rather than relying on a formula, teachers need to be able to employ and combine a variety of strategies to engage these diverse strengths. One such strategy uses children's intellectual strengths as levers through domains. Another looks to broach domains through entry points that are harmonious with students' styles. Other strategies play on the fact that the stuff of a domain is distributed among different resources in rich contexts. Apprenticeships and collaborative learning have brought many of these approaches together. Other existing pedagogies are likely to exist, however, that combine the richness of domains with the various strengths of learners and thereby enable children to engage, understand, and excel. We encourage administrators and policy makers to allow teachers the time to develop and explore these and other approaches.

FORMS OF CURRICULUM AND ASSESSMENT THAT ENGENDER UNDERSTANDING

It is evident that children who have competences or learning styles that are not synchronous with those called on in schools will have difficulty enhancing their competences and mastering school material. In addition, it is apparent that children whose physical and emotional needs go unmet will also have problems learning. What is less obvious is that many children who *do* have intellectual strengths, social supports, and even grades typical of "successful" students are not necessarily excelling. Again, our definition of excellence rests on high-level *performances of understanding*. These require an individual to apply facts, skills, and principles to complex problems successfully in domains not previously encountered.

> ...many children who *do* have intellectual strengths, social supports, and even grades typical of "successful" students are not necessarily excelling.

Some of the clearest evidence that successful students often fail to understand comes from research on learning in physics. In one study, investigators asked Johns Hopkins' students who had varying amounts of formal physics coursework to solve problems involving the concept of velocity. Students were given a diagram consisting of a pendulum made up of a ball tied to the end of a string. They were asked to indicate what path the ball would take if the string were cut when the ball had travelled halfway through its course (i.e., when the string is at 90 degrees to the surface below it). More than half the students who had a year or more of formal instruction in physics drew a line showing the ball dropping straight down (Caramazza, McCloskey, and Green, 1981). In other research using a task-analysis approach, an MIT undergraduate was asked to play a videogame in which a creature was to be guided across a computer screen according to the laws of Newtonian physics. The students had trouble abandoning the same Aristotelian principles that elementary school children relied on to play the game (DiSessa, 1982).

Although these successful college students were taught and could talk about Newton's laws, they did not demonstrate performances of understanding. Instead, their "naive physics and classroom physics stood side by side but unrelated" (DiSessa, 1982, p. 59). With problems of a type they had not encountered before and been explicitly tutored to solve, they did not summon up domain principles but reverted to childlike knowledge.

A less rigorously studied example illustrates lack of understanding in the realm of social sciences. Among those who have been admitted to leading universities are at least some students who harbor simplistic stereotypes about various racial and ethnic groups. Increasingly, some of these college students have resorted to acts of violence and vandalism against those they perceive as not belonging (Farrell, 1988; Wilkerson, 1988).

It is likely that these students had a reasonably thorough exposure to American history, the civil rights movement, the idea of equal rights, and political science. They may be well aware of affirmative action and other programs that attempt to increase diversity on college campuses. They may even realize that many of those they deem not to belong are as well or better qualified as they are. Yet, despite their previous education, such students reveal little ability to restrain naive and even primitive behavior. Among the many deficits in their understanding is an inability to apply the principle that minorities have a right not to be dominated by the majority.

We believe that students do not demonstrate performances of understanding because they are usually asked only for rote, ritualistic, or conventional performances (Gardner, 1991a). By this, we mean that their performances are limited to the routines of symbol manipulation they learn in school. Successful "A" students can plug variables into formulae, and can manipulate formulae in a way called on in traditional testing (see Chi, Glaser, and Rees, 1982). Outside of an exam format, however, many physics students are stumped. The social sciences present a similar picture. No doubt at least some of those who violated others' rights could compose an essay on democracy or the Constitution; yet in genuine social interactions many students revert to thinking in simplistic stereotypes.

Why do so many students seem stuck in conventional performances rather than demonstrating performances of understanding? Part of the answer has to do with issues discussed in the preceding section. Students are often called on to use a limited range of intelligences and are rewarded for their quantitative-logical styles. Also, too few students have experienced domains as they operate beyond school walls. There, the problems are not always clear cut and not always assigned. Information about when to invoke knowledge and principles is not contained in "the question" (Csikszentmihalyi, 1988). We believe this state of affairs exists largely because of the kind of testing Americans have come to rely on.

> **Students are often called on to use a limited range of intelligences and are rewarded for their quantitative-logical styles.**

Standardized tests have one primary virtue: They make it possible readily to compare students, or school districts, or even countries. This technology has been very convenient for colleges looking for comparable indicators across districts, families in search of prestigious public schools, and policy makers who like to beat the drum of international competitiveness. Unfortunately, it has not been notably beneficial for students or teachers.

Standardized tests show which children can answer fragmented, puzzlelike problems in a short period of time. Because such tests often carry such high stakes, they warp classroom practice (Fredericksen and Collins, 1989). They encourage teachers to look toward "test-taking skills," and to use short-answer tests and other practices that bear little relationship to high achievement in authentic domains.

Furthermore, these tests are not "intelligence fair." They evaluate all students primarily on the basis of linguistic and logical-mathematical intelligences, and they reward facility with abstract notations rather than the range of skills that go into genuine domains. Tests like these cannot reveal how well a child can use spatial and bodily-kinesthetic competences to solve mechanical problems. At best, they ask children to solve two-dimensional visual rotation problems. They test competences relevant to the mechanical domain only insofar as they require the student to use a pencil to fill in exam bubbles.

If educators are looking to foster excellent dancers, anthropologists, teachers, physicists, mechanics, historians, and other practitioners, standardized tests are not very helpful. What we need instead are what Fredericksen and Collins (1989) have called "systemically valid" assessments. These induce "curricular and instructional changes that foster the development of the cognitive traits that the test is designed to measure" (Fredericksen and Collins, 1989, p. 1).

We see promise for excellence in curriculum and assessment that allow students to develop and deploy the wide array of their strengths in genuine domains over time. The work of Project Spectrum is one such effort for preschoolers and early elementary-age children. Spectrum assumes that each child is capable of developing his or her strengths in one or more domains. To help parents and educators uncover this potential, the project makes use of intelligence-fair assessment and curriculum. Thus, children work with materials that are directly linked to the abilities being assessed. Jay was not asked to talk about or draw machinery or to fill in bubbles. Instead, he worked to fit together the pieces of the machines in front of him. This accomplishment clearly and fairly demonstrated his bodily-kinesthetic and spatial skills, as well as his ability to concentrate when engaged in mechanical tasks. Similarly, language is not evaluated by asking children to generate rhymes or repeat words. Rather, children play with a "storyboard" containing lively animals, people, and scenery and are encouraged to use these as prompts for storytelling.

> Spectrum assumes that each child is capable of developing his or her strengths in one or more domains.

Furthermore, Spectrum is not a one-shot assessment that is kept secret until the moment of administration. Instead, its materials are organized in learning centers around the classroom. The learning centers are designed to help children use their competences in a range of domains, among these mathematics, science, visual arts, dance, athletics, creative language, and reporting. As in authentic learning in all domains, children develop by working with these materials regularly.

The blurring of curriculum and assessment helps teachers, parents, and researchers gain a better idea of a child's strengths.

Teachers and researchers observe the children throughout the year. They periodically collect samples of their work and complete observation checklists. Occasionally a child is scored on performance in a specific domain, for example, in using creative language with the storyboard. This information is not evaluated with the aim of ranking and ordering children—a primary aim of standardized testing. Rather, the result is a "Spectrum Profile," intended to help those concerned with the child's development. The profile is a short, narrative, nontechnical report that describes the child's strengths. It suggests activities that parents can carry out as a follow-up to those in the classroom to support a child's strengths and build up areas that are less strong. Along with the profile, parents received the "Parent Activities Handbook" with concrete examples of activities they can structure using readily available and inexpensive materials (Krechevsky, 1991; Gardner and Hatch, 1990).

> The blurring of curriculum and assessment helps teachers, parents, and researchers gain a better idea of a child's strengths.

We also see promise for excellence in project-based curriculum and assessments that focus on genuine, rather than ritualistic, performances in a domain. The work of our video-portfolio research project is aimed in this direction. Its researchers are currently exploring how teachers help to foster and assess projects in five "nonprivileged" elementary schools in New England and the Midwest.

Based on our work with teachers, project members are developing description and evaluation sheets. These lay out critical dimensions of projects and presentations in different domains. For example, they provide a taxonomy of different resources that might be useful for a research report in history. The taxonomy is not intended to dictate which resources a teacher requires or a student uses. Nor is it a net to catch students whose projects fail to meet the standards for use of resources. Rather, its purpose is to enable ongoing discussion between teachers and students about the many resources that exist and to select from these ones that may be appropriate to a given project. Instead of just going reflexively to an encyclopedia or a magazine, children can learn about and use many kinds of resources just as historians do. Different resources are available for different competences: Interviewing, touring sites, and reading may all be used and are useful in different projects.

Because projects take place over time, a successful project usually demands sustained engagement. This is one ingredient for excellence. Because projects require effort and planning, they counter the notion of "you've either got it or you don't." Rather, success comes through drafts, revisions, and reflection. Another virtue of projects is that their goal or outcome need not be captured wholly or even partly in language or mathematics.

> Because projects take place over time, a successful project usually demands sustained engagement.

Depending on the domain, a child can work through ideas in symbolic forms that rely on other intelligences: in sketches or three-dimensional models, in gesture, or in music. Thus, projects permit a child to make use of a variety of ways of knowing. Furthermore, by working over time and using different underlying competences, both facile symbol manipulators and those with other strengths are less likely to deliver ritualized performances and more likely to demonstrate performances of understanding.

In the opening section of this paper, we saw how project work helped Kimberly engage her bodily-kinesthetic, musical, and interpersonal intelligences. Her ability to demonstrate understanding in dance and drama using these intelligences earned her acceptance into an arts magnet program. Another example can be drawn from the work of Shirley Brice Heath (1983), mentioned earlier.

Heath taught ethnography skills to a fifth-grade science class, in which nearly all the students were rural black boys who were working far below grade level in science. She then had them use these skills over eight weeks to find out how successful local gardeners' explanations and methods could be understood in terms of scientific theories and practices. To figure this out, the boys gathered information from newspaper clippings and science books, and they interviewed local growers. They also conducted their own gardening experiments. Finally, they produced a booklet containing charts, photographs, descriptions, and scientific explanations of the growers' produce and methods.

Thus, throughout the project, the students could tap their various intelligences, bring them to bear on the problem, and help each other. They could also use a full range of learning styles. For example, they employed experiential and narrative styles in interviewing and gathering life histories. In experimenting, they may have used a quantitative as well as an experiential entry point. They could access foundational approaches in grappling with folk and scientific theories about gardening. The aesthetic style was called on in designing the booklet and cataloging illustrations of plant species.

> Throughout the project, the students could tap their various intelligences, bring them to bear on the problem, and help each other.

Heath actively worked to get the youngsters to build links between local folk knowledge and explanations, and science's theory, experimentation, use of multiple sources of evidence, and verification. Thus, unlike the physics students' knowledge, which was frozen in the symbols of classroom instruction and testing, the boys' knowledge was flexible. They could "translate" explanations back and forth between folk knowledge and scientific knowledge (Heath, 1983, p. 321). It is also crucial to note that the project had meaning for the boys because it broke down barriers between the school and the community. This was evident beyond the classroom walls, since members of the community who rarely had contact with the school before came to visit and volunteer information.

At the end of the eight-week project, all 23 children passed a "standardized unit science test." None had ever passed such a test in his entire school career (Heath, 1983, p. 321). No doubt passing the exam was an important accomplishment in these youngsters' school life. We believe, however, that if the aim of education is understanding, such an accomplishment is gravy. The heart of their accomplishment lies in their high-level performance in the domains of botany and cultural anthropology. They had flexible knowledge of the principles, facts, and skills in these areas and could use them to answer many previously unencountered and complex questions. In short, they showed they could excel.

CONCLUSION AND RECOMMENDATIONS

This paper has set out a definition of excellence and asserts two interacting levels that are needed for excellence to occur. Excellence rests on many factors at the individual level as well as many at the social level. Within individuals there is an array of intelligences and learning styles. These need to be developed by extended and meaningful engagement in authentic domains. This engagement allows individuals to use a domain's facts, skills, and practices in a flexible way to solve new problems. When they regularly use this flexibility to solve complex problems in a domain, they have achieved excellence.

> **If schools seek to support excellence, they must be designed to involve diverse competences over time in genuine domain practices.**

But engagement is not just a matter of what is in the head. Many aspects of the wider society and of schools can promote or hinder sustained engagement. These include myths and practices that render domains more accessible to some than to others. It also includes dissonances or harmonies between schools and communities. Within the schools, matters of pedagogy, curriculum, and assessment are crucial. If schools seek to support excellence, they must be designed to involve diverse competences over time in genuine domain practices.

Clearly, excellence is more readily defined than realized. Nevertheless, we see some reasons for optimism. By allowing that excellence is based in many components, rather than just one or two, we can begin to construct designs that make excellence possible for more American schoolchildren. We have noted ways to support excellence en route to this point, but emphasize below recommendations that apply especially to schools.

1. Recognize that excellence is not one thing. Rather, it requires a broad range of human competences and is realized in diverse domains.

2. Excellence also requires a social environment that supports the long-term development of individuals' competences. Developing children's competences often builds on synchronous forces between schools and other social institutions. Thus,

school structure and governance should foster a synergistic alignment of school, family, and community.

3. Encourage and support teachers in efforts to develop diverse competences over time through cooperative learning, cognitive apprenticeships, and projects.

4. Encourage teachers to take advantage of the reality that domains of knowledge are complex bodies of facts, principles, and practices and not small splotches of ink on paper. Support them in efforts to design curricula and pedagogies that build on genuine practices in a domain and that are meaningful to students and members of their community.

5. Provide forms of assessment that are fair to those with diverse strengths and that help them to develop. Assessment needs to be ongoing and to use the media or symbol systems that are sensible for the competences and domains it is testing. It should provide feedback that is beneficial to students, parents, and teachers.

6. Seek as a marker of excellence performances of understanding: those in which children flexibly apply facts, principles, and skills of a domain to solve problems they have not encountered before.

Finally, we wish to underscore that excellence is not a single point of arrival. It is better to think of it as a series of steps or degrees, marked by performances of understanding. These steps are undertaken by those who have opportunities to take risks and who are supported through failures and successes in their efforts to reach high standards. The steps are spurred on by engagement, reflection, and commitment both on the part of individual students and those concerned with their development.

REFERENCES

Armstrong, J. (1980). *Participation of Women in Mathematics: An Overview.* Denver, CO: Education Commission of the States.

Ascher, C. (1988). "Improving the School-Home Connection for Poor and Minority Urban Students." *The Urban Review, 20*(2): 109–23.

Bailyn, B. (1960). *Education in the Forming of American Society.* Chapel Hill: University of North Carolina Press.

Barrett, J. (1990). "The Case for More School Days." *The Atlantic, 266*(5): 78–106.

Bastian, A., Fruchter, N., Gittell, M., Greer, C., and Haskins, K. (1986). *Choosing Equality: The Case for Democractic Schooling.* Philadelphia: Temple University Press.

Berger, R. (1991). "Building a School Culture Where Quality is Cool." *Harvard Education Letter, 7*(2): 5–7.

Binet, A. and Simon, T. (1973). "New Methods for the Diagnoses of the Intellectual Level of Subnormals," *L'annee Psychologique, 12.* In E. S. Kite (trans.), *The Development of Intelligence in Children* (pp. 37–90). New York: Arno Press. (Original work published in 1905.)

Birch, H. and Gussow, J. (1970). *Disadvantaged Children: Health, Nutrition, and School Failure.* New York: Harcourt Brace Jovanovich.

Bloom, B. (1985). *Developing Talent in Young People.* New York: Ballantine.

Boring, E. (1923). "Intelligence as the Tests Test It." *The New Republic, 34*: 35–36.

Brown, A. L. (1990). *Distributed Expertise in the Classroom.* Paper presented at the Annual Meeting of the American Educational Research Association, Boston, MA, April 1990.

Brown, A. L. and Palincsar, A. S. (1989). "Guided, Cooperative Learning and Individual Knowledge Acquisition," in L. B. Resnick (ed.), *Knowing, Learning, and Instruction: Essays in Honor of Robert Glaser.* Hillsdale, NJ: Lawrence Erlbaum.

Brown, J. S., Collins, A., and Duguid, P. (1989). "Situated Cognition and the Culture of Learning." *Educational Researcher, 18*(1): 32–42.

Caramazza, A., McCloskey, M., and Green, B. (1981). "Naive Beliefs in 'Sophisticated' Subjects: Misconceptions about Trajectories of Objects." *Cognition, 9*: 37–75.

Chi, M., Glaser, R., and Rees, E. (1982). "Expertise in Problem Solving," in R. Sternberg (ed.), *Advances in the Psychology of Human Intelligence.* Hillsdale, NJ: Lawrence Erlbaum.

Chipman, S., Brush, L., and Wilson, D. (1985). *Women and Mathematics: Balancing the Equation.* Hillsdale, NJ: Lawrence Erlbaum.

Cohen, D. (1989). "'Joining Forces': An Alliance of Sectors Envisioned to Aid the Most Troubled Young." *Education Week,* March 15, 1989, pp. 7–12.

Collins, A., Brown, J. S., and Newman, S. E. (1989). "Cognitive Apprenticeship: Teaching the Crafts of Reading, Writing, and Mathematics," in L. B. Resnick (ed.), *Knowing, Learning, and Instruction: Essays in Honor of Robert Glaser.* Hillsdale, NJ: Lawrence Erlbaum.

Comer, J. (1980). *School Power.* New York: The Free Press.

Comer, J. (1984). "Home-School Relationships as They Affect the Academic Success of Children." *Education and Urban Society, 16*(3): 323–37.

Comer, J. (1988a). "Educating Poor Minority Children." *Scientific American, 259*(5): 42–48.

Comer, J. (1988b). "Effective Schools: Why They Rarely Exist for At-Risk Elementary School and Adolescent Students," in *School Success for Students at Risk: Analysis and Recommendations of the Council of Chief State School Officers.* Orlando, FL: Harcourt Brace Jovanovich.

Commission on Minority Participation in Education and American Life. (1988). *One Third of a Nation.* Washington, DC: American Council on Education and Education Commission of the States.

Csikszentmihalyi, M. (1987). "Society, Culture, and Person: A Systems Theory of Creativity," in R. Sternberg (ed.), *The Nature of Creativity.* Cambridge: Cambridge University Press.

Csikszentmihalyi, M. (1988). "Motivation and Creativity: Toward a Synthesis of Structural and Energetic Approaches to Cognition." *New Ideas in Psychology, 6*(2): 159–76.

Csikszentmihalyi, M. (1990). "Literacy and Intrinsic Motivation." *Daedalus, 119*(2): 115–40.

Csikszentmihalyi, M. and Robinson, R. (1986). "Culture, Time, and the Development of Talent," in R. J. Sternberg (ed.), *Conceptions of Giftedness.* Cambridge: Cambridge University Press.

DiSessa, A. (1982). "Unlearning Aristotelian Physics: A Study of Knowledge-Based Learning." *Cognitive Science, 6*: 37–75.

Eysenck, H. (1981). *The Intelligence Controversy.* New York: Wiley.

Farrell, C. (1988). "Black Students Seen Facing 'New Racism' on Many Campuses." *Chronicle of Higher Education,* January 27, 1988, pp. A1, A36–8.

Feldman, D. (1980). *Beyond Universals in Cognitive Development.* New York: Ablex.

Feldman, D. (1986). *Nature's Gambit.* New York: Basic Books.

Fine, M. (1986). "Why Urban Adolescents Drop into and out of Public High School." *Teachers College Record, 87*(3): 393–409.

Fine, M. (1988). "De-institutionalizing Educational Inequity: Contexts That Constrict and Construct the Lives and Minds of Public-School Adolescents," in *School Success for Students at Risk: Analysis and Recommendations of the Council of Chief State School Officers.* Orlando, FL: Harcourt Brace Jovanovich.

Fordham, S. and Ogbu, J. (1986). "Black Students' School Success: Coping with the Burden of 'Acting White.'" *The Urban Review, 18*(3): 176–206.

Fredericksen, J. and Collins, A. (1989). "A Systems Theory of Educational Testing." *Educational Researcher, 18*(9): 27–32.

Freire, P. (1989). *Learning to Question: A Pedagogy of Liberation.* New York: Continuum.

Gardner, H. (1983). *Frames of Mind: The Theory of Multiple Intelligences.* New York: Basic Books.

Gardner, H. (1987). "An Individual-centered Curriculum," in *The Schools We've Got, the Schools We Need.* Washington, DC: Council of Chief State School Officers and the American Association of Colleges of Teacher Education.

Gardner, H. (1988). "Creativity: An Interdisciplinary Perspective." *Journal of Creativity Research, 1:* 8–26.

Gardner, H. (1989). *To Open Minds: Chinese Clues to the Dilemma of Contemporary Education.* New York: Basic Books.

Gardner, H. (1990). "The Difficulties of School: Probable Causes, Possible Cures." *Daedalus, 119*(2): 85–113.

Gardner, H. (1991a). *The Unschooled Mind: How Children Think and How Schools Should Teach.* New York: Basic Books.

Gardner, H. (1991b). *Intelligence in Seven Phases.* Paper delivered at the Centennial of the Harvard Graduate School of Education, September 1991. In H. Gardner (1993), *Multiple Intelligences: The Theory in Practice.* New York: Basic Books.

Gardner, H. (1991c). "The School of the Future," in J. Brockman (ed.), *Ways of Knowing: The Reality Club, 3.* Englewood Cliffs, NJ: Prentice-Hall.

Gardner, H. and Hatch, T. (1990). "Multiple Intelligences Go to School: Educational Implications of the Theory of Multiple Intelligences." *Educational Researcher, 18*(8): 147–50.

Gardner, J. W. (1961). *Excellence: Can We be Equal and Excellent Too?* New York: Harper and Brothers.

Giroux, H. (1988). *Schooling and the Struggle for Public Life: Critical Pedagogy in the Modern Age.* Minneapolis: University of Minnesota Press.

Goodnow, J. J. (1990). "The Socialization of Cognition: What's Involved?" in J. Stigler, R. A. Schweder, and G. Herdt (eds.), *Cultural Psychology: Essays on Comparative Human Development.* Cambridge: Cambridge University Press.

Goody, J. and Watt, I. (1963). "The Consequences of Literacy," in P. Giglioli (ed.), *Language and Social Context.* Harmondsworth, Middlesex: Penguin.

Gould, S. J. (1981). *The Mismeasure of Man.* New York: Norton.

Green, M. (1987). *Minorities on Campus: A Handbook for Enhancing Diversity.* Washington, DC: American Council on Education.

Greeno, J. (1990). *Number Sense as Knowing in a Conceptual Domain.* Palo Alto: Institute for Research in Learning.

Guilford, J. P. (1967). *The Nature of Human Intelligence.* New York: McGraw Hill.

Hamilton, S. (1990). *Apprenticeship for Adulthood: Preparing Youth for the Future.* New York: The Free Press.

Hatano, G. (1991). "Sharing Cognition through Collective Comprehension Activity," in L. Resnick, J. M. Levine, and S. Teasley (eds.), *Perspectives on Socially Shared Cognition.* Washington, DC: American Psychological Association.

Hayes, J. R. (1985). "Three Problems in Teaching General Skills," in J. Segal, S. Chipman, and R. Glaser (eds.), *Thinking and Learning Skills,* Vol. 1. Hillsdale, NJ: Lawrence Erlbaum.

Heath, S. B. (1983). *Ways with Words.* New York: Cambridge University Press.

Heath, S. B. and McLaughlin, M. W. (1987). "A Child Resource Policy: Moving Beyond Dependence on School and Family." *Phi Delta Kappan, 68*(8): 576–80.

Henderson, A. (1987). *The Evidence Continues to Grow: Parent Involvement Improves Student Achievement.* Columbia, MD: National Committee for Citizens in Education.

Herman, J. and Yeh, J. (1983). "Some Effects of Parent Involvement in Schools." The *Urban Review, 15*(1): 11–17.

Hofstadter, R. (1963). *Anti-Intellectualism in American Life.* New York: Alfred A. Knopf.

Horowitz, H. (1987). *Campus Life: Undergraduate Cultures from the End of the Eighteenth Century to the Present.* New York: Alfred A. Knopf.

Jackson, P. (1968). *Life in Classrooms.* New York: Holt, Rhinehart, and Winston.

Jackson, P. (1986). *The Practice of Teaching.* New York: Teachers College Press.

Jensen, A. (1969). "How Much Can We Boost IQ and Scholastic Achievement?" *Harvard Educational Review, 39*(1): 1–123.

Kahle, J. B. (ed.). (1985). *Women in Science: A Report from the Field.* London: Falmer Press.

Keating, D. (1984). "The Emperor's New Clothes: The 'New Look' in Intelligence Research," in R. Sternberg (ed.), *Advances in the Psychology of Human Intelligence, Vol. 2*: 1–45. Hillsdale, NJ: Lawrence Erlbaum.

Kornhaber, M. and Gardner, H. (1991). "Critical Thinking Across Multiple Intelligences," in S. Maclure and P. Davies (eds.), *Learning to Think; Thinking to Learn*. Proceedings of the 1989 OECD Conference Organized by the Centre for Educational Research and Innovation. Oxford: Pergamon Press.

Krechevsky, M. (1991). "Project Spectrum: An Innovative Assessment Alternative." *Educational Leadership, 48*(5): 43–48.

Krechevsky, M. and Gardner, H. (1990). "The Emergence and Nurturance of Multiple Intelligences," in M. J. A. Howe (ed.), *Encouraging the Development of Exceptional Abilities and Talents*. Leicester: British Psychological Society.

Lave, J. (1988). *Cognition in Practice: Mind, Mathematics, and Culture in Everyday Life*. Cambridge: Cambridge University Press.

LeVine, R. A. and White, M. I. (1986). *Human Conditions: The Cultural Basis of Educational Development*. New York and London: Routledge and Kegan Paul.

Lewis, M. (1979). *The Culture of Inequality*. New York: New American Library.

Lightfoot, S. L. (1978). *Worlds Apart: Relationships between Families and Schools*. New York: Basic Books.

Lightfoot, S. L. (1980). "Exploring Family-School Relationships: A Prelude to Curricular Designs and Strategies," in R. L. Sinclair (ed.), *A Two-Way Street: Home School Cooperation in Curriculum Decisionmaking*. Boston: Institute for Responsive Education.

Malkus, U., Feldman, D., and Gardner, H. (1988). "Dimensions of Mind in Early Childhood," in A. D. Pelligrini (ed.), *Psychological Bases of Early Childhood Education*. Chichester: Wiley.

Ogbu, J. (1978). *Minority Education and Caste: The American System in Cross-Cultural Perspective*. New York: Academic Press.

Olson, D. (1977). "From Utterance to Text. The Bias of Language in Speech and Writing." *Harvard Educational Review, 47*: 257–81.

Olson, L. (1988). "Children Flourish Here: Eight Teachers and a Theory Changed a School." *Education Week*, January 27, 1988, pp. 1, 18–19.

Orfield, G. (1988). "Race, Income, and Educational Inequality: Students and Schools at Risk in the 1980s," in *School Success for Students at Risk: Analysis and Recommendations of the Council of Chief State School Officers*. Orlando, FL: Harcourt Brace Jovanovich.

Orfield, G. and Peskin, L. (1990). "Metropolitan High Schools: Income, Race, and Inequality," in D. E. Mitchell and M. E. Goertz (eds.), *Education Politics for the New Century*. London and New York: Falmer Press.

Palincsar, A. S. (1989). "Less Charted Waters." *Educational Researcher, 18*(4): 5–7.

Patterson, J. T. (1986). *America's Struggle Against Poverty.* Cambridge: Harvard University Press.

Pea, R. D. (1990). *Distributed Intelligence and Education.* Paper presented at the Annual Meeting of the American Educational Research Association, Boston, MA, April 1990.

Perkins, D., Crismond, D., Simmons, R., and Unger, C. (in preparation). *Inside Understanding.*

Perkins, D. and Salomon, G. (1987). "Transfer and Teaching Thinking," in J. Bishop, J. Lochhead, and D. Perkins (eds.), *Thinking: Progress in Research and Teaching.* Hillsdale, NJ: Lawrence Erlbaum.

Polanyi, M. (1958). *Personal Knowledge: Towards a Post-Critical Philosophy.* London: Routledge and Kegan Paul.

Powell, A. G., Farrar, E., and Cohen, D. (1985). *The Shopping Mall High School: Winners and Losers in the Educational Marketplace.* Boston: Houghton Mifflin.

Quality Education for Minorities Project. (1990). *Education That Works: An Action Plan for the Education of Minorities.* Cambridge: Massachusetts Institute of Technology.

Resnick, L. (1987). "Learning In School and Out." *Educational Researcher, 16*(9): 13–20.

Rogoff, B. (1990). *Apprenticeships in Thinking: Cognitive Development in Social Context.* New York and Oxford: Oxford University Press.

Ryan, W. (1976). *Blaming the Victim.* New York: Vintage Books.

Sarason, S. (1983). *Schooling in America: Scapegoat and Salvation.* New York: The Free Press.

Sizer, T. (1984). *Horace's Compromise.* Boston: Houghton Mifflin.

Sniderman, P. (1989). *Race and Inequality: A Study in American Values.* Chatham, NJ: Chatham House Publishers.

Spearman, C. (1927). *The Abilities of Man.* New York: Macmillan.

Sternberg, R. (1990). *Metaphors of Mind: Conceptions of the Nature of Intelligence.* Cambridge: Cambridge University Press.

Stevenson, H. (1990). *Contexts of Achievement: A Study of American, Chinese, and Japanese Children.* Chicago: University of Chicago Press.

Terman, L. (1916). *The Measurement of Intelligence: An Explanation of and a Complete Guide for the Use of the Stanford Revision and Extension of the Binet-Simon Intelligence Scale.* Boston: Houghton Mifflin.

Terman, L. (1919). *The Intelligence of School Children*. Boston: Houghton Mifflin.

Terman, L. (1923). *Intelligence Tests and School Reorganization*. Yonkers-on-Hudson, NY: World Book Company.

Thomas, G. E. and Hirsch, D. J. (1989). "Blacks," in A. Levine (ed.), *Shaping Higher Education's Future*. San Francisco: Jossey-Bass.

Thurstone, L. (1938). *Primary Mental Abilities*. Chicago: University of Chicago Press.

Trubowitz, S. (1984). *When a College Works with a Public School*. Boston: Institute for Responsive Education.

Tuchman, B. (1982). *Practicing History*. New York: Ballantine Books.

Walters, J. and Gardner, H. (1985). "The Development and Education of Intelligences," in F. Link (ed.), *Essays on the Intelligence*. Washington, DC: Curriculum Development Associates.

White, M. (1987). *The Japanese Educational Challenge: A Commitment to Children*. New York: The Free Press.

Wilkerson, I. (1988). "Campus Blacks Feel Racism's Nuances." *The New York Times*, April 17, 1988, pp. 1, 34–35.

Wilson, R. and Justiz, M. J. (1987/1988). "Minorities in Higher Education: Confronting a Time Bomb." *Educational Record, 68*(4): 8–14.

Wilson, S. H. (1983). "Strengthening Connections between Schools and Communities: A Method of Improving Urban Schools." *Urban Education, 18*(2): 153–77.

Wilson, W. J. (1987). *The Truly Disadvantaged: The Inner City, the Underclass, and Public Policy*. Chicago: Chicago University Press.

Wineburg, S. (1989). "Remembrance of Theories Past." *Educational Researcher, 18*(4): 7–10.

Acknowledgments: Publication of this landmark paper would not have been possible without the contributions of many people. First, gratitude is owed to Edmund Gordon, who coordinated the New York State "Standards of Excellence" project for which this paper was originally written. Dr. Gordon's wise and experienced leadership guided that project in pragmatic and useful directions, so that it could make a real difference to New York schools. For support of the research discussed in this paper, we would like to thank the William T. Grant Foundation, the Lilly Endowment, the Rockefeller Brothers Fund, the Rockefeller Foundation, and the Spencer Foundation. Finally, we thank NCREST editor Elizabeth Lesnick and communications director Diane Harrington for polishing the draft and producing this volume.

Section 3

... to Practice

ndergirding Gardner's theory of multiple intelligences is the belief that "there is no recipe for a multiple intelligences education," but rather "some notions about an education framed in the 'spirit' of multiple intelligences." Gardner further envisions "an ensemble of scholastic visions . . . teased out or constructed from . . . the theory of multiple intelligences," providing a "countervision that categorizes and celebrates the astonishing range of the human mind" (Gardner, 1993, p. 66).

To take an emergent theory and put it into practice is no easy task. The implementation of any theory is impacted by the interpretive filter of the innovators. In the case of multiple intelligences, a variety of programs and models are at various stages of conception and development.

Showcased in this section are five articles that focus on the practical applications of Gardner's "frames of mind." While Gardner seems willing to let practitioners create the actual hands-on programs, he is pragmatically involved in a number of projects that shepherd his theory along those practical lines.

In the opening article, "Multiple Intelligences Go to School: Educational Implications of the Theory of Multiple Intelligences," Howard Gardner and Thomas Hatch review three separate projects: at the junior/senior high level (Arts PROPEL); at the elementary level (the Key School in Indianapolis); and at the preschool/kindergarten level (Project Spectrum). The authors critique the early results of these programs and leave the doors open for future revisions.

Tina Blythe and Howard Gardner lay out their vision of an MI school that focuses on deep understanding in "A School for All Intelligences." They share ideas from several pilot projects and describe how the community provides fertile ground for learning. In addition, Blythe and Gardner develop the concepts of "thematic ties" and "museums" where children are free to explore and expand their intelligences, and conclude with a call for a "full-court press" of support from community leaders and the entire educational arena.

Developing a thoughtful classroom through the application of multiple intelligences theory forms the foundation for yet another practical discussion in which Gardner joins colleagues Noel White and Tina Blythe. In their thought-provoking essay, "Multiple Intelligences Theory: Creating the Thoughtful Classroom," the authors question how to make sense of the peaks and valleys in students' abilities without lowering standards or blaming teachers for a challenge that occurs naturally in classrooms across the country. Their premise of providing multiple paths to understanding and their mandate for diversifying assessment encourage further investigation.

The two articles that close this section describe multiple intelligences projects. In "Multiple Intelligences in Action," Bruce Campbell explains the model he uses in his multiage classroom of third, fourth, and fifth graders to immerse students in the multiple intelligences through a network of seven learning centers. His description of the projects and their alignment to district and curriculum goals sheds light on the accountability factors involved.

In an example of a more extensive project, Patricia Bolanos, principal at Key Elementary School, tells how she and her staff are successfully applying Gardner's theory as a model for a whole school. The MI project began in 1987 with the Key Elementary School and was extended in 1993 to include a local middle school. In her article, "From Theory to Practice: Indianapolis' Key School Applies Howard Gardner's Multiple Intelligences Theory to the Classroom," Bolanos inspires visionary planning as she discusses the Key School's plans for the future.

Led by Gardner's own vision of how multiple intelligences theory is best put into practice, this set of articles provides a variety of ideas for implementation—from project designs, Arts PROPEL, and Project Spectrum developed by theoretical researchers to the dynamic ideas and projects of practitioners in classrooms and schools.

REFERENCE

Gardner, H. (1993). *Multiple intelligences: The theory in practice.* New York: Basic Books.

Multiple Intelligences Go to School: Educational Implications of the Theory of Multiple Intelligences

by Howard Gardner and Thomas Hatch

A new approach to the conceptualization and assessment of human intelligences is described. According to Gardner's Theory of Multiple Intelligences, each human being is capable of seven relatively independent forms of information processing, with individuals differing from one another in the specific profile of intelligences that they exhibit. The range of human intelligences is best assessed through contextually based, "intelligence-fair" instruments. Three research projects growing out of the theory are described. Preliminary data secured from Project Spectrum, an application in early childhood, indicate that even 4- and 5-year-old children exhibit distinctive profiles of strength and weakness. Moreover, measures of the various intelligences are largely independent and tap abilities other than those measured by standard intelligence tests.

Despite swings of the pendulum between theoretical and applied concerns, the concept of intelligence has remained central to the field of psychology. In the wake of the Darwinian revolution, when scientific psychology was just beginning, many scholars became interested in the development of intelligence across species. The late 19th and early 20th centuries were punctuated by volumes that delineated levels of intelligence across species and within the human species (Baldwin,

From *Educational Researcher*, vol. 18, no. 8, p. 4–10, November 1989. © 1989 by the American Educational Research Association. Reprinted with permission.

1895; Hobhouse, 1915; Romanes, 1892). Francis Galton (cousin of Charles Darwin) was perhaps the first psychologically oriented scientist to try to measure the intellect directly. Though Galton (1870) had a theoretical interest in the concept of intelligence, his work was by no means unrelated to practical issues. A committed eugenicist, he sought to measure intelligence and hoped, through proper "breeding," to increase the overall intelligence of the population.

During the following half century, many of the most gifted and influential psychologists concerned themselves with the nature of human intelligence. Although a few investigators were interested principally in theoretical issues, most seasoned their concerns with a practical orientation. Thus Binet (Binet & Simon, 1916) and Terman (1916) developed the first general-purpose intelligence tests in their respective countries; Yerkes (Yerkes, Bridges, & Hardwick, 1915) and Wechsler (1939) created their own influential instruments. Even scientists with a strong theoretical bent, like Spearman (1927) and Thurstone (1938), contributed either directly or indirectly to the devising of certain measurement techniques and the favoring of particular lines of interpretation.

> **For the most part, the burgeoning interest in cognitive matters bypassed the area of intelligence.**

By midcentury, theories of intelligence had become a staple of psychology textbooks, even as intelligence tests were taken for granted in many industrialized countries. Still, it is fair to say that, within scientific psychology, interest in issues of intelligence waned to some extent. Although psychometricians continued to perfect the instruments that purported to measure human intellect and some new tests were introduced (Guilford, 1967), for the most part, the burgeoning interest in cognitive matters bypassed the area of intelligence.

This divorce between mainstream research psychology and the "applied area" of intelligence might have continued indefinitely, but, in fact, by the late 70s, there were signs of a reawakening of interest in theoretical and research aspects of intelligence. With his focus on the information-processing aspects of items in psychological tests, Robert Sternberg (1977, 1982, 1985) was perhaps the most important catalyst for this shift, but researchers from a number of different areas of psychology have joined in this rediscovery of the centrality of intelligence (Baron, 1985; Brown & Campione, 1986; Dehn & Schank, 1982; Hunt, 1986; Jensen, 1986; Laboratory of Comparative Human Cognition, 1982; Scarr & Carter-Salzman, 1982; Snow, 1982).

THE THEORY OF MULTIPLE INTELLIGENCES

A decade ago Gardner found that his own research interests were leading him to a heightened concern with issues of human intelligence. This concern grew out of two disparate factors, one primarily theoretical, the other largely practical.

As a result of his own studies of the development and breakdown of cognitive and symbol-using capacities, Gardner (1975, 1979, 1982) became convinced that the Piagetian (Piaget, 1970) view of intellect was flawed. Whereas Piaget (1962) had conceptualized all aspects of symbol use as part of a single "semiotic function," empirical evidence was accruing that the human mind may be quite modular in design. That is, separate psychological processes appear to be involved in dealing with linguistic, numerical, pictorial, gestural, and other kinds of symbolic systems (Gardner, Howard, & Perkins, 1974; Gardner & Wolf, 1983). Individuals may be precocious with one form of symbol use, without any necessary carryover to other forms. By the same token, one form of symbol use may become seriously compromised under conditions of brain damage, without correlative depreciation of other symbolic capacities (Wapner & Gardner, 1979). Indeed, different forms of symbol use appear to be subserved by different portions of the cerebral cortex.

> As a result of his own studies...Gardner became convinced that the Piagetian view of intellect was flawed.

On a more practical level, Gardner was disturbed by the nearly exclusive stress in school on two forms of symbol use: linguistic symbolization and logical-mathematical symbolization. Although these two forms are obviously important in a scholastic setting, other varieties of symbol use also figure prominently in human cognitive activity within and especially outside of school. Moreover, the emphasis on linguistic and logical capacities was overwhelming in the construction of items on intelligence, aptitude, and achievement tests. If different kinds of items were used, or different kinds of assessment instruments devised, a quite different view of the human intellect might issue forth.

These and other factors led Gardner to a conceptualization of human intellect that was more capacious. This took into account a wide variety of human cognitive capacities, entailed many kinds of symbol systems, and incorporated as well the skills valued in a variety of cultural and historical settings. Realizing that he was stretching the word *intelligence* beyond its customary application in educational psychology, Gardner proposed the existence of a number of relatively autonomous *human intelligences*. He defined intelligence as the capacity to solve problems or to fashion products that are valued in one or more cultural settings and detailed a set of criteria for what counts as a human intelligence.

> **Gardner's definition and his criteria deviated significantly from established practices in the field of intelligence.**

Gardner's definition and his criteria deviated significantly from established practices in the field of intelligence (however, see Guilford, 1967; Thurstone, 1938). Most definitions of intelligence focus on the capacities that are important for success in school. Problem solving is recognized as a crucial component, but the ability to fashion a product—to write a symphony, execute a painting, stage a play, build up and manage an organization, carry out an experiment—is not included, presumably because the aforementioned capacities cannot be probed adequately in short-answer tests. Moreover, on the canonical account, intelligence is presumed to be a universal, probably innate, capacity, and so the diverse kinds of roles valued in different cultures are not considered germane to a study of "raw intellect."

For the most part, definitions and tests of intelligence are empirically determined. Investigators search for items that predict who will succeed in school, even as they drop items that fail to predict scholastic success. New tests are determined in part by the degree of correlation with older, already accepted instruments. In sharp contrast, existing psychometric instruments play no role in Gardner's formulation. Rather, a candidate ability emerges as an intelligence to the extent that it has recurred as an identifiable entity in a number of different lines of study of human cognition.

To arrive at his list of intelligences, Gardner and his colleagues examined the literature in several areas: the development of cognitive capacities in normal individuals; the breakdown of cognitive capacities under various kinds of organic pathology; the existence of abilities in "special populations," such as prodigies, autistic individuals, *idiots savants*, and learning-disabled children; forms of intellect that exist in different species; forms of intellect valued in different cultures; the evolution of cognition across the millennia; and two forms of psychological evidence—the results of factor-analytic studies of human cognitive capacities and the outcome of studies of transfer and generalization. Candidate capacities that turned up repeatedly in these disparate literatures made up a provisional list of human intelligences, whereas abilities that appeared only once or twice or were reconfigured differently in diverse sources were abandoned from consideration.

> It is claimed that, as a species, human beings have evolved over the millennia to carry out at least these seven forms of thinking.

The methods and the results of this massive survey are reported in detail in Frames of Mind (Gardner, 1983) and summarized in several other publications (Gardner 1987a, 1987b; Walters & Gardner, 1985). Gardner's provisional list includes seven intelligences, each with its own component processes and subtypes (see Table 1). It is claimed that, as a species, human beings have evolved over the millennia to carry out at least these seven forms of thinking. In a biological metaphor, these may be thought of as different mental "organs" (Chomsky, 1980); in a computational metaphor, these may be construed as separate information-processing devices (Fodor, 1983). Although all humans exhibit the range of intelligences, individuals differ—presumably for both hereditary and environmental reasons—in their current profile of intelligences. Moreover, there is no necessary correlation between any two intelligences, and they may indeed entail quite distinct forms of perception, memory, and other psychological processes.

Table 1
The Seven Intelligences

Intelligence	End-States	Core Components
Logical-mathematical	Scientist Mathematician	Sensitivity to, and capacity to discern, logical or numerical patterns; ability to handle long chains of reasoning.
Linguistic	Poet Journalist	Sensitivity to the sounds, rhythms, and meanings of words; sensitivity to the different functions of language.
Musical	Composer Violinist	Abilities to produce and appreciate rhythm, pitch, and timbre; appreciation of the forms of musical expressiveness.
Spatial	Navigator Sculptor	Capacities to perceive the visual-spatial world accurately and to perform transformations on one's initial perceptions.
Bodily-kinesthetic	Dancer Athlete	Abilities to control one's body movements and to handle objects skillfully.
Interpersonal	Therapist Salesman	Capacities to discern and respond appropriately to the moods, temperaments, motivations, and desires of other people.
Intrapersonal	Person with detailed, accurate self-knowledge	Access to one's own feelings and the ability to discriminate among them and draw upon them to guide behavior; knowledge of one's own strengths, weaknesses, desires, and intelligences.

Although few occupations rely entirely on a single intelligence, different roles typify the "endstates" of each intelligence. For example, the "linguistic" sensitivity to the sounds and construction of language is exemplified by the poet, whereas the interpersonal ability to discern and respond to the moods and motivations of other people is represented in the therapist. Other occupations more clearly illustrate the need for a blend of intelligences. For instance, surgeons require both the acuity of spatial intelligence to guide the scalpel and the dexterity of the bodily-kinesthetic intelligence to handle it. Similarly, scientists often have to depend on their linguistic intelligences to describe and explain the discoveries made using their logical-mathematic intelligence, and they must employ interpersonal intelligence in interacting with colleagues and in maintaining a productive and smoothly functioning laboratory.

> **Although few occupations rely entirely on a single intelligence, different roles typify the "endstates" of each intelligence.**

THE EDUCATION AND ASSESSMENT OF INTELLIGENCES

Until this point, we have been reviewing the history of intelligence research, admittedly from the perspective of the Theory of Multiple Intelligences (hereafter MI Theory). Since the publication of *Frames of Mind* (Gardner, 1983), we and our colleagues have been involved in investigating its implications. On the one hand, we seek to determine the scientific adequacy of the theory (for a discussion of some of the scientific questions raised by the theory, see Gardner, 1983, chapter 11, and Walters & Gardner, 1986). On the other hand, in our view, a principal value of the multiple intelligence perspective—be it a theory or a "mere" framework—lies in its potential contributions to educational reform. In both cases, progress seems to revolve around assessment. To demonstrate that the intelligences are relatively independent of one another and that individuals have distinct profiles of intelligences, assessments of each intelligence have to be developed. To take advantage of students' multiple intelligences, there must be some way to identify their strengths and weaknesses reliably.

Yet MI Theory grows out of a conviction that standardized tests, with their almost exclusive stress on linguistic and logical skills, are limited. As a result, the further development of MI Theory requires a fresh approach to assessment, an approach consistent with the view that there are a number of intelligences that are developed—and can best be detected—in culturally meaningful activities (Gardner, [1992]). In the remainder of the paper, we describe our approach to assessment and broadly survey our efforts to assess individual intelligences at different age levels. In addition, we report some preliminary findings from one of our projects and their implications for the confirmation (or disconfirmation) of MI Theory.

If, as argued, each intelligence displays a characteristic set of psychological processes, it is important that these processes be assessed in an "intelligence-fair" manner. In contrast to traditional paper-and-pencil tests, with their inherent bias toward linguistic and logical skills, intelligence-fair measures seek to respect the different modes of thinking and performance that distinguish each intelligence. Although spatial problems can be approached to some degree through linguistic media (like verbal directions or word problems), intelligence-fair methods place a premium on the abilities to perceive and manipulate visual-spatial information in a direct manner. For example, the spatial intelligence of children can be assessed through a mechanical activity in which they are asked to take apart and reassemble a meat grinder. The activity requires them to "puzzle out" the structure of the object and then to discern or remember the spatial information that will allow reassembly of the pieces. Although linguistically inclined children may produce a running report about the actions they are taking, little verbal skill is necessary (or helpful) for successful performance on such a task.

> Intelligences are always conceptualized and assessed in terms of their cultural manifestation in specific domains of endeavor...

Whereas most standard approaches treat intelligence in isolation from the activities of a particular culture, MI theory takes a sharply contrasting tack. Intelligences are always conceptualized and assessed in terms of their cultural manifestation in specific domains of endeavor and with reference to particular adult "end states." Thus, even at the preschool level, language capacity is not assessed in terms of vocabulary, definitions, or similarities, but rather as manifest in story telling (the novelist) and reporting (the journalist). Instead of attempting to assess spatial skills in isolation, we observe children as they are drawing (the artist) or taking apart and putting together objects (the mechanic).

Ideally, one might wish to assess an intelligence in a culture-independent way, but this goal has proved to be elusive and perhaps impossible to achieve. Cross-cultural research and studies of cognition in the course of ordinary activities (Brown, Collins, & Duguid, 1989; Laboratory of Comparative Human Cognition, 1982; Lave, 1988; Rogoff, 1982; Scribner, 1986) have demonstrated that performances are inevitably dependent on a person's familiarity and experience with the materials and demands of the assessments. In our own work, it rapidly became clear that meaningful assessment of an intelligence was not possible if students had little or no experience with a particular subject matter or type of material. For example, our examination of bodily-kinesthetic abilities in a movement assessment for preschoolers was confounded by the fact that some 4-year-olds had already been to ballet classes, whereas others had never been asked to move their bodies expressively or in rhythm. This recognition reinforced the notion that bodily-kinesthetic intelligence cannot be assessed outside of a specific medium or without reference to a history of prior experiences.

Together, these demands for assessments that are intelligence fair, are based on culturally valued activities, and take place within a familiar context naturally lead to an approach that blurs the distinctions between curriculum and assessment. Drawing information from the regular curriculum ensures that the activities are familiar; introducing activities in a wide range of areas makes it possible to challenge and examine each intelligence in an appropriate manner. Tying the activities to inviting pursuits enables students to discover and develop abilities that in turn increase their chances of experiencing a sense of engagement and of achieving some success in their society.

PUTTING THEORY INTO PRACTICE

In the past 5 years, this approach to assessment has been explored in projects at several different levels of schooling. At the
junior and senior high school level, Arts
PROPEL, a collaborative project with the
Educational Testing Service and the Pittsburgh Public School System, seeks to assess growth and learning in areas like music, imaginative writing, and visual arts,
which are neglected by most standard
measures (for further details, see
Gardner, [1989]; Wolf, 1989; Zessoules,
Wolf, & Gardner, 1988). Arts PROPEL
has developed a series of modules, or
"domain projects," that serve the goals of
both curriculum and assessment. These projects feature sets of
exercises and curriculum activities organized around a concept
central to a specific artistic domain—such as notation in music,
character and dialogue in play writing, and graphic composition
in the visual arts. The drafts, sketches, and final products generated by these and other curriculum activities are collected in
portfolios (sometimes termed "process-folios"), which serve as
a basis for assessment of growth by both the teacher and the
student. Although the emphasis thus far has fallen on local
classroom assessments, efforts are also under way to develop
criteria whereby student accomplishment can be evaluated by
external examiners.

> Arts PROPEL has developed a series of modules, or "domain projects," that serve the goals of both curriculum and assessment.

At the elementary level, Patricia Bolanos and her colleagues
have used MI theory to design an entire public school in downtown Indianapolis (Olson, 1988). Through a variety of special
classes (e.g., computing, bodily-kinesthetic activities) and enrichment activities (a "flow" center and apprentice-like "pods"),
all children in the Key School are given the opportunity to discover their areas of strength and to develop the full range of intelligences. In addition, over the course of a year, each child ex-
ecutes a number of projects based on schoolwide themes such
as "Man and His Environment" or "Changes in Time and
Space." These projects are presented and videotaped for subsequent study and analysis. A team of researchers from Harvard
Project Zero is now engaged in developing a set of criteria

whereby these videotaped projects can be assessed. Among the dimensions under consideration are project conceptualization, effectiveness of presentation, technical quality of project, and originality, as well as evidence for cooperative efforts and distinctive individual features.

A third effort, Project Spectrum, codirected by David Feldman of Tufts University, has developed a number of curriculum activities and assessment options suited to the "child-centered" structure of many preschools and kindergartens (for details, see Hatch & Gardner, 1986; Krechevsky & Gardner, in press; Malkus, Feldman, & Gardner, 1988; Ramos-Ford & Gardner, in press; Wexler-Sherman, Feldman, & Gardner, 1988). At present, there are 15 different activities, each of which taps a particular intelligence or set of intelligences. Throughout the year, a Spectrum classroom is equipped with "intelligence-fair" materials. Miniature replicas and props invite children to deploy linguistic intelligence within the context of story telling; household objects that children can take apart and reassemble challenge children's spatial intelligence in a mechanical task; a "discovery" area including natural objects like rocks, bones, and shells enables children to use their logical abilities to conduct small "experiments," comparisons, and classifications; and group activities such as a biweekly creative movement session can be employed to give children the opportunity to exercise their bodily-kinesthetic intelligence on a regular basis.

> **Project Spectrum has developed a number of curriculum activities and assessment options suited to the "child-centered" structure of many preschools and kindergartens.**

Provision of this variety of "high-affordance" materials allows children to gain experiences that engage their several intelligences, even as teachers have the chance unobtrusively to observe and assess children's strengths, interests, and proclivities. More formal assessment of intelligences is also possible. Researchers can administer specific games to children and apply detailed scoring systems that have been developed for research purposes. For instance, in the bus game, children's ability to organize numerical information is scored by noting the extent to which they can keep track of the number of adults and children getting on and off a bus. Adults and children and on and off constitute two different dimensions. Thus, a child can receive one of the following scores: 0—no dimensions recorded; 1—disorganized recording of one dimension (either adults and children or on and off); 2—labeled, accurate recording of one dimension; 3—disorganized recording of two dimensions; 4—disorganized recording of one dimension and labeled, accurate recording of one dimension; or 5—labeled, accurate recording of two dimensions (for further information, see Krechevsky, Feldman, & Gardner, in press).

> A consideration of a broader range of talents brings to the fore individuals who previously had been considered unexceptional or even at risk for school failure.

We have also created a related instrument, the Modified Spectrum Field Inventory, that samples several intelligences in the course of two 1-hour sessions. Although this inventory does not draw directly from the curriculum, it is based on the kinds of materials and activities that are common in many preschools. In addition, related materials from the Spectrum curriculum can be implemented in the classroom to ensure that the children will be familiar with the kinds of tasks and materials used in the inventory.

PRELIMINARY RESULTS FROM PROJECT SPECTRUM

Although none of these programs is in final form, and thus any evaluation must be considered preliminary and tentative, the results so far at the pilot sites seem promising. The value of rich and evocative materials has been amply documented. In the classrooms in Pittsburgh, Indianapolis, and Boston, teachers report heightened motivation on the part of the students, even as students themselves appreciate the opportunity to reflect on their own growth and development. Moreover, our programs with both older and younger children confirm that a consideration of a broader range of talents brings to the fore individuals who previously had considered unexceptional or even at risk for school failure.

As for the assessment instruments under development, only those of Project Spectrum have been field tested in classrooms. In 1987–1989, we used these instruments in two different settings to investigate the hypothesis that the intelligences are largely independent of one another. To examine this hypothesis, we sought to determine (a) whether young children exhibit distinct profiles of intellectual strengths and weaknesses and (b) whether or not performances on activities designed to tap different intelligences are significantly correlated. In the 1987–1988 academic year, 20 children from a primarily White upper middle-income population took part in a yearlong Spectrum program. In the 1988–1989 academic year, the Modified Spectrum Field Inventory was piloted with 15 children in a combined kindergarten and first-grade classroom. This classroom was in a public school in a low-to-middle-income school district.

In the preschool study, children were assessed on 10 different activities (story telling, drawing, singing, music perception, creative movement, social analysis, hypothesis testing, assembly, calculation and counting, and number and notational logic) as well as the Stanford-Binet Intelligence Scale, Fourth Edition. To compare children's performances across each of the activities, standard deviations were calculated for each activity. Children who scored one or more standard deviations above the mean were judged to have a strength on that activity; those who scored one or more standard deviations below the mean were considered to have a weakness on that activity. This analysis revealed that these children did not perform at the same level across activities and suggested that they do not have distinct intellectual profiles. Of the 20 children, 15 demonstrated a strength on at least one activity, and 12 children showed a weakness on one or more activities. In contrast, only one child was identified as having no strengths or weaknesses, and her scores ranged from - .98 to +.87 standard deviations from the mean.

> To compare children's performances across each of the activities, standard deviations were calculated for each activity.

These results were reinforced by the fact that, for the most part, children's performances on the activities were independent. Using Spearman rank-order correlations, only the number activities, both requiring logical-mathematical intelligence, proved significantly correlated with one another ($r = .78$, p

<.01). In the other areas, music and science, where there were two assessments, there were no significant correlations. Conceivably, this result can be attributed to the fact that the number activities, both of which involved calculation, shared more features than the music activities (singing and music perception) or the science activities (hypothesis-testing and mechanical skill). Of course, the small sample size also may have contributed to the absence of powerful correlations among measures.

A comparison of the Spectrum and Stanford-Binet assessments revealed a limited relationship between children's performances on these different instruments. Spearman rank-order correlations showed that only performances on the number activities were significantly correlated with IQ (dinosaur game, $r = .69$, $p < .003$; bus game, $r = .51$, $p < .04$). With its concentration on logical-mathematic and linguistic skills, one might have expected a significant correlation with the Spectrum language activity as well. Conceivably, there was no significant correlation because the Stanford-Binet measures children's vocabulary and comprehension, whereas Spectrum measures how children *use* language within a story-telling task.

> The Stanford-Binet measures children's vocabulary and comprehension, whereas Spectrum measures how children *use* language within a story-telling task.

In the second study, eight kindergartners (four boys and four girls) and seven first graders (five girls and two boys) were assessed on the seven activities of the Modified Spectrum Field Inventory (MSPFI). This inventory, based on the activities developed for the yearlong Spectrum assessments of preschoolers, consists of activities in the areas of language (storyboard), numbers and logic (bus game), mechanics (assembly), art (drawing), music (xylophone games), social analysis (classroom model), and movement (creative movement). These assessments were administered in two 1-hour sessions. Each activity was videotaped, and children were scored by two independent observers. Spearman rank-order correlations between the scores of the two observers ranged from .88 (language) to .97 (art) and demonstrated the interrater reliability of these scores.

As in the first study, strengths and weaknesses were estimated using standard deviations. Unlike the findings from the earlier study, however, these results revealed that some children performed quite well and others performed quite poorly across many of the activities. It appears that the small sample size and wide age ranges may have contributed to this result. Of the five first-grade girls, none demonstrated a weakness in any area; all showed at least one strength, with one girl having strengths in six of the seven areas.

> An examination of children's ranks on each of the activities revealed a more complex picture.

The two first-grade boys showed no strengths, and both demonstrated weaknesses in three areas. Of the kindergartners, only two showed any strengths, with all but one of the other children showing at least one weakness. Quite possibly, these results reflect differences in developmental level, and perhaps gender differences as well, that did not obtain in the preschool sample and that may have overpowered certain individual differences. It is also conceivable that a more extended exposure to, and greater familiarity with, the Spectrum materials and activities, as in the yearlong Spectrum program, may have made the individual differences among younger children more visible.

Nonetheless, an examination of children's ranks on each of the activities revealed a more complex picture. Although the first-grade girls dominated the rankings, all but two children in the sample were ranked among the top five on at least one occasion. All but one child also scored in the bottom five on at least one activity. Considered in this way, children did exhibit relative strengths and weaknesses across the seven activities.

To determine whether or not performance on one activity was independent of performance on the other activities, we standardized each of the scores with a mean = 0 and standard deviation = 1 (Sattler, 1988) and performed Spearman rank-order correlations. Because of the superior performance of the first-grade girls, the performances of kindergartners and first graders were computed separately. Consideration of the kindergartners alone revealed only one correlation, between art and social analysis, that approached significance ($r = .66$, $p < .071$).

For the sample of first graders, including the "high"-scoring girls, there were a number of significant correlations: language and assembly ($r = .77$, $p < .04$), language and numbers ($r = .81$, $p < .027$), movement and social analysis ($r = .77$, $p < .04$), and assembly and numbers ($r = .79$, $p < .034$).

With the exception of the performance of the first graders in the second study, these results are reasonably consistent with the claims of MI Theory. For younger children, performances on the Spectrum activities were largely independent, relative strengths and weaknesses were uncovered, and there was a significant correlation between preschoolers' performances on the Spectrum activities and the Stanford-Binet in one of the two areas where it would be expected. Further investigations need to be conducted to establish norms, to identify strengths and weaknesses consistently, and to examine fully the effects of age and gender on the Spectrum activities.

CONCLUSION

In this essay, we have sketched the background and the major claims of a new approach to the conceptualization and assessment of human intelligence. Put forth in 1983, the theory of multiple intelligences has inspired a number of research-and-development projects that are taking place in schools ranging from preschool through high school. Until now, our focus has fallen largely on the development of instruments that can assess strengths and weaknesses in an "intelligence-fair" way. This research-and-development process has proved time consuming and costly. The measures must involve materials that are appealing and familiar to children; there is little precedent for developing scoring systems that go beyond linguistic and logical criteria; and materials appropriate for one age group, gender, or social class may not be appropriate for others. Of course, it should be recalled that huge amounts of time and money have already been invested in standard psychometric instruments, whose limitations have become increasingly evident in recent years.

> **Until now, our focus has fallen largely on the development of instruments that can assess strengths and weaknesses in an "intelligence-fair" way.**

Once adequate materials have been developed, it becomes possible to begin to address some of the theoretical claims that grow out of MI Theory. We have presented here some preliminary findings from one of our current projects. These results give some support to the major claims of the theory, inasmuch as children ranging in age from 3 to 7 do exhibit profiles of relative strength and weakness. At the same time, even these preliminary data indicate that the final story on Multiple Intelligences may turn out to be more complex than we envisioned. Thus, the rather different profile of results obtained with our two young populations indicates that, in future research, we must pay closer attention to three factors: (a) the developmental appropriateness of the materials; (b) the social class background, which may well exert an influence on a child's ability and willingness to engage with diverse materials; and (c) the exact deployment of the Spectrum materials and assessment instruments in the classroom.

> **Even these preliminary data indicate that the final story on Multiple Intelligences may turn out to be more complex than we envisioned.**

Some critics have suggested that MI Theory cannot be disconfirmed. The preliminary results presented here indicate some of the ways in which its central claims can indeed be challenged. If future assessments do not reveal strengths and weaknesses within a population, if performances on different activities prove to be systematically correlated, and if constructs (and instruments) like the IQ explain the preponderance of the variance on activities configured to tap specific intelligences, then MI Theory will have to be revamped. Even so, the goal of detecting distinctive human strengths, and using them as a basis for engagement and learning, may prove to be worthwhile, irrespective of the scientific fate of the theory.

Note: The research described in this article has been generously supported by the Grant Foundation, the Lilly Endowment, the Markle Foundation, the Rockefeller Brothers Fund, the Rockefeller Foundation, the Spencer Foundation, the Bernard Van Leer Foundation, and the Office of Educational Research and Improvement's Center for Technology in Education at the Bank Street College of

Education. We thank our colleagues at the Eliot-Pearson Children's School and in the Somerville Public School system for their collaboration. For comments on an earlier draft of this paper, we are grateful to Robert Glaser, Robert Sternberg, Joseph Walters, and an anonymous reviewer.

REFERENCES

Baldwin, J. M. (1895). *Mental development in the child and the race.* New York: Macmillan.

Baron, J. (1985). *Rationality and intelligence.* New York: Cambridge University Press.

Binet, A., & Simon, T. (1916). *The development of intelligence in children.* Baltimore, MD: Williams & Wilkins.

Brown A. L., & Campione, J. C. (1986). *Academic intelligence and learning potential.* In R. J. Sternberg & D. Detterman (Eds.). *What is intelligence?* (pp. 39-49). Hillsdale, NJ: Erlbaum.

Brown, J. S., Collins, A., & Duguid, P. (1989). Situated cognition and the culture of learning. *Educational Researcher, 18*(1), 32–42.

Chomsky, N. (1980). *Rules and representations.* New York: Columbia University Press.

Dehn, N., & Schank, R. C. (1982). Artificial and human intelligence. In R. Sternberg (Ed.), *Handbook of human intelligence* (Vol. 1, pp. 352–391). New York: Cambridge University Press.

Fodor, J. (1983). *The modularity of mind.* Cambridge, MA: MIT Press.

Galton, F. (1870). *Hereditary genius.* New York: Appleton.

Gardner, H. (1975). *The shattered mind.* New York: Knopf.

Gardner, H. (1979). Developmental psychology after Piaget: An approach in terms of symbolization. *Human Development, 15,* 570–580.

Gardner, H. (1982). *Art, mind and brain.* New York: Basic Books.

Gardner, H. (1983). *Frames of mind.* New York: Basic Books.

Gardner, H. (1987a). Symposium on the theory of multiple intelligences. In D. N. Perkins, J. Lockhead, & J. C. Bishop (Eds.), *Thinking: The second international conference* (pp. 77–101). Hillsdale, NJ: Erlbaum.

Gardner, H. (1987b). Developing the spectrum of human intelligence. *Harvard Education Review, 57,* 187–193.

Gardner, H. ([Winter 1989]). Zero-based arts education: An introduction to Arts PROPEL. *Studies in Art Education,* [*30*, 71–83].

Gardner, H. ([1992]). Assessment in context: The alternative to standardized testing. In B. Gifford (Ed.), [*Policy perspectives on educational testing.* Norwell, MA: Kluwer Academic Publishers].

Gardner, H., Howard, V., & Perkins, D. (1974). Symbol systems: A philosophical, psychological and educational investigation. In D. Olson (Ed.), *Media and symbols* (pp. 37–55). Chicago: University of Chicago Press.

Gardner, H., & Wolf, D. (1983). Waves and streams of symbolization. In D. R. Rogers & J. A. Sloboda (Eds.), *The acquisition of symbolic skills* (pp. 19–42). London: Plenum.

Guilford, J. P. (1967). *The nature of human intelligence.* New York: McGraw-Hill.

Hatch, T., & Gardner, H. (1986). From testing intelligence to assessing competences: A pluralistic view of intellect. *Roeper Review, 8*, 147–150.

Hobhouse, L. T. (1915). *Mind in evolution.* London: Macmillan.

Hunt, E. (1986). The heffalump of intelligence. In R. J. Sternberg & D. Detterman (Eds.), *What is intelligence?* (pp. 101–107). Hillsdale, NJ: Erlbaum.

Jensen, A. R. (1986). Intelligence: "Definition," measurement, and future research. In R. J. Sternberg & D. Detterman (Eds.), *What is intelligence?* (pp. 109–112). Hillsdale, NJ: Erlbaum.

Krechevsky, M., Feldman, D., & Gardner, H. (in press). The Spectrum handbook.

Krechevsky, M., & Gardner, H. ([1992]). The emergence and nurturance of multiple intelligences. In M. J. A. Howe (Ed), *Encouraging the development of exceptional* [*skills*] *and talents.* [Concord, MA: Paul & Company Publishers Consortium.]

Laboratory of Comparative Human Cognition. (1982). Culture and intelligence. In R. Sternberg (Ed.), *Handbook of human intelligence* (Vol. 2, pp. 642–722). New York: Cambridge University Press.

Lave, J. (1988). *Cognition in practice.* Cambridge, England: Cambridge University Press.

Malkus, U., Feldman, D. H., & Gardner, H. (1988). Dimensions of mind in early childhood. In A. D. Pellegrini (Ed.), *Psychological bases of early education* (pp. 25–38). New York: Wiley.

Olson, L. (1988). Children flourish here: 8 teachers and a theory changed a school world. *Education Week, 18*(1), 18–19.

Piaget, J. (1962). *Play, dreams and imitation in childhood* (C. Gattegno & F. M. Hodgson, Trans.). New York: Norton.

Piaget, J. (1970). *Science of education and the psychology of the child* (D. Coltman, Trans.) New York: Orion.

Ramos-Ford, V., & Gardner, H. (in press). Giftedness from a multiple intelligences perspective. In N. Colangelo & G. Davis (Eds.), *The handbook of gifted education.*

Rogoff, B. (1982). Integrating context and cognitive development. In M. Lamb & A. Brown (Eds.), *Advances in developmental psychology* (Vol. 2, pp. 125–169). Hillsdale, NJ: Erlbaum.

Romanes, G. J. (1892). *Animal intelligence.* New York: Appleton.

Sattler, J. M. (1988). *Assessment of children.* San Diego: Author.

Scarr, S., & Carter-Saltzman, L. (1982). Genetics and intelligence. In R. Sternberg (Ed.), Han*dbook of human intelligence* (Vol. 2, pp. 792–896). New York: Cambridge University Press.

Scribner, S. (1986). Thinking in action: Some characteristics of practical thought. In R. Sternberg & R. K. Wagner (Eds.), *Practical intelligence: Origins of competence in the everyday world.* New York: Cambridge University Press.

Snow, R. E. (1982). Education and intelligence. In R. Sternberg (Ed.), *Handbook of human intelligence* (Vol. 2, pp. 493–585). New York: Cambridge University Press.

Spearman, C. E. (1927). *The abilities of man: Their nature and measurement.* New York: Macmillan.

Sternberg, R. (1977). *Intelligence, information processing, and analogical reasoning.* Hillsdale, NJ: Erlbaum.

Sternberg, R. J. (Ed.). (1982). *Handbook of human intelligence.* New York: Cambridge University Press.

Sternberg, R. J. (1985). *Beyond IQ.* New York: Cambridge University Press.

Terman, L. M. (1916). *The measurement of intelligence.* Boston: Houghton Mifflin.

Thurstone, L. L. (1938). *Primary mental abilities.* Chicago: University of Chicago Press.

Walters, J., & Gardner, H. (1985). The development and education of intelligences. In F. Link (Ed.), *Essays on the intellect* (pp. 1–21). Washington, DC: Curriculum Development Associates.

Walters, J., & Gardner, H. (1986). The theory of multiple intelligences: Some issues and answers. In R. Sternberg & R. Wagner (Eds.), *Practical intelligence: Origins of competence in the everyday world* (pp. 163–182). New York: Cambridge University Press.

Wapner, W., & Gardner, H. (1979). A study of spelling in aphasia. *Brain and Language, 7,* 363–374.

Wechsler, D. (1939). *The measurement of adult intelligence.* Baltimore, MD: Williams & Wilkins.

Wexler-Sherman, C., Feldman, D., & Gardner, H. (1988). A pluralistic view of intellect: The Project Spectrum approach. *Theory Into Practice, 28,* 77–83.

Wolf, D. P. (1989, April). What's in it? Examining portfolio assessment. *Educational Leadership,* [46, 35–39].

Yerkes, R. M., Bridges, J. W., & Hardwick, R. S. (1915). *A point scale for measuring mental ability.* Baltimore, MD: Warwick and York.

Zessoules, R., Wolf, D., & Gardner, H. (1988). A better balance: Arts PROPEL as an alternative to discipline-based art education. In J. Burton, A. Loderman, & P. London (Eds.), *Beyond discipline-based art education.* University Council on Art Education.

A School for All Intelligences

by Tina Blythe and Howard Gardner

Recent discussions about the restructuring of schools focus on ways in which institutional settings and teacher roles can enhance student learning. This is an important concern, but the issue of curriculum content—what should be taught and why—is still relatively neglected. Our research group, Harvard Project Zero, has been examining these questions through the lens of the theory of multiple intelligences. We would like to describe this theory, some of the research projects it has engendered, and its implications for elementary and secondary education.

The theory of multiple intelligences (MI theory) challenges the prevailing concept of intelligence as a single possessor to deal more or less effectively with virtually any situation. MI theory paints a more variegated and contextualized picture, positing a number of intelligences. Based on Gardner's empirical work with normal and gifted children, as well as on studies of brain-injured adults, it defines an intelligence as the capacity to solve problems or fashion products which are valued in one or more cultural settings.

> **MI theory proposes that people use at least seven relatively autonomous intellectual capacities...to approach problems and create products.**

REALMS OF INTELLIGENCE

As described in Gardner's 1983 book *Frames of Mind*, MI theory proposes that people use at least seven relatively autonomous

From *Educational Leadership*, vol. 47, no. 7, p. 33–37, April 1990. © 1990 by the Association for Supervision and Curriculum Development. Reprinted with permission.

intellectual capacities—each with its own distinctive mode of thinking—to approach problems and create products. These include linguistic, musical, logical-mathematical, spatial, bodily-kinesthetic, interpersonal, and intrapersonal intelligences. Although they are not necessarily dependent on each other, these intelligences seldom operate in isolation. Every normal individual possess varying degrees of each of these intelligences, but the ways in which intelligences combine and blend are as varied as the faces and the personalities of individuals.

MI theory suggests some compelling alternatives to current educational practices in several areas.

1. **Range of abilities addressed.** According to MI theory, it is important for education to address other human abilities and talents besides the linguistic and logical-mathematical intelligences which have long been the primary focus of most schools (Gardner 1987b).

2. **Learning environment.** By acknowledging the wide variety of valuable—and independent—domains, MI theory calls for an attendant shift in instructional conditions. Typical classroom procedures rely heavily on linguistic and logical-mathematical symbol systems. However, one cannot develop musical intelligence, for example, merely by talking and writing about music. Sustained, hands-on practice with the procedures, materials, and problems of such a domain are crucial to achieving deep knowledge within it. Hence, MI theory places an emphasis on learning in context, particularly via apprenticeships.

3. **Assessment measures.** MI theory challenges the viability of standardized, machine-scored, multiple-choice assessments, which by their very nature appraise students' knowledge through the filter of the linguistic and logical-mathematical intelligences. Each intelligence needs to be assessed directly, in contexts which call it into play (Gardner [1992]).

4. **Concept of learner.** By proposing that each person possesses a distinctive combination of intelligences, MI theory emphasizes the highly individualized ways in which people learn. It calls into question the prevailing policy of educating all students in the same subjects with the same methods and materials. To students with high degrees of spatial intelligence, for example, the history of an era might best be introduced through art, architecture, and/or geography. For students with high interper-

sonal or linguistic intelligences, biographies and dramatic reenactments might prove better vehicles (Gardner 1987a).

RECENT RESEARCH PROJECTS

At Project Zero, we have begun to explore these alternatives in a series of research projects, each addressing specific facets of education at the primary, middle, and secondary levels. Project Spectrum, a collaboration with David Feldman of Tufts University, developed intelligence-fair assessment measures to identify and describe the various intellectual strengths exhibited by preschoolers (Krechevsky and Gardner [1992]). These evaluation measures—number games, storytelling activities, creative movement exercises—double as part of the classroom curriculum and as free-play activities. As in other initiatives, we deliberately blur the traditional line between curriculum and assessment, thus enabling students to be assessed in natural, familiar, and non-threatening contexts.

Arts PROPEL, a collaborative research project with the Educational Testing Service and the Pittsburgh Public School System, assesses middle and high school students' growth and achievement in artistic endeavors (Gardner 1989a). By working through "domain projects" and compiling their own portfolios, students learn to reflect on and evaluate their work in music, creative writing, and visual arts.

Carried out in collaboration with Robert J. Sternberg at Yale University, the Practical Intelligence for Schools project (PIFS) has developed meta-curricular units that can be infused into the curriculum typically taught in middle school classes. These infused units help students to focus on problems which predictably arise in the traditional content areas of mathematics, social studies, and reading and writing (Krechevsky and Gardner [1990]). Typical problems include how to take notes, how to revise an essay, and how to use resources for a term paper. The units encourage students to identify their own intellectual strengths and abilities and to draw on them as they tackle academic problems.

OUR VISION OF AN MI SCHOOL

These and other pilot studies provide glimpses of what a school might accomplish if it were to embrace MI theory at all levels of operation. Because no such school exists as yet, we offer here our personal vision of what such a school would be like. Details from our pilot studies fill out this picture; they represent the initial steps schools are now taking toward nurturing the development of multiple intelligences in all children.

The school we envision commits itself to fostering students' deep understanding in several core disciplines. It encourages students' use of that knowledge to solve the problems and complete the tasks that they may confront in the wider community. At the same time, the school seeks to encourage the unique blend of intelligences in each of its students, assessing their development regularly in intelligence-fair ways. To achieve these goals, the school draws inspiration from the educational successes of non-school enterprises. Modeling the fresh and engaging approach of children's museums, the school creates an atmosphere in which students feel free to explore novel stimuli and unfamiliar situations. In the spirit of traditional apprenticeships, it promotes students' sustained and guided efforts on individual projects. Students and teachers collaborate in an environment that is at once unconstrained and purposeful.

> The school seeks to encourage the unique blend of intelligences in each of its students, assessing their development regularly in intelligence-fair ways.

Our school day reflects these ideals. In the mornings, students study the traditional subject areas but in untraditional ways. Almost all the work in mathematics, social studies, reading and writing, and science takes the form of student projects. Students explore particular aspects of material in depth, addressing problems that confront professionals in the discipline. For instance, they might attempt to make sense of conflicting reports about a single historical event or to define a scientific problem and then informatively explore it by carrying out small-scale experiments (Gardner 1989b).

Arts PROPEL provides a model for this kind of learning via projects. The domain projects developed for this study provide a rich series of exercises to help students focus on a particular aspect of an art form (composition in the visual arts, characterization in play-writing, rehearsal in music). Students work through these projects, keeping their drafts, revisions, final products, and observations in a portfolio (a better name might be "process-folio"). This documentation of the student's creative growth serves as a catalyst for her own reflections on herself as learner and fledgling artist. The student's work is assessed by examining the final product, her thinking in forming it, and her plans for subsequent projects.

> **Students work through these projects, keeping their drafts, revisions, final products, and observations in a portfolio.**

The second half of our school day is a natural extension of the first. During this time, students and teachers venture out into the community for further contextual exploring and learning. The younger children and their teachers often travel to a children's museum, a playground, or a special participatory demonstration at the local theater, symphony, or art museum. These excursions differ from typical field trips because classes return to the same spots many times over the course of the year. Students can continue projects begun in previous visits (perhaps working on a sculpture at the local art museum or continuing study on the life cycle of the crabs at the aquarium) or hone their skills in favorite activities (examining butterfly specimens at the children's museum or playing the tympany at the symphony demonstrations). Teachers prepare students for these experiences by planning related in-class projects and discussions and debrief them afterward in parallel ways.

Such educational bridges could be constructed with programs like a current Project Spectrum initiative which seeks to create thematic ties between preschool curricula and museum exhibits through the use of kits. Organized around topics which intrigue young schoolchildren, these kits provide activities which can be used in school, museum, and home settings to stimulate a range of intelligences. The "Night and Day" kit, for example, includes a game board (featuring children's usual night and day activities) which facilitates exploration of number concepts. Books and related storyboards stimulate language skills, and "shadow games" encourage students' active investigation of the concepts of "light" and "dark."

Whether at the museum or our enriched school environment, children are allowed to explore freely and encouraged to ask questions. Teachers, aides, and other adults (including those who staff the field trip sites) jot down notes (or make mental ones to be written down later) about the children they are watching. Which students show interest or skill in particular activities or exhibits? What sorts of questions do students ask? What tasks do they have difficulty with?

> Whether at the museum or our enriched school environment, children are allowed to explore freely and encouraged to ask questions.

Project Spectrum employs a similar in-school technique for compiling information about a student's intellectual proclivities. In a Spectrum classroom, students are provided with a variety of rich materials designed to stimulate particular intelligences. A treasure hunt game helps to develop children's abilities to make logical inferences. Assembly activities involving simple mechanical objects draw upon their fine motor skills. A storyboard composed of an ambiguous landscape and imaginative figures and objects (a king, a dragon, a jewel box) fosters children's skills in using descriptive language, dialogue, and narration. Over the year, teachers and observers make notes about the activities students gravitate toward and the progress they make in working with the materials. At the end of the year, parents receive a Spectrum Report: a short essay detailing the child's intellectual profile, along with suggested home or community activities that might foster growth in areas of particular strength or weakness.

These reports play a prominent role in the MI-based school. Teachers and parents observe how the child carries out tasks and projects in the classroom, on field trips, and at home and put their notes into the files the school's assessment team keeps on each child. Video documentation of the student's projects, activities, and personal observations and preferences is also a possibility—and is in fact being carried out at the Key School, an Indianapolis public school strongly influenced by MI theory (Olson 1988). A record of the student's own preferences completes the collection. When a student reaches 3rd grade, he and his parents meet with a member of the assessment team to review the variety of strengths and preferences he has exhibited thus far. Together, they choose the three apprenticeships he will pursue within the school and community in the coming years.

Like the Key School, our school not only takes its students into the community but also brings the community to its students. Community members volunteer to share their expertise in some craft or occupation by working with a small group of students who have expressed interest in it. In addition, a "flow period" gives students time to play with games, activities, and ideas that appeal to them (while observers take note of their preferences and strengths). The important point here is that students can explore interests and abilities not necessarily tapped by the typical school curriculum.

> A "flow period" gives students time to play with games, activities, and ideas that appeal to them.

In our school, older students carry on this intellectual exploration in a more structured way. While continuing to spend mornings carrying out the projects of the basic core curriculum, they devote their afternoons to the apprenticeships they chose as 3rd graders. They study intensively with "master" teachers, members of the community who possess expertise in a particular area. Each student pursues an academic discipline, a physical activity, and an art or craft. Just as in the early years, when their school encompassed numerous exploratory opportunities in the wider community, now the workplaces and studios of their various masters become another richly contextualized extension of the classroom.

Adults in the community can participate in two ways. Some become masters; they devote time to working intimately with an apprentice. Others, while not working directly with apprentices, provide ideas for particular projects which advanced apprentices can carry out with minimal guidance from their masters. Such projects might include designing and painting murals for particular buildings or businesses, developing a more efficient record-keeping system for the public library, or composing music for a school event. Each adult meets with a member of the school's community liaison team, which keeps names of potential masters and projects in the community/school opportunities bank. These are shared with the assessment team as it guides students in selecting their apprenticeships. In addition, the community liaison team monitors the progress of the apprenticeships and projects, intervening constructively if problems arise.

WHAT'S NEXT?

Whatever the fate of these pilot projects, MI theory has the potential to dramatically alter the ways in which we think about schools and about education. However, we cannot realistically expect schools as they are now to assume the full burden for educating such a range of human intelligences. To restructure education, we must enlarge the circle of responsible individuals.

> We cannot realistically expect schools as they are now to assume the full burden for educating such a range of human intelligences.

Only a "full-court press" of support from parents, community leaders, neighborhood organizations and institutions, concerned adults from all walks of life, and broad-minded educators will help our communities achieve viable schools for the future (Gardner [1991, in press]).

There are many possible schools, given the diversity of resources, both human and material, that make up individual communities. And since MI theory is, at most, a charter and not a cookbook, this is all to the good. However, we suspect that all MI-inspired schools will share at least a few important features. Even traditional subjects will be taught in a variety of ways, thereby addressing the varied intelligences of students and their teachers. Assessment will be intelligence-fair and will take place, as much as possible, in the context of the rich and engaging projects that make up the daily curriculum. As a result of such a regimen, we expect that students will end up having a stronger and more fruitful understanding of themselves—their strengths, their distinctive approaches, the particular vocational and avocational roles for which they might be suited.

Many individuals have now entered into discussions of school reform; some are drawn from the domain of educational

research, others from the practical world of classrooms. Too often, the gulf between educational theory and practice remains
unchallenged. In the long run, there is nothing so practical as a
good theory, but a theory without the opportunity for real-life
implementation will soon fade away. At Project Zero, we seek to
span this gulf. By working together as equal partners on projects
of mutual interest, educators and researchers can form productive collaborations through which we can effectively restructure
our schools, leading ultimately to the fuller realization of our
children's rich potential.

*Author's note: The research described in this article has been gen-
erously supported by the Grant Foundation, the Lilly Endowment,
the McDonnell Foundation, the Rockefeller Brothers Fund, the
Rockefeller Foundation, the Spencer Foundation, and the Bernard
Van Leer Foundation.*

REFERENCES

Gardner, H. (1983). *Frames of Mind: The Theory of Multiple Intelligences.* New York: Basic Books.

Gardner, H. (1987a). "An Individual-Centered Curriculum." In *The Schools We've Got, the Schools We Need.* Washington, D.C.: Council of Chief State School Officers and the American Association of Teacher Education.

Gardner, H. (1987b). "Developing the Spectrum of Human Intelligences." *Harvard Educational Review* 57: 187–193.

Gardner, H. (1989a). "Zero-Based Arts Education: An Introduction to Arts PROPEL." *Studies in Art Education: A Journal of Issues and Research* 30(2):71–83.

Gardner, H. (November 8, 1989b). "The Academic Community Must Not Shun the Debate on How to Set National Educational Goals." *The Chronicle of Higher Education,* A52.

Gardner, H. ([1991]). "The School of the Future." In [*Ways of Knowing, No. 3:*] *The Reality Club,* edited by J. Brockman. New York: The Education Foundation.

Gardner, H. ([1992]). "Assessment in Context: The Alternative to Standard-ized Testing." In [*Policy Perspectives on Educational Testing*], edited by B. Gifford. Boston: Kluwer.

Gardner, H. ([In press]). "Four Factors for Reforming Education." *On The Beam*.

Krechevsky, M. and H. Gardner. ([1990]). "Enhancing Scholastic Performance: An Infusion Approach." In *Developmental Perspectives on Teaching and Learning Thinking Skills*, edited by D. Kuhn. Basel, [Switzerland]: S. Karger.

Krechevsky, M. and H. Gardner. ([1992]). "The Emergence and Nurturance of Multiple Intelligences." In *Encouraging the Development of Exceptional [Skills] and Talents*, edited by [M.J.] Howe. Leicester, U.K.: The British Psychological Society.

Olson, L. (January 27, 1988). "Children Flourish Here." *Education Week*, 1.

Multiple Intelligences Theory: Creating the Thoughtful Classroom

by Noel White, Tina Blythe, and Howard Gardner

Sophia roams around her kindergarten classroom, teasing classmates and disrupting games until it's her turn during story time. Then she becomes quickly absorbed in long and intricate tales of her own making. Rui, shy and inarticulate in his seventh grade English class, performs gracefully and compellingly in the school play. Lynn can't focus on any math problem for more than thirty seconds, but practices basketball for hours with methodical concentration, discipline, and dedication. They are puzzling, these students—and classrooms teem with them. Their inconsistent performances defy easy labels such as "under-achiever," "slow," and "learning disabled." Their strengths belie the less-than-satisfactory grades that cover their report cards. As these students become older and their schools more departmentalized, the chances that their teachers will see and value their particular strengths decrease dramatically. Even if he or she doesn't "catch" a student in some moment of greatness, a teacher who has to give a failing mark often does so with the nagging sense that the student is smarter than the grade indicates.

> A teacher who has to give a failing mark often does so with the nagging sense that the student is smarter than the grade indicates.

From *If Minds Matter: A Foreword to the Future,* vol. 2, edited by Art Costa, James Bellanca, and Robin Fogarty, p. 127–134. © 1992 by IRI/Skylight Publishing. Reprinted with permission.

How do we begin to make sense of the peaks and valleys in these students' abilities? How do we address their failures in the classroom? Is there a way—or even a reason—to recognize and reward their strengths? Can such recognition further the cause of the traditional goals of public schooling, namely reading, writing, and arithmetic?

For their appealing answers to such difficult questions, the alternative theories of intelligence espoused by Robert Sternberg (1985), Stephen Ceci (1990), David Feldman (1986), and others have been gaining popularity in educational circles. Despite their differences, these theories all assert that humans exhibit intelligent behavior in a wide variety of ways. People are not simply "smart" or "dumb." They vary in their intellectual strength depending on the context in which they are working. In the cases of Sophia, Rui, and Lynn, these theories might suggest that nothing is wrong with the students, but rather they have talents that traditional classrooms seldom tap.

> Educational standards do not have to be lowered for them, but should be expanded to offer a wider variety of opportunities for success.

Educational standards do not have to be lowered for them, but should be expanded to offer a wider variety of opportunities for success. Teachers have not failed, but they may need to direct their talents to a diversified curriculum. At the same time, these students' strengths, once identified, could be used in the service of more traditional goals. This chapter explores some of the ways the theory of "multiple intelligences," developed by Howard Gardner and colleagues, has been used to approach traditional schooling from a more complex and, we argue, a more fruitful perspective.

MULTIPLE INTELLIGENCES THEORY

Gardner's theory of multiple intelligences maintains that we all possess several different and independent capacities for solving problems and creating products (Gardner, 1983, 1991a). Gardner and his colleagues gleaned the evidence for these capacities, or "intelligences," from many varied sources: empirical work with normal and gifted children; investigations of brain-damaged adults; and studies of idiot savants, prodigies, and other special populations. These data yield evidence for at least seven discrete domains of human achievement.

Linguistic intelligence involves not only ease in producing language, but also sensitivity to the nuances, order, and rhythm of words. Poets exemplify this intelligence in its mature form. Students who enjoy playing with rhymes, who pun, who always have a funny story to tell, who quickly acquire other languages — including sign language—and who write copious notes to their friends in class all exhibit linguistic intelligence.

Logical-mathematical intelligence entails the ability to reason either deductively or inductively, and to recognize and manipulate abstract patterns and relationships. Scientists, mathematicians, and philosophers all rely on this intelligence. So do the students who "live" baseball statistics or who carefully analyze the components of problems—either personal or school-related—before systematically testing solutions.

Musical intelligence includes sensitivity to pitch, timbre, and rhythm of sounds, as well as responsiveness to the emotional implications of these elements. While composers and instrumentalists clearly exhibit this intelligence, so do the students who seem particularly caught by the birds singing outside the classroom window, or who constantly tap out intricate—if irritating—rhythms on the desk with their pencils.

Spatial intelligence is the ability to create visual-spatial representations of the world and to transfer those representations either mentally or concretely. Well-developed spatial capacities are needed for the work of architects, sculptors, and engineers. The students who turn first to the graphs, charts, and pictures in their textbooks, who like to "web" their ideas before writing a paper, and who fill the blank space around their notes with intricate patterns are also using their spatial intelligence.

Bodily-kinesthetic intelligence involves using the body to solve problems, to create products, and to convey ideas and emotions. Athletes, surgeons, dancers, choreographers, and crafts people all use bodily-kinesthetic intelligence. The capacity is also evident in students who relish gym class and school dances, who prefer to carry out class projects by making models rather than writing reports, and who pitch their crumbled papers with annoying accuracy and frequency into wastebaskets across the room.

Interpersonal intelligence is the ability to understand other people, to notice their goals, motivations, intentions, and to work effectively with them. Teachers, parents, politicians, psychologists, and salespeople rely on interpersonal intelligence to carry out their work. Students exhibit this intelligence when they thrive on small-group work, when they notice and react to the moods of their friends and classmates, and when they tactfully convince the teacher of their need for extra time to complete the homework assignment.

Intrapersonal intelligence is personal knowledge turned inward to the self. This form of intellect entails the ability to understand one's own emotions, goals, and intentions. Although it is difficult to assess who has this capacity and to what degree, evidence can be sought in students' uses of their other intelligences—how well they seem to be capitalizing on their strengths, how cognizant they are of their weaknesses, and how thoughtful they are about the decisions and choices they make. The two personal intelligences are, perhaps, the hardest to observe and, at the same time, are the most important to success in any societal domain.

Each person exhibits a unique intellectual profile with preferred methods of approaching and solving problems.

Along with positing these seven capacities, Multiple Intelligences theory makes some important assertions about the way these intelligences develop and manifest themselves.

First, every normal individual possesses all seven intelligences, but in varying degrees of strengths. Each person exhibits a unique intellectual profile with preferred methods of approaching and solving problems. Thus, a standardized approach to education faces the serious problem of inevitably neglecting many students. Sophia, Rui, and Lynn, for example, would have scant opportunity to make use of their strengths in a traditional classroom, where certain aspects of linguistic and logical-mathematical intelligence are regnant while other forms of intelligence are largely ignored.

Second, intelligences are educable. Although determined to some extent by genetic predisposition, the development of intelligences is also a matter of culture and education. Traditionally, our culture has valued language and logic skills, so it has developed educational curricula and methods that favor students gifted in these two domains. According to Multiple Intelligences theory, even students not gifted in these domains can improve, but they may need to begin by drawing on their stronger intelligences. Lynn, for example, might sit easier in math class if the work involved opportunities to play with physical representations of problems or the manipulation of basketball statistics rather than isolated numbers. And if we decide to value other skills, they too can be accommodated and educated within our schools.

Third, each intelligence can be mobilized for a variety of tasks and goals. For example, Sophia's linguistic intelligence enables her to tell stories and to invent the rhyming nicknames with which she teases classmates. Furthermore, intelligences almost never operate in isolation; most goals and tasks involve a number of intelligences working together. For example, Sophia's storytelling reveals her linguistic abilities as well as her bodily-kinesthetic and logical intelligences. This is evidenced in her manipulation of the toy figures she uses to represent a story's characters and in her creation of a cause-and-effect plot for her stories.

> **Sophia's linguistic intelligence enables her to tell stories and to invent the rhyming nicknames with which she teases classmates.**

Fourth, intelligences manifest themselves in specific domains with particular types of materials and problems. A person cannot develop fully or assess accurately one intelligence through the medium of another. For instance, a student's musical intelligence cannot be developed merely by discussing music—although, if the student is linguistically gifted, talking could be a good place to start. At some point, the student will need to experiment with the tools of the domain—for example, by playing an instrument, composing a melody, or beating a rhythm. By the same token, assessing the student's progress in music cannot be done solely through pencil-and-paper short-answer tests.

THEORY INTO PRACTICE

The particulars of Multiple Intelligences theory are not set in stone. Further research may modify our description of intelligences, may suggest different labels, or may identify altogether new intelligences. But these particulars are not as important as the basic implication that intellectual development involves more than a single, genetically determined capacity. This basic understanding complicates our picture of the factors at play in any educational setting. If we examine school through the lens of Multiple Intelligences theory, the typical classroom becomes a complex web of numerous strengths, weaknesses, opportunities, and dead ends. Students do not simply vary from one to another; they vary along several different dimensions. Teachers, too, are strong in some intelligences but not others, and they need to engage students who, for the most part, bear intelligence profiles different from theirs. When viewed through Multiple Intelligences theory, the standard curriculum itself has fortes, such as language and logic, and deficiencies—for example, many capacities receive only cursory acknowledgment in the form of gym, art, and music classes. All of these—students, teachers, and curriculum—interact in ways that are complicated, sometimes productive, and sometimes not.

> ...the typical classroom becomes a complex web of numerous strengths, weaknesses, opportunities, and dead ends.

Given this complex picture of school, Multiple Intelligences theory suggests educational practices that diverge considerably from the current push toward standardization of curriculum, pedagogy, and assessment. In particular, Multiple Intelligences theory calls for broadening the school curriculum to emphasize the divergent paths students can take toward understanding and for diversifying assessment. The following pages describe some examples of how these ideas might play out in the classroom.

BROADENING THE SCHOOL CURRICULUM

If students are to develop the full range of their potential, they need to be exposed early and often to a wide variety of activities and materials. Only the most gifted prodigies can develop their talents to any extent in the absence of external encouragement. One suspects, for example, that Mozart would have found a way to make music even if his father hadn't himself been an ambitious musician. However, Sophia might never have discovered, much less developed, her ability to create stories had not her teacher given her the time and the encouragement to do so.

In order to create a model for enabling very young children to explore their various intelligences and interests, multiple intelligences researchers worked with teachers to develop Project Spectrum (Krechevsky & Gardner, 1990b). In a Spectrum classroom, students visit "learning centers," where they can choose freely from a variety of hands-on activities that permit them to experiment with the materials of each domain. For example, imaginative figures and story boards aid students in storytelling, engaging their linguistic abilities. Sorting and assembling simple mechanical devices allow for the development of spatial and bodily-kinesthetic skills. Throughout the year, the teacher makes notes about which activities students gravitate toward, as well as the progress they make in working with the various materials. At the year's end, the teacher produces a report that details each student's intellectual profile and offers suggestions for activities which would encourage a child's strengths and shore up that child's weaknesses.

Of course, it is important for students—not just their parents and teachers—to understand their own intellectual profiles. Toward this end, activities involving reflection need to accompany these explorations. In Spectrum classrooms, students as young as four years old are asked to identify the activities that they like most, as well as the ones they think they do best. Older students write in journals, create charts, or discuss their strengths with other students. Such reflection fosters the development of intrapersonal intelligence, a capacity that enables students to draw more readily on their strengths when solving future problems.

Self-knowledge is not the only benefit of a more inclusive curriculum. Motivation is another important by-product (Csikszentmihalyi, 1990). Students who are encouraged to develop their strengths are more likely to enjoy their work and to persevere when they encounter difficulties in these domains. Such perseverance and the attendant increase in the students' skill builds both confidence and competence for dealing with more complex problems as they arise.

MULTIPLE PATHS TO UNDERSTANDING

Broadening the curriculum does not imply that traditional goals need to be disregarded. However, Multiple Intelligences theory does suggest that there may be more than one way to achieve those goals. Because each student has different strengths for experiencing the world, a presentation of the curriculum which emphasizes only language and logic will not be equally successful for all students. Each student will thrive depending on how he or she experiences the new materials. Some students need visual and physical representations of concepts. Some students prefer abstract mind-work. Some need ideas explained verbally in several different ways. Some students benefit when a classmate explains materials. Some work best when given the opportunity to play for some time with materials, as in a science lab, before they discover the key information. Others want to be told the answer directly.

> Experienced and successful teachers often cater to a range of students by teaching each part of the curriculum in many different ways.

Making the match between the standard curriculum and each student's proclivities is not easy, but progress can be achieved with the efforts of teachers and students. Teachers can take an active role by shaping their presentations of the curriculum to fit the needs of a wider range of students. Experienced and successful teachers often cater to a range of students by teaching each part of the curriculum in many different ways. They tend to revisit a key concept or theme often and with variations to provide several opportunities for students to approach a concept from different perspectives. In multiple intelligences terms, this variety provides the multiple paths to understanding necessary to engage the multiple intelligences that students bring to the classroom.

A Project Approach

One of the most common and most effective ways to provide multiple opportunities for students to use their strengths is through working on projects (Gardner, 1991b). Projects can allow students to choose topics or approaches that fit their interests (Olson, 1988). Projects also provide opportunities for extended work with peers, which develops interpersonal skills. Given the opportunity to present their information in forms other than writing, students can develop and display musical, spatial, and kinesthetic skills.

Public elementary school teachers in Indianapolis, Indiana created The Key School around Gardner's Multiple Intelligences theory. It makes projects an important part of each student's experience. Students in the Key School learn about multiple intelligences and are required to take regular classes in physical education, computers, art, music, and a foreign language, as well as the standard reading, writing, and arithmetic. They draw on these diverse experiences to create three major projects each year. Several elements of the projects encourage students to draw on and to develop multiple intelligences: the Key School's general course-work, which feeds into the projects; the encouragement to be creative and personal in developing projects; working on projects for extended periods of time; cooperating with others; performing or presenting their projects to classmates; and documenting the process and product on videotape, which captures much more than written documentation. With its focus on extended projects that emphasize a range of skills, including linguistic, musical, and interpersonal, the Key School has a lively and productive atmosphere. It differs enormously from schools that emphasize practice for written, standardized tests of language and logic. Students at the Key School acquire the "basic skills" required of public education, but they do so through multiple paths that take advantage of their personal and creative energies.

> **Students at the Key School acquire the "basic skills" required of public education, …through multiple paths that take advantage of their personal and creative energies.**

Teachers, school curriculum, and administrators are not the only ones responsible for matching student intelligences with curricular goals. Students can be encouraged to take some of the responsibility for shaping their school experience. Students can learn to adapt the curriculum to their needs, and to use their own strengths to better serve the demands of school. Most students stumped by a writing assignment or dismayed by the prospect of failing yet another math exam might give up or might overcome the difficulty only if the teacher intervenes. The student who approaches an assignment as if there is only one way to go about the task has little hope once stuck. Students with the perspective of multiple intelligences have a better chance by understanding that there are many approaches to writing and a variety of ways to gain insight into math. If students have had the opportunity to learn something about their own intelligences, then they have a better chance to find approaches that will work for them when facing tough assignments.

Training Practical Intelligence

The difficulty is that not all students know they can take responsibility for their learning by drawing on their own strengths and interests, and not all students know how. Put another way, some students have "practical intelligence." That is, they understand themselves well enough to know how their own ways of working are unique, and they understand school well enough to recognize how they can best utilize personal abilities—and overcome disabilities—to fit the varying demands of school tasks. Many students, however, do not possess the practical intelligence that would allow them to maneuver successfully through their school careers. The Practical Intelligence for School (PIFS) project developed curricular materials to help students take more responsibility for their learning (Krechevsky & Gardner, 1990a; Walters, Blythe, & White, [1993]).

Study skills curricula often help when and where students do not need it, disconnected from their daily schoolwork.

Many efforts—generally called study skills curricula—already exist to teach practical skills. The PIFS project differs from these efforts in several respects. Study skills curricula often help when and where students do not need it, disconnected from their daily schoolwork. Proceeding on Multiple Intelligences theory's assertion that intelligences manifest themselves in specific domains with particular types of materials and problems, PIFS lessons consider practical knowledge in the context of the academic problems students face daily. Practical intelligence is not something more to be learned on top of reading, writing, and arithmetic. Rather, practical skills such as being organized, managing time, understanding one's best work styles, and understanding the school system at large are integrally mixed with and complicated by the process of learning these subjects. Study skills curricula often present single or simple solutions to complex problems, thereby failing to serve the needs of many students. Following Multiple Intelligences theory, the PIFS curriculum gives students opportunities in the course of their regular lessons to recognize that they have unique ways of going about schoolwork. In this manner, PIFS lessons help students establish personal, workable solutions to their own difficulties.

DIVERSIFYING ASSESSMENT

An important part of any plan to encourage a variety of abilities and to provide multiple paths between those abilities and the standard curriculum, is the broadening of assessment conceptions (Gardner, 1990a). Even educators who appreciate their students' different needs and strengths often give grades that credit only a narrow range of skills, mainly those that exploit language and logic. The scope of assessment can be expanded without severely altering classroom culture. Common school experiences, such as science laboratories and social studies projects, can be supplemented with notebooks, journals, portfolios, review conferences, videos, or other kinds of records. These supplements broaden the focus of both teachers and students. The most common student products, such as tests, papers, and oral presentations, highlight mainly linguistic and logical skills. Such products leave out other important skills students may have and which certainly are important for students' overall growth.

The scope of assessment can be expanded without severely altering classroom culture.

To examine how assessment can include a wider range of intelligences, the Arts PROPEL project, a collaboration among Harvard Project Zero, the Educational Testing Service, and Pittsburgh Public Schools, has done considerable work toward making portfolios a practical and educational part of the classroom (Gardner, 1990b). By building portfolios over time, PRO-PEL classes encourage an examination of the evolution and range of students' thinking. Documenting the process that students undertake when they write, paint, or prepare for tests, these assessments generate more opportunities to recognize and encourage strengths that may not be evidenced in the final product (Winner et al., in press).

Building on the notion of portfolios, but taking care to focus on more than polished final products, Arts PROPEL calls its assessment devices "processfolios." A processfolio is a record of learning that captures a student's process of creation. The activity of focus may be in any domain: music, drama, science, English, history, or the like. Processfolios can include pieces that represent different styles, mastery of specific skills, and examples of pivotal works in progress. Unlike tests, processfolios can preserve examinations of problems that students find important, that may have several answers, or that require original and sustained research (Wolf, 1988). The Arts PROPEL processfolios sample a wide range of skills, among them are craft, pursuit (revision and development over time), expressiveness, inventiveness, self-assessment, use of criticism, the capacity to make distinctions among works, awareness of physical properties of materials, ability to work independently or collaboratively, and use of resources. Students develop critical intrapersonal and interpersonal skills by reviewing their processfolios with the teacher and with one another. Classrooms involved with the Arts PROPEL project recognize and encourage a larger range of student talents than classrooms relying only on such assessments as standard written tests and papers.

> **Processfolios can include pieces that represent different styles, mastery of specific skills, and examples of pivotal works in progress.**

On a smaller scale, classes that extensively feature the informal assessments naturally integrated into activities, such as class discussions, self-monitoring, small-group work, and peer reviewing, also tend to promote a more productive range of thinking in students. By interacting with people other than the teacher, students have the opportunity to see ideas from many different perspectives and to gauge their own learning. Similar to portfolios, devices such as journals and videotapes can record the process of these important learning experiences as well as their results. When students have opportunities to review their learning, especially with peers, they develop a wider range of skills and begin assuming more responsibility in shaping their own educational experiences.

CONCLUSION

Theories that expand our notions of intelligence have offered some hope for understanding the successes and the failures of students like Sophia, Rui, and Lynn. Gardner's theory of multiple intelligences argues that these students may have great potential, both in school and adult life. Drawing on the basic notion that students bring multiple abilities with them to school, and that school can offer a much richer range of opportunities than is commonly emphasized, several ongoing efforts have shown how the perspective of Multiple Intelligences theory can help more students capitalize on their skills. The ultimate goal of these efforts is to reach beyond the schools and into later life.

> If we declare our educational goal to be preparing children for productive adult lives, we have an obligation to help students develop all of their intelligences.

Even more than school success, performance in any vocation or avocation depends on a combination of intelligences. One has only to reflect on the disparate duties performed by teachers, lawyers, mechanics, artists, doctors, parents, engineers, and business people to see that much more than linguistic or logical-mathematical intelligence is needed for success in any of these occupations. If we declare our educational goal to be preparing children for productive adult lives, we have an obligation to help students develop all of their intelligences. By more closely mirroring the complexities of adult life, including its demand for multiple and intertwined skills, school can better prepare our youth to assume responsibility for our world—and, in the future, their world.

We would like to express our gratitude to the William T. Grant Foundation, the Lilly Endowment, the MacArthur Foundation, the James S. McDonnell Foundation, the Pew Charitable Trusts, the Rockefeller Brothers' Fund, the Rockefeller Foundation, and the Spencer Foundation for their generous support of the work described in this chapter. We would also like to thank the students, teachers, and administrators who have been invaluable sources of information and enthusiasm in our research.

REFERENCES

Ceci, S. (1990). *On intelligence, more or less.* Englewood Cliffs, NJ: Prentice Hall.

Csikszentmihalyi, M. (1990). *Flow: The psychology of optimal experience.* New York: Harper & Row.

Feldman, D. H. (1986). *Nature's gambit: Child prodigies and the development of human potential.* New York: Basic [Books].

Gardner, H. (1991a). *Intelligence in seven phases.* Paper presented at the 100th Anniversary of Education at Harvard, Cambridge, MA.

Gardner, H. (1991b). *The unschooled mind: How children think and how schools should teach.* New York: Basic [Books].

Gardner, H. (1990a). Assessment in context: The alternative to standardized testing. In B. R. Gifford & M. C. O'Connor (Eds.), *Changing assessments: Alternative views of aptitude, achievement, and instruction* (pp. 77–119). Boston: Kluwer.

Gardner, H. (1990b). *The assessment of student learning in the arts.* Paper presented at the Conference on Assessment in Arts Education, Bosschenhooft, the Netherlands.

Gardner, H. (1983). *Frames of mind: The theory of multiple intelligences.* New York: Basic [Books].

Krechevsky, M., & Gardner, H. (1990a). Approaching school intelligently: An infusion approach. In D. Kuhn (Ed.), *Developmental perspectives on teaching and learning thinking skills* (pp. 79–94). Basel, [Switzerland]: Karger.

Krechevsky, M., & Gardner, H. (1990b). The emergence and nurturance of multiple intelligences. In M. J. A. Howe (Ed.), *Encouraging the development of exceptional abilities and talents* (pp. 222–245). Leicester, England: British Psychological Society.

Olson, L. (1988, January 27). Children "flourish" here. *Education Week*, pp. 1, 18–21.

Sternberg, R. J. (1985). *Beyond I.Q.: A triarchic theory of human intelligence.* New York: Cambridge University.

Walters, J., Blythe, T., & White, N. ([1993]). PIFS: Everyday cognition goes to school. In H. Reese & J. Puckett (Eds.), [*Mechanisms of everyday cognition*]. Hillsdale, NJ: Lawrence Erlbaum.

Winner, E. (in press). Arts PROPEL: An introductory handbook. In E. Winner (Ed.), *Arts PROPEL Handbook Series* (vol. 1). Princeton, NJ: Educational Testing Service; Cambridge, MA: Harvard Project Zero.

Wolf, D. P. (1988). Opening up assessment. *Educational Leadership, 45*(4), 24–29.

Multiple Intelligences
in Action

by Bruce Campbell

lthough many teachers are interested in innovative education theories that suggest ways to optimize student learning, they often find it difficult to make the transition from
theory to practice. Howard Gardner's theory of multiple intelligences offers an intriguing theory for classroom practice. In his
book *Frames of Mind: The Theory of
Multiple Intelligences* (1983), Gardner
defines intelligence as the ability to find
and solve problems and create products
of value in one's culture. He points out
that the concept of intelligent behavior
varies from culture to culture. Linguistic
intelligence and logical/mathematical intelligence, for example, are generally es-
teemed in Western culture. To an Afri-
can tribesman, however, musical intelligence may be equally
important. To a Polynesian navigator, spatial intelligence is
critical, and for a family of high-wire artists, finely tuned kinesthetic intelligence is necessary.

> Howard Gardner's
> theory of multiple
> intelligences offers an
> intriguing theory for
> classroom practice.

A cognitive psychologist at Harvard University, Gardner is
not the first to recognize multiple human abilities. He is, however, the first to acknowledge diverse competencies as forms of
human intelligence. The seven intelligences he has identified
are: Linguistic, Logical/Mathematical, Spatial or Visual, Musical, Kinesthetic and what he calls the Personal Intelligences—
Interpersonal and Intrapersonal.

From *Childhood Education*, vol. 68, no. 4, p. 197–200, Summer 1992. © 1992
by the Association for Childhood Education International. Reprinted with
permission.

The program described here is one educator's attempt to implement Gardner's concept of seven human intelligences into daily teaching. In this model, used successfully with 3rd- through 5th-graders, the curriculum is based on student interests. Seven learning centers offer thematic multimodal learning activities engaging the seven intelligences. A flexible daily schedule is provided to better meet student needs. Such a program decentralizes the classroom, empowering students to take a proactive role in their education as well as transforming the teacher's function from director to facilitator. Both students and teacher have opportunities to develop their multiple intelligences as they learn together.

> **Seven learning centers offer thematic multimodal learning activities engaging the seven intelligences.**

THE FOUR-STEP MODEL

The classroom program is based on a four-step instructional sequence: the main lesson, centers (based on multiple intelligences), sharing and reviewing and individual projects implementing the multiple intelligences.

The Main Lesson

Each school day begins with a main lesson, a 15- to 20-minute multimodal overview of the topic to be studied that day. Since the curriculum is thematic, daily main lessons are drawn from the theme being studied. The major units are developed based on student interests that have been organized into related areas. Examples of such themes include outer space, animals, foreign countries and legends. Frequently these thematic units address more than one group of interests. If there were several foreign countries on the chart as well as diverse art forms, for example, a unit entitled "Art Around the World" might be developed. Or, if animals as well as the environment were listed, a unit on the impact of environmental problems on animals might emerge.

Once a unit has been identified, teacher and students divide it into focal points that become the main lessons. The daily lesson in a unit on outer space might focus on comets; in a unit on animals, marsupials; in a unit on "Art Around the World," Chinese block printing; in a unit on animals and the environment, how water pollution affects whales. Generally, the daily lessons follow some sequence with one topic leading to the next. The next lesson following comets, for example, might cover other objects orbiting the sun (e.g., asteroids and planets). Each main lesson consists of a lecture prepared and presented by either the teacher or a student, including visuals, possibly kinesthetic activities and provocative questions. Some questions may be answered in the main lesson, but many are left for students to explore.

Centers Based on Multiple Intelligences

The greatest part of the children's school day is spent in seven learning centers. Based on the seven intelligences identified by Gardner, these areas reflect seven modes of learning. The centers are named after the intelligences (see Figure 1).

Figure 1
Seven Learning Centers Based on the Theory of Multiple Intelligences

William Shakespeare .... Linguistic
Albert Einstein .... Logical/Mathematical
Thomas Edison .... Kinesthetic
Pablo Picasso .... Visual/Spatial
Ray Charles .... Musical
Mother Teresa .... Interpersonal
Emily Dickinson .... Intrapersonal

Following the main lesson and brief instructions for the day's activities, students break into small groups to work at the centers. Learning activities in each center explore the main lesson's topic in seven different ways. Students build models, dance, read, write, compose songs, solve mathematical problems, illustrate and collaborate on small group projects. All of the centers' activities are thematically connected to the main lesson, providing continuity and focus for students.

The groups, which stay together for one month, work in each center for approximately 25 minutes. A bell indicates when to move to the next station. On a daily basis, each student is responsible for completing individual as well as group center assignments. A *flow time,* or free-work period, provides time for any unfinished assignments to be completed. Because the centers are based on multiple ways of working, each student can find at least one area of strength. As a result, everyone is successful in one way or another.

> **Because the centers are based on multiple ways of working, each student can find at least one area of strength.**

These sample activities demonstrate the kinds of work students encounter at the seven centers:

• **William Shakespeare Center.** Students read, write and learn in many traditional modes. They analyze and organize information in written form.

• **Albert Einstein Center.** Students work with math games, manipulatives, mathematical concepts, science experiments, deductive reasoning and problem-solving.

• **Thomas Edison Center.** Students build models, dramatize events and dance in ways that relate to the content of that day's subject matter.

• **Pablo Picasso Center.** Students explore a subject area using diverse art media, manipulatives, puzzles, charts and pictures.

• **Ray Charles Center.** Students learn in rhythmical ways. They compose and sing songs about the subject matter, learn to play instruments, make their own instruments and listen to pre-recorded music.

• **Mother Teresa Center.** Students develop cooperative learning skills as they solve problems, answer questions, create learning games, brainstorm ideas and discuss the day's topic collaboratively.

• **Emily Dickinson Center.** Students develop thinking skills as they explore the present area of study through research, reflection, individual projects and writing.

Numerous opportunities allow students to have regular input into their learning and take an active role in planning daily activities. Sometimes the small groups plan one center for the rest of the class, or each group may plan all of its own center activities. Sometimes, teacher and students concur at a whole-group planning session. One final option is that individual students can contract to use the center time in more personally meaningful ways.

While students are at work in the centers, teacher time is spent with individuals or small groups. Teacher activities might include helping students in one group learn a new skill, tutoring those with reading or math difficulties, assisting a gifted student with a challenging research topic or advising a small group in designing a structure or creating a dance. Additionally, the teacher often meets with individual students, evaluating work, suggesting opportunities for improvement and giving positive feedback.

> **While students are at work in the centers, teacher time is spent with individuals or small groups.**

Sharing & Reviewing

After center work, time is set aside each day for students to share their learning. Poems are read, art work displayed, songs sung, structures exhibited, dances and skits performed and posters, murals and charts displayed. Sharing is voluntary, but most students participate in one way or another. Everyone enjoys this time, since students can display work from their areas of strength.

Students also keep a daily log to record what they learn and accomplish each day. Serving several purposes, the log reinforces student learning, enhances retention and helps students summarize and synthesize their school work. By the end of the year, the log furnishes students with memories and is an effective tool for sharing a child's school experiences with parents and other interested adults.

Reviewing each day's lesson involves not only sharing and the daily log, but also discussion. What was learned about this topic? Why is it important? What does it have to do with real life? Where does it lead? What do you want to learn next? Such questions are discussed at the end of the day or the following day prior to the main lesson. The review creates a larger context for the daily lesson and center activities. An important part of the learning process, the review brings a meaningful closure to each lesson by reinforcing information for long-term memory and allowing students to demonstrate what they have learned.

Projects

At the centers, students develop many skills by learning in diverse modes. After centers and sharing, however, students work on independent projects of their choice. It is here that some of the most profound learning occurs. Project time each afternoon is really an extension of center time. The difference is that the projects are generally unrelated to the unit being studied, and the format is entirely student-centered and self-directed. Here students apply the strategies and skills they are developing in the centers.

> As the school year progresses and areas of expertise emerge, more and more emphasis is placed on independent work.

Approximately every three weeks, students begin a project either independently or with one or two classmates on a topic of their choice. The requirements include doing independent research, learning five to ten concepts and preparing a multimodal presentation to teach the class about their topic. At the end of the three-week period, students demonstrate their research through songs, skits, posters and other forms of artwork or visuals, videotapes, computer-generated information, surveys, class participation activities, raps, constructions, puzzles and problems for their classmates. These reflect the same types of multiple intelligences activities they are doing in the learning centers.

The skills developed during centers then emerge in highly personal and relevant ways in the independent projects. Students learn *how to learn* and can demonstrate their knowledge in many ways. The high quality of the independent projects illustrates the importance of student choice. Yet, without the multiple intelligences centers, it is questionable whether student projects would be so creative and informative. As the school year progresses and areas of expertise emerge, more and more emphasis is placed on independent work. For some children, however, the structured learning of the centers remains crucial for their success.

In summary, a typical day begins with the main lesson presented to the whole class by the teacher or a student. Directions are given for work at the seven centers and students break into their groups and work for 15- to 25-minute sessions in each center. A short time is taken to share and review work produced at the centers. Last, approximately one hour is set aside for work on independent projects. Naturally, other activities go on in an ordinary school day—recess, special programs and more—but generally the bulk of the day is occupied as described here.

TEACHER PREPARATION AND PLANNING

Although initial planning for such diverse activities can be challenging and time consuming, it soon becomes no more difficult than preparing for a more traditional program. It is important to realize that the teacher does not plan seven centers each day. Many activities are continued for more than one day, perhaps for as long as a month. At the Mother Teresa Center, for example, a group may be developing a board game to learn geography that could take one to two weeks. It could take a few days to build a model or diorama at the Thomas Edison Center or write, edit and rewrite a composition at the Emily Dickinson Center.

Moreover, as the teacher attempts to create depth so that students can develop skills in the various centers, activities tend to build on each other. At the Pablo Picasso Center in a unit about cities, for example, students may go through a series of lessons in which they develop drawing skills using city scenes for practice. This series of lessons is a form of long-term planning that minimizes the day-to-day process of finding activities for each center.

Since students themselves are sometimes involved in the planning process, the teacher's role is simplified accordingly. With practice, the teacher becomes more skilled at planning in multimodal ways and finds it requires less effort. Finally, whenever teachers work as teams, different teachers can prepare different centers. Regardless of who does the planning, the goal is always to integrate the activities for each center with the main lesson. A sample lesson is shown in Figure 2.

A multiple intelligences classroom requires many resources; consequently, preparing lessons may present new challenges in the early stages since more diverse materials are needed. As technology becomes more accessible, these needs can be met through software programs, CD-ROMs and laser disks. Tape decks and filmstrip projectors are also frequently used. The school library or media center offers additional reference materials. Finally, certain basic art supplies are necessary.

Figure 2
A Sample Multiple Intelligences Lesson with Centers

Main Lesson: *Comets.* A short lecture is given with pictures and diagrams describing comets, their size, composition and orbits. Students act out a kinesthetic activity where some portray the sun and others assume the different parts of the comet and "walk" through the comet's orbit around the sun.

Centers
William Shakespeare. Students read about comets from science books, library books on astronomy or encyclopedias and answer diverse levels of questions about their reading.

Albert Einstein. Using graph paper and rulers, students draw a series of comets to different scales: with the tail 10x as long as the head, 50x as long, 100x as long and 500x as long.

Thomas Edison. Students make their own comets with marshmallows, sticks and ribbons for comet tails. When completed, students walk through a geometrically correct comet orbit.

Pablo Picasso. Using glue and glitter, students make comets on colored paper, correctly labeling all of the parts.

Ray Charles. Using the melody *Twinkle, Twinkle, Little Star* or one of their own choice, groups write a song about comets containing information they have learned.

Mother Teresa. In a group, students design a board game that requires knowledge of comets to play successfully. When completed, students will play their own games as well as those created by other groups.

Emily Dickinson. Individually, students write imaginary stories about the exploration of an approaching comet from spaceships they are piloting. The stories must demonstrate knowledge about comets as well as thinking skills.

ACCOMMODATING DISTRICT CURRICULUM GOALS

Questions typically asked are, "What about the basics?" and "When are social studies and science taught?" The basics and other subjects are taught every day. Students read and write at most centers, as well as in their independent projects. Well-informed of curriculum guidelines, the teacher attempts to keep every student at his/her appropriate skill level. The class may not study direct objects on page 126 of the language arts book on a specific day. By year's end, however, most students know how to write a sentence with a direct object because the teacher works with individual students on a day-to-day basis.

Many stories in the reading text are integrated with thematic units, as are social studies and science chapters. Students read other textbook stories or units at their leisure. The 3rd-grade science text, for example, features a unit on astronomy. While working on outer space, chapters in the science text are read at the William Shakespeare Center. Over the course of the year, most district curriculum becomes integrated into thematic units.

When subjects are not easily integrated (e.g., math or language), the teacher will break from the center format and provide a lesson on a new concept to the whole class. Students seldom object, and the continuity of the interdisciplinary program is not jeopardized.

RESEARCH RESULTS

In an attempt to ascertain the effects of such an instructional model, an action research project was conducted during the 1989–1990 school year. The teacher kept a daily journal with specific entries recording the following:

- General daily comments
- Daily evaluation of how focused or "on-task" students were
- Evaluation of transitions between center activities
- Explanation of any discipline problems
- Self-assessment—how teacher time was used
- Tracking of three individuals, previously identified as students with behavior problems

In addition, a Classroom Climate Survey was administered 12 times during the year, a Student Assessment Inventory of work at the seven centers was administered 9 times during the year and a Small Group Attitudinal Survey was administered 8 times during the year.

Briefly, the research data revealed the following:

• Students developed increased responsibility and independence during the year and their self-direction and motivation were apparent to numerous classroom visitors. The students became skilled at developing their own projects, gathering necessary resources and materials and making well-planned presentations.

> By year's end, every student identified at least six centers that were favorites where they felt skilled.

• Students previously identified as having serious behavior problems showed rapid improvement during the first six weeks of school. By mid-year, they were making important contributions to their groups. By year's end, they had assumed positive leadership roles that had not formerly been evident.

• All students developed and applied new skills. In the fall, most students described only one center as a favorite where they felt confident. (The distribution among the seven centers was relatively even.) By mid-year, most identified three to four favorite centers. By year's end, every student identified at least six centers that were favorites where they felt skilled. Moreover, they were all making multimodal presentations of independent projects including songs, skits, visuals, poems, games, surveys, puzzles and group participation activities.

• Cooperative learning skills improved in all students. Since so much of the center work was collaborative, students became highly skilled at listening, helping each other, sharing leadership in different activities, accommodating group changes and introducing new classmates to the program. They learned not only to respect each other, but also to appreciate and call on the unique gifts and abilities of their classmates.

• Academic achievement improved as measured by both classroom and standardized tests. MAT scores from the previous year's students were above state and national averages in all areas. Retention was high on a classroom year-end test of all areas studied during the year. Methods for recalling information were predominantly musical, visual and kinesthetic, indicating the influence of the different intelligences. Students who had previously been unsuccessful in school became successful achievers in new areas.

In summary, students' learning improved. Many students stated they enjoyed school for the first time. As the school year progressed, new skills emerged. Some students discovered musical, artistic, literary, mathematical and other new-found capacities. Others became skilled leaders. In addition, self-confidence and motivation increased significantly. Finally, students developed responsibility, self-reliance and independence as they took an active role in shaping their own learning experiences.

> Students' learning improved. Many students stated they enjoyed school for the first time.

ROLE OF THE TEACHER

The teacher's role transforms in this type of program, requiring different skills from those needed when lecturing in front of a class. The teacher must learn to observe students from seven different perspectives and gather resources to facilitate learning that is center- and project-based. The teacher also finds that he/she is working *with* students, rather than for them, exploring what they explore, discovering what they discover and often learning what they learn. Satisfaction is gleaned from student enthusiasm for learning and independence, rather than test scores and ability to sit quietly. Most important, in planning for such diverse modes of learning, the teacher becomes more creative and multimodal in his/her own thinking and learning. A teacher might well ask: Who is changing the most, students or teachers?

SUCCESS OF A MULTIPLE INTELLIGENCES MODEL

The reasons for the program's academic and behavioral success appear to be twofold. First, every student has an opportunity to specialize and excel in at least one area of human intelligence. Usually, however, it is three or four. In the four years since this program was initiated, not one student has been unable to find an area of success. By learning subject matter in different ways, each student has multiple chances of understanding and retaining academic information. Because of the input students have into the program, their learning experiences are personally meaningful.

Second, many student needs are met through this program. Intellectual needs are met through constant challenge in their daily activities, and emotional needs are met by working closely with others at times and independently at other times. Students develop diverse strengths and come to better understand themselves as individuals.

Such a program emphasizes learning and learning how to learn rather than teaching. Students' interests and developmental needs dictate the direction of the program. Such a model adapts to students rather than expecting students to adapt to it. Experience indicates that by teaching and learning through a student-centered multiple intelligences program, many school problems are reduced and the learning experience for students and teachers alike is optimized.

REFERENCE

Gardner, H. (1983). *Frames of mind: The theory of multiple intelligences.* New York: Basic Books.

From Theory to Practice: Indianapolis' Key School Applies Howard Gardner's Multiple Intelligences Theory to the Classroom

by Patricia J. Bolanos

Ten years ago the founders of the Key School began to study Howard Gardner's theory of multiple intelligences. First, we used it as a basis for a curriculum guide for gifted and talented students. Then, we concluded we could benefit a wide range of students, from slow learners to gifted, by applying the seven areas of intelligence to the classroom. Thus began the creation of the Key School from scratch.

We garnered community support and the approval of James A. Adams, then the superintendent of the Indianapolis Public Schools. With funding from a local foundation, we planned for one year.

When it opened in 1987, the school's goal was to give equal emphasis to the seven areas of intelligence. This idea separates the innovators from the modifiers. If you take equal status seriously,

> We concluded we could benefit a wide range of students, from slow learners to gifted, by applying the seven areas of intelligence to the classroom.

From *The School Administrator,* vol. 51, no. 1, p. 30–31, January 1994. © 1994 by the American Association of School Administrators. Reprinted with permission.

then the staff must include persons who are qualified to teach a specific discipline, e.g., instrumental music, and develop schedules to equalize the instructional time across the seven areas. Classroom generalists cannot teach effectively in all these areas.

Our current staffing pattern at the Key Elementary School includes seven classroom generalists, full-time specialists in the visual arts, instrumental music, and physical education, a media specialist, a resource teacher, and two teachers on special assignment—the flow activity teacher and the community resource teacher. These two positions were designed to make possible grounded research in intrinsic motivation and community involvement.

One other position is extremely critical to our success in the research and development of video portfolios: the non-licensed video specialist. Her major responsibility is to document all the students' theme-based projects and maintain the school's video archives.

> **The staffing and the scheduling reflect the priority to provide all children equal emphasis in all seven areas of intelligence.**

To give more than lip service to multiple intelligences theory requires an investment in a staff that not only is qualified to teach the particular disciplines, but also can schedule adequate time for them to teach what they know. The staffing and the scheduling reflect the priority to provide all children equal emphasis in all seven areas of intelligence.

The theory of multiple intelligences stimulates a wide range of interpretations. Many educators use it as a new veneer over old practice. Arts in education, gifted and talented education, and learning styles are examples of educational approaches that use the theory to justify what already is being done.

The mental model we promote starts with multiple intelligences theory, makes a value judgment of equal emphasis on all seven areas, and establishes a priority by focusing on the student's area of strength. Consequently, the staff includes more specialists than normally is the case at the elementary level. The schedule is balanced to provide equitable time to all students with instruction across the seven areas of intelligence.

STIMULATING MOTIVATION

In September 1993, with the support of superintendent Shirl E. Gilbert II, we opened a middle school, the Key Renaissance School, in downtown Indianapolis. The Renaissance School is an extension of the Key School elementary program in all ways: equal emphasis on the seven areas of intelligence, theme-based interdisciplinary curriculum, multi-aged heterogeneous classes, projects, video portfolios, authentic assessment, and exit-level performance standards.

We want to prepare students of the Key Renaissance School to become future community leaders in business, government, education, the arts, technology, and the sciences. These students will become the pathfinders for Indianapolis in the 21st century. Significantly the school is located in the heart of the business district.

We are establishing mentorships in the larger community for our eighth grade students. After identifying each student's area of highest interest, we match him or her with an adult role model. A student who demonstrates through his or her projects a strength and intrinsic motivation in activities reflecting spatial intelligence might be matched with a mentor from the city planning department.

> After identifying each student's area of highest interest, we match him or her with an adult role model.

We believe time, energy, and resources are best directed toward helping each student discover his or her particular areas of highest interest where intrinsic motivation supports the extra work required to build that strength. A full-time staff member, the service apprenticeship teacher, coordinates this work.

Our plans for these students do not end with the middle school program. We have permission to develop a high school. Our ultimate goal is to create a total learning community (kindergarten through 12th grade). Once the middle school is firmly in place, the high school will be phased in over a four-year period.

Allow me to speculate about the future Key Renaissance High School. I have a persistent vision of students applying their knowledge in the community and working to become high-performance adults.

The current reality is that large, departmentalized urban high schools have values and priorities that are very different from the values and priorities of the Key Renaissance School. Little that now operates in the high schools fits with what we are creating. We are forced to design another type of high school. If the intent to link the individual with the community is pursued actively during the high school years, there is a far greater chance for success with a higher percentage of students.

If these students are to be imprinted with the history of the city of Indianapolis and groomed to become future community leaders, we believe a major emphasis must be placed on life in this community. All persons are expected to contribute with their strength(s) to the common good.

Two specific strategies at the high school level help achieve this goal. One is requiring apprenticeships in a chosen area of strength for all students; the other is meeting a set of eight performance standards. To graduate, high school students must document in a profile portfolio their participation and applied knowledge regarding eight human commonalties identified by Ernest Boyer as the goals of general education (see chart on the next page).

All the work from kindergarten through eight grade leads up to this challenge of each student documenting his or her applied knowledge in the context of the total learning community. The idea is for each individual with strengths to contribute to the common good in a focused community of believers.

For our culture, this idea is to prepare young citizens for active lives as adults in a diverse democratic society.

UNIQUE OPPORTUNITY

Peter Senge has written convincingly in his book, *The Fifth Discipline: The Art and Practice of the Learning Organization*, about the role of a leader as designer. This overview of the Key Renaissance School reflects my primary role as designer in the creation of a total learning community.

This challenge of creation contains enough work in curriculum, instruction, and assessment to require another 10

Goals of a General Education at the Key School

Human Commonality	Applied Knowledge
Shared Life Cycle	In-depth work with elderly, young children, or infirmed
Shared use of symbols	A major multi-media composition—sound, graphics, text
Shared membership in groups	Participation in school governance, sports, community or religious groups
Shared values and beliefs	A major project related to excellence, mutual trust and respect, diversity, and responsible citizenship
Shared sense of time and space	A major project on the history of Indianapolis or ethnic groups' contributions
Shared producing and consuming	A major project related to marketing and economics
Shared relationship with nature	A major project on environmental concerns and stewardship
Shared sense of the aesthetic	A major composition, production, or performance

years of hard labor to reach fruition. Few educators have an opportunity to engage in the collaborative work of establishing a new type of school from the bottom up, kindergarten through 12th grade.

On second thought, maybe the opportunity wasn't really offered—more accurately, it was hammered out of the granite mountain of urban education. Persistence is the password to success.

For All Children

With his theory of multiple intelligences, Gardner seeks to broaden the idea of intelligence to more naturally embrace the differences in all children. He writes, "Anyone who has spent a significant amount of time with children, whether as teacher, counselor, therapist, or family member, will have been struck by the vast differences among children.... As if by edict, all of these differences had mysteriously been ruled out of court, and all children were assessed and arrayed along a single, rather narrow dimension called 'intelligence.' In my view, the intuition that there was something fundamentally askew about such an approach, and that there was a need for a counterview that categorized and celebrated the astonishing range of the human mind, strongly fueled the excitement about MI theory" (Gardner, 1993, p. 65–66).

To accentuate the idea that all children are served equally by the theory of multiple intelligences, Section Four features three articles that give a sample of the vast differences in children and the ways MI theory can help all children learn. In "Different Child, Different Style: Seven Ways to Reach and Teach All Children," Kathy Faggella and Janet Horowitz wisely advise teachers to use Gardner's theory to "encourage those 'at promise' in a particular intelligence, provide intervention for those 'at risk,' and help all students find their own niche in learning and in life." The authors share characteristics of each form of intelligence and offer practical strategies for reinforcing the strengths of all students.

Thomas Armstrong's piece, "Learning Differences—Not Disabilities," advocates education based on how children *can* learn and makes a convincing case for the use of a multiple intelligences approach with all children, especially with children labeled "learning disabled." He coins the term "dysteachia" as the inability or unwillingness of educators to incorporate a broad array of teaching strategies to reach all children.

To round out the section, Dona Matthews looks at the gifted population and applies a multiple intelligences approach to their needs. In her appraisal, Matthews presents theoretical support and contradictory empirical findings, and concludes that although there is little hard evidence in cognitive research literature, "a system that takes into account an individual's aptitude across MI's seven domains would make infinitely more sense in terms of identifying who needs special programming." Matthews recommends the integrative possibilities and theoretical breadth that MI may have for the field of gifted education.

REFERENCE

Gardner, H. (1993). *Multiple intelligences: The theory in practice.* New York: Basic Books.

Different Child, Different Style: Seven Ways to Reach and Teach All Children

by Kathy Faggella and Janet Horowitz

D o you have a student who loves to tell stories or one who always seems to be asking questions? Is one of your students always moving around while another prefers quiet time alone? You might be surprised to find that the traits you observe in your students this year might actually be expressions of different forms of intelligence.

In his book, *Frames of Mind*, Harvard psychologist Howard Gardner concludes that all normal individuals are capable of at least seven forms of intellectual accomplishment. In other words, according to Gardner, humans don't have one overall intelligence, but at least seven distinct ones: linguistic, logical-mathematical, spatial, musical, bodily-kinesthetic, interpersonal, and intrapersonal. We each possess all seven, though one or more may be stronger than others. This tendency toward greater strengths in certain types of intelligence over others can make a difference in many areas of our lives: from preferred learning styles, to the things that interest us both in school and out, to our career choices later in life.

You can put this research on intelligence to work in your classroom.

You can put this research on intelligence to work in your classroom. By being more aware of your students' learning

From *Instructor*, vol. 100, no. 2, p. 49–54, September 1990. © 1990 by Scholastic Inc. Reprinted with permission.

styles, you can encourage those "at promise" in a particular intelligence, provide intervention for those "at risk," and help all students find their own niche in learning and in life. Bear in mind that while every child possesses all seven intelligences, some are stronger in certain areas than others. And some students will have very pronounced strengths in one or two intelligences. Here's how to recognize the characteristics of each form of intelligence and how to supply the materials, activities, and experiences that will reinforce these strengths in your students.

THE LINGUISTIC LEARNER

Characteristics: Loves to read books, write, and tell stories. Has a good memory for names, places, dates, and trivia information.

Materials: Word-making tools, such as a typewriter, word processor, tape recorder, alphabet stamps; as well as many books, records, book-tape sets, and periodicals.

Activities: Storytelling, oral reading, creative writing, audiotaping, written and oral direction games, and joke telling. This child will excel in social studies activities involving dates and places, and will enjoy writing reports and essays.

Special Outings: Trips to the library, a bookstore, or a newspaper office. This child will enjoy a prose or poetry reading and a talk with an author.

THE LOGICAL-MATHEMATICAL LEARNER

Characteristics: Excels at math. Has strong problem-solving and reasoning skills. Asks questions in a logical manner.

Materials: Collections of objects to sort; items to explore, like old wind-up clocks, telephones, kitchen gadgets, magnets, magnifiers; and games that encourage deductive thinking.

Activities: Experimenting, exploring, categorizing, classifying, working with numbers, questioning. This child will enjoy breaking codes, solving mysteries, and writing word problems or coded riddles for other children to solve.

Special Outings: Introduce this student to people in the math, computer, and technical world. Visit museums and science and computer fairs.

THE SPATIAL LEARNER

Characteristics: Needs a mental or physical picture to best understand new information. Does well with maps, charts, and diagrams. Likes mazes and puzzles. Has a good imagination: can design, draw, and create things. Daydreams.

Materials: Lots of visuals: maps, charts, illustrations, films, slides, and photographs; provide mazes, puzzles, and construction toys.

Activities: Will be comfortable with organizing visual information. Map making, chart construction, and media presentations are appropriate activities. This child prefers drawing and painting projects and can conjure up vivid mental pictures of stories.

Special Outings: Take a trip to an art museum or planetarium. Visit with craftspeople, architects, and artists of all kinds.

THE MUSICAL LEARNER

Characteristics: Responds to music. Remembers melodies, notices pitch and rhythm. Is aware of surrounding sounds, such as the nearly inaudible ticking of a watch or a bird singing outside.

Materials: Musical instruments, computerized sound systems, percussion objects, records, tapes, compact discs, and other materials for making music, including taping equipment.

Activities: Needs music activities, including rhythm exercises. Learning often comes easier if things are set to music or to a beat. This child can gain information through ballads and other song lyrics.

Special Outings: Visit music and instrument stores, meet musicians and songwriters, and attend concerts, recitals, operas, and musicals.

Seven Styles of Learning

TYPE	LIKES TO	IS GOOD AT	LEARNS BEST BY
LINGUISTIC LEARNER "The Word Player"	read write tell stories	memorizing names, places, dates, and trivia	saying, hearing and seeing words
LOGICAL/MATHEMATICAL LEARNER "The Questioner"	do experiments figure things out work with numbers ask questions explore patterns and relationships	math reasoning logic problem solving	categorizing classifying working with abstract patterns/relationships
SPATIAL LEARNER "The Visualizer"	draw, build, design and create things daydream look at pictures/slides watch movies play with machines	imagining things sensing changes mazes/puzzles reading maps, charts	visualizing dreaming using the mind's eye working with colors/pictures
MUSICAL LEARNER "The Music Lover"	sing, hum tunes listen to music play an instrument respond to music	picking up sounds remembering melodies noticing pitches/rhythms keeping time	rhythm melody music
BODILY/KINESTHETIC LEARNER "The Mover"	move around touch and talk use body language	physical activities (sports/dance/acting) crafts	touching moving interacting with space processing knowledge through bodily sensations
INTERPERSONAL LEARNER "The Socializer"	have lots of friends talk to people join groups	understanding people leading others organizing communicating manipulating mediating conflicts	sharing comparing relating cooperating interviewing
INTRAPERSONAL LEARNER "The Individual"	work alone pursue own interests	understanding self focusing inward on feelings/dreams following instincts pursuing interests/goals being original	working alone individualized projects self-paced instruction having own space

THE BODILY-KINESTHETIC LEARNER

Characteristics: Is good at physical activities. Has a tendency to move around, touch things, and gesture.

Materials: Hands-on craft materials, such as wood, clay, fabric, yarns, and manipulatives like blocks. This child will find swings, ladders, slides, riding toys, and other gym equipment especially appealing.

Activities: Shines in physical skills, both fine and large motor. This child likes craft activities and drawing and can express him- or herself through dance, drama, and movement.

Special Outings: Attend sporting and dance events and participate in programs that encourage physical movement. Talks with dancers, sports personalities, and craftspeople are great for this child.

THE INTERPERSONAL LEARNER

Characteristics: Strong leadership skills. Understands people and is sociable. Skilled at organizing, communicating, mediating, negotiating.

Materials: People are the most important resource. Arrange desks and chairs to encourage discussion. Have tape machines available to record interviews and other discourse.

Activities: The ultimate group worker, this child often needs to talk to or even teach others in order to learn. Discussions, interviews, debates, and verbal problem-solving sessions are good activities. Encourage sharing and cooperation through group work.

Special Outings: Social and cultural events. This child might like to meet newscasters, politicians, actors, salespeople, and others who communicate directly with people.

THE INTRAPERSONAL LEARNER

Characteristics: Has a strong sense of self. Is confident, a bit of a dreamer, and often prefers working alone. Good instincts about strengths and abilities. Follows through on interests and goals, asking for help as needed.

Materials: Space for solitude. Include books and films about people who have "done their own thing" in the class collection. Make sure that some of the classroom games and collections are suitable for individual work.

Activities: Provide individualized activities such as independent research projects or cumulative writing projects. Allow this child time alone to work on special interests such as writing poetry, putting together a collection, creating artwork, or even thinking.

Special Outings: Spend time on quiet walks, encouraging thinking and mediating. This child might like to meet people who have successfully pursued unusual goals.

PUTTING IT ALL TOGETHER

You might be wondering how you can provide materials, activities, and experiences that consider individual students' learning styles, enhance special inclinations and abilities, and cover your curriculum at the same time. Here's one way you might integrate the seven areas of intelligence into a common elementary course of study: colonial American history.

The linguistic child will gather information from reading the text. This child might also enjoy reading biographies of historical figures; writing stories about the people and events of the colonial period; or creating broadsides, one-page newspapers tacked to the sides of colonial buildings that often included balladlike poetry to tell the public of current events.

The logical-mathematical child will enjoy conducting research. This child could turn information about the time period into a trivia game for the rest of the class. A time line would be another good project.

The spatial learner will learn more about colonial history from films, maps, and charts, or a trip to an historical site. If you read *Johnny Tremain* to the class, this child's imagination will paint vivid pictures of the patriots. Have him or her illustrate parts of the book.

The kinesthetic child will also love a trip to a museum or historic home, especially if it has a hands-on orientation. Creating crafts of the time or preparing a pantomime of activities done will be good projects for this child.

The musical child can learn from 18th-century music and dance. Recordings and pictures will help him or her get to know the lifestyles of the colonists. Rather than write a report, this child might compose a ballad relating the history of this time period.

The interpersonal learner might want to discover historical facts by setting up interviews with linguistic classmates who have read biographies of colonial history makers. Planning a colonial party with games, songs, dances, and foods would be just the thing for this child.

The intrapersonal child might choose one aspect of colonial life and research it in depth. This child might enjoy spending time in the library, pursuing this project independently at his or her own pace, asking for help if it becomes too difficult.

TEACHER STRENGTH

As you've no doubt seen, providing opportunities to stimulate children in the ways they learn best might mean that more than one type of project is going on in your classroom at any one time. To pull it all off, you'll need to examine your own strengths and weaknesses in each of the intelligences and recognize when you have to call on specialists and resource people from your school or community.

> To pull it all off, you'll need to examine your own strengths and weaknesses in each of the intelligences...

Ask the librarian to suggest colorful books, informative films, and trips that will engage children in learning more about particular subjects. Team up with the art teacher to learn about crafts and other art forms. Incorporate music, song, and dance by involving the music teacher in your studies. Ask the physical education teacher to include games, dances, and movements related to a field of study in gym class.

Check around the school. Is there a teacher, administrator, or other staff person who has a special interest in a subject your students are studying and would like to share it with them?

Know the resources, including people, available in your community. Your geographic area may offer hands-on history, science, art, and math challenges. Invite people who have succeeded in fields related to the different intelligences to discuss their occupations and how they relate to the topics you're studying.

Most of all, remember that we are all different. And within the uniqueness of each person lies the excitement of knowing others who expand our view of the world. When we recognize and foster our students' different interests and styles, we let them know that they have valuable contributions to make to their own lives and to our world.

Learning Differences— Not Disabilities

by Thomas Armstrong

I don't believe in learning disabilities. I realize saying that will probably upset a lot of people. Learning disabilities have become as acceptable to educators as diseases are to physicians.

In my way of thinking, though, education has no place for learning "diseases." Instead of focusing on *deficiencies*—what kids *can't* do—education should be based on *growth*—how kids *can* learn. But so far, in all the thousands of tests and programs developed in the past 20 years to "remediate" frustrated learners, I've seen very little attention paid to how LD kids can learn and grow.

Mary Poplin, the former editor of the *Learning Disability Quarterly*, noted this omission in a farewell address to her readership a few years ago:

> The horrifying truth is that in the four years I have been editor of *LDQ*, only one article has been submitted that sought to elaborate on the talents of the learning disabled. . . . Why do we not know if our students are talented in art, music, dance, athletics, mechanical repair, computer programming, or are creative in other nontraditional ways? . . . It is because, like regular educators, we care only about competence in its most traditional and bookish sense.[1]

This narrow conception of competence has excluded a broad range of children, who are learning *different*, but who are called learning *disabled.*

From *Principal*, vol. 68, no. 1, p. 34–36, September 1988. © 1988 by the National Association of Elementary School Principals. Reprinted with permission.

I did my doctoral dissertation on the strengths of LD children. In the process, I discovered a few things that might surprise you. I learned that kids labeled "LD" are often nonverbally creative; better than average at visual-spatial tasks; and talented in mechanical, architectural, musical, and athletic pursuits. Some are even highly talented in specific language and mathematical areas.[2]

Why isn't this information more widely recognized and acted on? One reason, as Mary Poplin points out, is that special education is especially prone to a problem that afflicts *all* of public education: Schools have become worksheet wastelands. Classroom teachers spend too much time on paper-and-pencil tasks and not enough time on active learning that engages the total individual.

> Special education is especially prone to a problem that afflicts *all* of public education: Schools have become worksheet wastelands.

This heavy reliance on dittos and textbooks reinforces a habit of thinking about schoolwork solely as bookwork. Harvard University's Howard Gardner, author of *Frames of Mind,*[3] had it right when he said that there are at least seven different kinds of intelligence and that our schools are only dealing with two of them: linguistic and logical-mathematical intelligence. In other words, the child who reads, spells, computes, and reasons well goes to the head of the class.

Concentration on only these abilities, though, ignores the dominant strengths of perhaps the majority of children in the classroom. Many children are not so gifted in linguistic or logical-mathematical intelligence, but may be talented in one or more of five other intelligences: musical, spatial, bodily-kinesthetic, interpersonal, and intrapersonal. All too often, such children are at risk of being unjustly labeled "learning disabled."

The abilities these kids possess simply never get a chance to be displayed in the classroom. There seems to be no room for the young mechanical wizard, or the child who can dance well, or the ham who performs skits brilliantly, or the "street-wise" playground leader who turns "school dumb" in class. From such students, we have created the "six-hour disabled child," who functions below grade level during school hours, but learns much better away from school.

There are hundreds of thousands of kids like this in our schools. What can we do to help them?

First, we've got to find out what they're good at and help them develop their strengths in the classroom. Ironically, we now do this for gifted children, who are *least* in need of having their talents identified. It is far more critical for "LD" children to have a chance to shine in some area.

Gardner's theory of multiple intelligences serves as an excellent framework for finding the strengths in *all* kids, including the gifted and learning different. Keeping in mind that all children possess each of the seven intelligences to some degree and that there are different ways to be intelligent even within a single category, here is what to look for in the classroom:

> **Gardner's theory of multiple intelligences serves as an excellent framework for finding the strengths in *all* kids.**

The *linguistic child* is word-oriented; a good storyteller and writer; a trivia expert; an avid reader who thinks in words and loves verbal play (tongue twisters, puns, riddles).

The *logical-mathematical child* is concept-oriented; the little scientist who loves experiments, testing hypotheses, and discovering logical patterns in nature; a good math student.

The *spatial child* is image- and picture-oriented; a daydreamer; an artist, designer, or inventor; attracted to visual media; adept at spatial puzzles (Rubik's cube, three-dimensional tick tack toe); creates visual patterns.

The *musical child* is rhythm- and melody-oriented; may sing or play a musical instrument; sings little songs in class; becomes animated and may study better when music is playing.

The *bodily-kinesthetic child* is physically-oriented; excels in athletics or fine-motor areas like crafts; achieves self-expression through body action (acting, dancing, mime); touches things to learn about them.

The *interpersonal child* is socially-oriented; has strong leadership abilities; mediates disputes; can be an excellent peer teacher; enjoys group games and cooperative learning.

The *intrapersonal child* is intuitively-oriented; is strong-willed and self-motivated; prefers solitary hobbies and activities; marches to the beat of a different drummer.

Since traditional instruction caters to linguistic and logical-mathematical learners, kids with strengths in the other five areas of intelligence aren't ordinarily taught according to their most natural ways of learning. Sitting quietly in a classroom is totally against the natural inclinations of bodily-kinesthetic children, who need to move in order to learn and who may thus be considered "hyperactive" (and unjustly medicated). Spatial children, who need vivid images and pictures to learn, are apt to be classified as "dyslexic" because they are dragged too quickly into the world of abstract numbers and letters.

> **Teachers need to make a conscious effort to connect math with the other intelligences.**

Such children seldom learn well in conventional classrooms and usually they continue to fail in remedial programs, which simply administer more concentrated doses of the same teaching approaches that were wrong from the start.

On the other hand, if we were to give learning-different kids *regular classroom instruction* appropriate to their native intelligences, we might not have to ship them out to special education in the first place. Here are some examples of how teachers in both special and regular education classes can adapt their teaching to Gardner's intelligences:

• Even though *reading* is a linguistic act, it's possible to structure a reading program for spatial children around color (Words in Color is one such program) or to build in music, movement, social cooperation, and independent reading to reach other intelligences.

• In *math* class, the logical-mathematical child is in his element. The linguistic child is safe, too, as long as problems are explained with words. Teachers need to make a conscious effort, though, to connect math with the other intelligences.

I taught multiplication tables musically by singing them to a twelve-bar blues melody and spatially by telling kids a vivid story about a man named Mr. As-Much, who had sons named Just, Twice, and Thrice; whatever Thrice As-Much touched tripled in quantity. I taught the threes tables kinesthetically by having the class count to 30, clapping (or jumping or raising their arms) on every third number. Cooperative learning or math games assisted the interpersonal learner, while the intrapersonal learner learned best through a self-paced instruction book or computer program.

   • Typical methods of learning *spelling* words include copying the word several times (a linguistic approach) or applying spelling rules (a logical-mathematical method based on regularities). Spatial approaches might include making pictures out of words (putting rays around the word "sun," for example) or mentally inscribing them on an imaginary blackboard. Kinesthetic learners might trace the word in clay or stand up when the vowels of a word are spelled. For musical learners, spellings can be sung or chanted (perhaps going up an octave to emphasize vowels or silent letters). Seven-letter words, for instance, work really well to the tune of "Twinkle, Twinkle, Little Star" — try it with "another."

   So you see, many roads lead to the same instructional objective if only we are willing to take them. Many teachers have objected that they can't teach to several learning styles with so many children in their classes, but the kinds of activities I have mentioned can be carried out with large groups of children.

Many roads lead to the same instructional objective if only we are willing to take them.

   All a teacher has to do is teach seven different ways on seven different days. On Monday, teachers can begin with a linguistic approach—God help us, with a worksheet if they really have to. On Tuesday, they can bring in imaginative or art activities to reach the spatial learners. On Wednesday, the class might practice the skill through energetic physical activity on the playground or more restrained physical activity in the classroom. On Thursday, they can relate the skill to music, and on Friday, to a computer program, which will appeal to the logical-mathematical minds. The next Monday, games will reach the sociable interpersonal learners. On Tuesday, a choice of different activities caters to the intrapersonal learner.

Thus, at the end of seven days, the teacher would have presented the skill through every child's strongest intelligence and bolstered children's less-developed intelligences as well.

Learning centers can also be keyed to this multivariate approach to learning. Teachers can arrange their classrooms to include a book nook (appealing to linguistic intelligence), a math lab and/or science center (logical-mathematical), a round table for games and discussions (interpersonal), a carpeted open space for movement activities (bodily-kinesthetic), a listening lab (musical), a partitioned quiet space (intrapersonal), and an art media center (spatial).

Remember when I said I didn't believe in learning disabilities? I suppose that if you pressed me, I'd admit that they do exist. But all of us have them.

Some of us have dysmusia. In other words, we can't whistle a tune. Maybe you or someone you know has dyspraxia, which can lead to a tendency for one's legs to get all twisted up on the dance floor. Others may have dyslexia, which is just Latin bafflegab for "trouble with words."

What I'm most concerned about, however, is "dysteachia," the unwillingness to adapt instruction to a broader conception of learning. Dysteachia threatens to banish many children to a barren future in special education classrooms.

The only way to combat dysteachia is for educators to reconceptualize learning abilities to include the strengths of millions of kids who will otherwise languish in remedial programs. Aren't we ready at last to let learning-different kids shine in their own way?

NOTES

1. Mary Poplin, "Summary Rationalizations, Apologies, and Farewell: What We Don't Know About the Learning Disabled," *Learning Disability Quarterly* 7 (Spring 1984): 133.

2. Thomas Armstrong, "Describing Strengths in Children Identified as "Learning Disabled" Using Howard Gardner's Theory of Multiple Intelligences as an Organizing Framework" (Ph.D. diss., California Institute of Integral Studies, 1987).

3. Howard Gardner, *Frames of Mind* (New York: Basic Books, 1983). See also, M. Scherer, "How Many Ways Is a Child Intelligent?" *Instructor* (January 1985).

Gardner's Multiple Intelligence Theory: An Evaluation of Relevant Research Literature and a Consideration of Its Application to Gifted Education

by Dona Matthews

*The notion of intelligence is conceptually and practically impor-
tant for those working in the field of gifted education. In this
paper, Gardner's theory of Multiple Intelligence is considered from
the perspective of its educational viability, especially in comparison
with the more traditional IQ-based construct of intelligence. Empirical and theoretical support and contradictory findings are
discussed, from the literature in cognitive science and gifted education. It is concluded that Multiple Intelligence theory, by virtue of
its integrative possibilities and its theoretical breadth, is worthy of
further investigation and consideration by gifted educators.*

*The author would like to thank Dan Keating for his academic
guidance and the Social Sciences and Humanities Research Council of Canada for their financial support.*

Howard Gardner's Multiple Intelligence (MI) construct
(Gardner, 1983) postulates intelligence as a profile
showing an individual's relative strengths and weaknesses
across seven domains, or intelligences. This is a radical departure from the culturally predominant IQ-based conceptualiza-

From *Roeper Review*, vol. 11, no. 2, p. 100–104, October 1988. © 1988 by the
Roeper Review. Reprinted with permission.

tion of the nature of intelligence, which places a supreme value on language and logical-mathematical skills. Within the MI framework, Gardner has "no objection to using the word 'talent' in place of intelligences, provided that it is recognized that language and logical-mathematical skills are themselves talents. It is the step of putting one or two sets of skills, talents, or intelligences 'on a pedestal' which is repugnant to me" (private correspondence with the author, June, 1988).

This particular factorial approach to an understanding of the nature of intelligence holds much appeal because of its breadth: MI theory comprises linguistic, logical-mathematical, spatial, bodily-kinesthetic, musical, interpersonal and intrapersonal domains of intelligence. In this inclusiveness, it offers an integrative structure for many of the current research foci in cognitive science and education:

1. *G*, or general intelligence theory, has often been criticized as being empirically and conceptually inadequate (Frederiksen, 1986; Keating & MacLean, 1987; Sternberg, 1985). MI offers a potentially more viable theory of cognitive functioning, particularly because it is based on and takes into account the nature of real-world intelligent behavior.

> **MI offers a potentially more viable theory of cognitive functioning, particularly because it is based on and takes into account the nature of real-world intelligent behavior.**

2. The notion of social intelligence, for which there is empirical support as a component or domain of intelligence (Ford, 1982; Sternberg & Smith, 1985), is incorporated into MI theory as interpersonal intelligence.

3. The MI construct provides a cognitive framework for the distinction between paradigmatic and narrative thinking (Bruner, 1985; Zukier, 1986), in that the two thinking modes appear to be differentiably applicable to the various intelligences. For example, paradigmatic (analytical) thinking is generally more useful in the logical-mathematical domain, whereas narrative (contextual) thinking may be more appropriate in the personal domains.

4. Generally speaking, women have not been as successful in their use of their gifted level abilities as have men (Block, 1984; Kaufmann, 1981). It may be that (for whatever reasons)

women think differently than men, as Gilligan (1982) and Benbow (in press), from very different perspectives, suggest. If so, women might be expected to function more optimally if alternative domains more representative of their particular strengths, such as Gardner's personal intelligences (suggested by Gilligan's "care" construct), were socially valued and educationally developed.

5. The artistically creative dimension of intellectual exceptionality, sometimes called talent rather than giftedness, has been problematic for educators, and is often ignored or glossed over in the identification and programming of giftedness (Gardner, 1982; Torrance, 1977). The framework provided by MI incorporates the artistically creative domains in its inclusion of musical, bodily-kinesthetic and spatial intelligences, and thus provides a theory-based educational context for their development.

6. The extensive research done in the mathematical domain by Julian Stanley and his colleagues in the Study of Mathematically Precocious Youth (SMPY) (Benbow & Stanley, 1983; Stanley & Benbow, 1986) surprisingly has been ignored by most educators. If intelligence was perceived as multiple, this research would be rendered more accessible, as well as being recognized as important in its generalizability to other domains. The SMPY findings fit very well into a theory of multiple intelligence in that they demonstrate domain-specific development and educational needs.

> **MI offers a theoretical framework...that is inherently adaptive to a wide spectrum of individual cognitive differences.**

7. Adaptiveness to individual differences is an important and ongoing theme in the special education literature (Berliner, 1985; Glaser, 1985). MI offers a theoretical framework, in its concept of intelligence as a profile of seven intelligences, that is inherently adaptive to a wide spectrum of individual cognitive differences.

The fact that MI is theoretically or practically appealing does not, of course, validate it, does not mean that it explains the way that cognitive functioning is really organized. What research exists in the cognitive science literature to support this as a viable construct of intelligence?

EMPIRICAL SUPPORT FOR MULTIPLE INTELLIGENCE

A qualitative longitudinal study is being conducted at Tufts and Harvard Universities by David Feldman and Howard Gardner (Feldman & Gardner, 1987) to explore the viability of MI. At this time, although the program is in process and there are no scientifically validated results, there are preliminary indications that the children in the study demonstrate domain-specific strengths and weaknesses, along the lines predicted by the theory.

Marion Porath (1988), in her research conducted with gifted children to assess neo-Piagetian developmental levels across the domains of logical reasoning, verbal ability and spatial-artistic cognition (corresponding closely to MI's logical-mathematical, linguistic, and spatial intelligences), found evidence of domain-specific functioning. She stated that "some distinguishing features of gifted children's thinking may be independent of a general/structural analysis and far ahead of both expectations for age and performance in other domains, [which] appears to support further the hypothesis of independence of domains" (p. 4). Her results suggest that individual developmental differences tend to be domain-specific along lines predicted by MI.

> ...results suggest that individual developmental differences tend to be domain-specific along lines predicted by MI.

Although Ford's study (1982) of social cognition's relationship to social behavior was methodologically somewhat problematic (for example, self-ratings were taken at face value), factor analytic results did suggest a social domain of functioning separate from a cognitive or general competence domain. This supports Gardner's notion of the existence of the personal intelligences as separate from and different than other cognitive competences.

Chi (1978, 1981, 1985), in her studies with child and adult chess experts, and her theoretical discussions of these, found domain-specific knowledge to be a significant influence on memory. Ericsson, Chase and Faloon (1980), in their digit span memory training research, found no learning transfer from digits to consonants. If memory, a basic cognitive processing function, is domain-specific, as these data tentatively suggest, this is further support for a theory of intelligence as domain-specific or multiple.

Some educators and researchers have worked with children who show exceptional ability in one domain. Most notable for the scientific rigor of their research in this regard are Julian Stanley and his associates at Johns Hopkins University, in their work with mathematically gifted students in the longitudinal SMPY (Stanley & Benbow, 1986), as mentioned above. Similarly, Jeanne Bamberger (1982, 1986) has done some important work with the musically gifted. It is interesting to note that the mathematical and musical domains have yielded robust research results that indicate unique developmental patterns and educational needs, and that these same domains are identified as Intelligences in the MI theory. The possibility is thereby suggested that the other intelligences are similarly independent, and that a profile of Gardner's seven intelligences might indeed be a useful way to conceptualize intelligence, particularly for educational purposes.

In factor analyses of research done with laypersons and experts in order to develop an implicit theory of intelligence, Sternberg, Conway, Ketron and Bernstein (1981) found three main factors emerging consistently throughout their studies: problem-solving, verbal ability and social competence. These three factors can be seen to correspond to three of the multiple intelligences: logical-mathematical, linguistic and interpersonal. The fact that Gardner's spatial, musical, bodily-kinesthetic and intrapersonal intelligences have not been included suggests at least two possible interpretations, other than their not being genuine intelligences: (a) that they have not been analytically considered by the researchers, and (b) people's conceptualization of intelligence is somewhat limited by conventional educational and psychological use and practice. In any case, this research by Sternberg et al. suggests that people see intelligence as factorial, and at least partially along the lines indicated by the MI theory.

THEORETICAL SUPPORT FOR MULTIPLE INTELLIGENCE

Jackson and Butterfield (1986), in discussing the need for theory-driven research in gifted education, and considering the relevant research in cognitive science, suggested that it might be efficacious to devote more teaching time with gifted students to the transmission of domain-specific knowledge, and less to metacognitive skills. This position is highly reminiscent of Keating's (1980) model for the development of creativity that is grounded on the acquisition of domain-specific knowledge bases. Similarly, Sternberg and Davidson (1985) suggested that Renzulli's (1978) depiction of giftedness as involving task commitment, creativity and high ability is meaningful, but that the meaning of these terms varies across domains. These theorists, in recommending a domain-specific focus when educating children with exceptional ability, are suggesting an approach that would tend to emerge from educational programming based on MI theory. The fact that these positions have come from other theoretical traditions, and were not put forward in order to support MI, can be seen as convergent support for the plausibility of this theory.

> These theorists...are suggesting an approach that would tend to emerge from educational programming based on MI theory.

Rabinowitz and Glaser (1985), in a discussion of giftedness from the perspective of cognitive theory and research, suggested that an understanding of highly competent performance must take into account the interactive nature of domain-specific knowledge-based processes and general cognitive strategies. This provides further support for a theory of multiple intelligences, while at the same time suggesting the possibility of a general, or interdomain, cognitive function. This kind of conceptualization might allow the integration of g with MI, providing the cognitive theory equivalent of Spearman's (1927) and Thurstone's (1938) earlier work in factorial intelligence.

In their discussion of a triarchic perspective on the role of mental speed in intelligence, Marr and Sternberg (1987) suggested that the degree to which mental speed is adaptive and intelligent varies across tasks and across individuals. In addition,

Sternberg (1986), in discussing a triarchic theory of intellectual giftedness, stated that giftedness is found in a multiplicity of forms, and varies from one person to another. Although in neither case is empirical evidence or domain-specific analysis provided, these positions can be seen as being theoretically consistent with the MI construct, in their affirmation of the importance of domain-specificity and individual differences.

Although Keating and Bobbitt (1978) were not specifically concerned with domain-specificity, they suggested that "Future research should attempt to tie specific processing parameters to different ability factors. The pattern of relationships may be especially interesting, since some processes may reasonably be expected to be associated more closely with certain psychometric abilities than others" (p. 166). Such an association between processing parameters and psychometric abilities (in clusters described by the various intelligences) would be predicted by MI theory.

> Such an association between processing parameters and psychometric abilities ...would be predicted by MI theory.

Feldman (1986), on the basis of his work as a developmentalist, and citing research with chess experts, musical prodigies, and creativity, states that giftedness must be viewed not statically or narrowly, but developmentally and in a domain-specific framework. "Performance," he states, "is virtually always domain specific" (p. 302). This is a strong recommendation of Gardner's developmentally-oriented multiple intelligence approach, and in fact, as mentioned above, Feldman is working with Gardner in Project Spectrum.

Along similar lines, Horowitz (1987), in discussing a lack of and need for theory-based research concerning developmental issues relating to giftedness, suggested that developmental needs are likely to vary across domains. Interestingly for purposes of the present discussion, the domains to which she refers as examples throughout the paper are the following: motor, which can be understood as bodily-kinesthetic in Gardner's theory; language, which can be seen as linguistic; musical; artistic, which requires concentrated spatial ability; mathematical; and social, which can be interpreted as interpersonal. The only one of the multiple intelligences not discussed is the intrapersonal, which is also the least developed in Gardner's discussions to date (Gardner, 1983; Walters & Gardner, 1985, 1986).

CONTRADICTORY EMPIRICAL FINDINGS

Case (1986), in a discussion of research that purportedly shows the interdomain equivalence of reasoning, defends the neo-Piagetian position that cognitive development is stage-related and not domain-specific or much related to individual differences. However, as is pointed out by Turnure (1986), Case has not demonstrated interdomain measure equivalence in his research. In fact there appears to be cross-domain task confounding, a lack of attention in this research to the importance of contextually appropriate measures being used in each domain. In addition, only group data were reported; individual patterns are not assessible from the data given, and so one can not tell if individuals show same-level reasoning on cross-domain tasks, or if cross-domain similarities just reflect a generalized function of age. Because of these methodological flaws, this research can be used neither to confirm nor disconfirm MI as a viable construct of intelligence.

Siegler (1986), in strategy choice research using an information-processing (associationist) model with group data, states that there are unities in reasoning across the task domains of addition, subtraction, multiplication, spelling and a balance scale test. These tasks appear to relate primarily to Gardner's logical-mathematical intelligence, with spelling as representative of the linguistic domain. Although this might initially seem to disconfirm a MI thesis, because the data are reported only by group it is, as with Case, impossible to tell from this study whether individuals tend to show unities in reasoning across domains. In fact, children of different ages were used on the different tasks because, Siegler states, using a single age would have failed to reveal parallel patterns of behavior. Thus, inadvertently, this research suggests interdomain developmental differences in strategy choices, and can be used to support, rather than disconfirm, MI.

Keating and Clark (1980), in a study of cognitive development in different domains, stated that their results (consistent with those of Keating [1978] in investigating social and academic domains) did not support an interpretation that physical and interpersonal reasoning are separate domains of reasoning, and in fact suggested that more interdomain similarities than differences were shown in the measures used.

However, they did find a developmental rate difference, in that subjects applied formal reasoning to interpersonal issues significantly later than to the impersonal physical world. This would tend to support Gardner's notion of interdomain developmental differences. Additionally, and perhaps even more significantly, as suggested by these researchers in their conclusion, it may be that, in order to obtain an understanding of domain differences, domain-specific tasks must be used in domain-specific modes of functioning. In this case, that means that social factors must be tested dynamically and interactively, in a social context. When social tasks with a large intellectual/analytic/reflective component are used, it makes sense, as these researchers suggest, that it might be difficult to distinguish between impersonal and interpersonal intelligences. This research, although appearing to disconfirm an MI theory, is valuable in its illumination of important methodological considerations for further research into MI or domain-specific cognitive functions.

> ...it may be that, in order to obtain an understanding of domain differences, domain-specific tasks must be used in domain-specific modes of functioning.

In their study designed as a validity investigation of cognitive processing research related to individual and developmental differences, Keating, List and Merriman (1985) obtained results that also might be seen to call into question a theory of domain-specific intelligences. In this carefully designed research, an analysis of their subjects' scores provided no significantly differentiable factors, although 3 tests each for verbal and spatial abilities were used, providing opportunities for both convergent and discriminant validation of the existence of cognitive factors.

However, a close look at the measures suggests some confounding of verbal and spatial factors that could well lead to lack of discrimination between spatial and verbal factors: letters were used in a spatial task and form-matching was used in a verbal task. Thus, although the results might initially appear to disconfirm the validity of a domain-specific theory of intelligence, they do not do so at all conclusively. In fact, as the researchers suggest, more than anything else the results invite further investigation, preferably "in the direction of using the sophisticated techniques of processing analysis to chart short-term (microgenetic) changes in the performance of important, real-world complex cognitive tasks: to study cognitive processing developmentally and contextually" (p. 169). As with the Keating and Clark (1980) study cited above, this research is more instructive in its sophistication of methodological techniques useful for the further investigation of MI than as a disconfirmation of the MI theory.

IN CONCLUSION

There is much in the way of direction and suggestion in the cognitive research literature, and little if anything in the way of hard evidence at this time, for Gardner's theory of Multiple Intelligence. However, that does not mean that it is a flimsy proposition. It is very difficult, if not impossible, to prove empirically a theory of cognitive functioning like Multiple Intelligence. The psychometric, correlational and cognitive processing approaches have all been shown to be ambiguous and arbitrary when one is attempting to analyze complex real-world (beyond the laboratory) behavior and attributes (Cole & Means, 1981; Keating & MacLean, 1987). As an interesting example of this, Baltes, Nesselroade and Cornelius (1978), in a multivariate modeling analysis, demonstrated equivalent proof of environmental, genetic and mixed models of individual and developmental differences in cognitive processing, using obtained data structures of psychometric performance variance. Their results strongly suggest that it is inappropriate to infer causes of cognitive variance from psychometric data.

Perhaps, then, experimental data, difficult to collect, and ambiguous and arbitrary in analysis, are not even appropriate as tools in the confirmation of a theory of intelligence. Stanley and

Benbow (1986) argue the necessity for case study clinical research methods, rather than rigorously controlled experiments, when working with people. They cite Burt (1975, p. 138) as having stated this point especially clearly: "With human beings, when the problem is primarily psychological, statistical studies of populations should always be supplemented by case studies of individuals: early histories will often shed further light on the origin and development of this or that peculiarity" (p. 370).

In a similar vein, Feldman (1986), Horowitz (1987), Keating, List and Merriman (1985), and Keating and MacLean (1987), all state that what is needed at this time, in order to further understand the nature of individual and developmental cognitive differences, are theories and research methods which address questions of the individual's developmental history.

...it becomes clear that IQ is relatively useless in the identification of giftedness, and completely irrelevant in programming for it.

It is, in fact, an early and developmental case study approach, combined with some psychometric testing and as much scientific control as possible, that Feldman and Gardner (1987) are currently using in their MI research with Project Spectrum.

From a practical perspective, if intelligence is observed to be differentially distributed among multiple domains, more a profile of various abilities than a unitary and general innate quality of a person, it becomes clear that IQ is relatively useless in the identification of giftedness, and completely irrelevant in programming for it. A system that takes into account an individual's aptitudes across MI's seven domains would make infinitely more sense in terms of identifying who needs special programming, and what to do with these individuals, than a system that measures IQ and puts the high scorers together with a hodge-podge of "enriched" programming.

In an educational system wherein intelligence was conceptualized as multiple, a child demonstrating exceptional mathematical intelligence, for example, could be given accelerated and enriched mathematical instruction, along the lines of the SMPY research findings. Similarly, an individual whose exceptional intelligence lay in musical and artistic domains, but whose mathematical intelligence was average, could be given the direction and guidance that she requires to develop her special abilities, without having the frustration of participation in mathematics classes for "gifted" students. The MI framework, used intelligently, can lead to identification and programming policies that assess children's unique giftedness and offer appropriate educational modifications.

Cultural differences, including those attributable to ethnicity, language, race and socio-economic status, constitute an important and contentious topic in the field of special education. MI theory was developed with cultural differences very much in mind, and in fact an important factorial-inclusion criterion for Gardner in developing the theory was cross-cultural relevance.

> An important factorial-inclusion criterion for Gardner in developing the theory was cross-cultural relevance.

The issue of relative culture-fairness of MI and IQ can best be understood by considering the theoretical underpinnings of each approach. Subtests are chosen for inclusion in IQ tests not because they are theoretically the best possible tests of certain well-defined intellectual abilities, but because they work well psychometrically to differentiate the individuals in the normative sample. This automatically biases the test against those individuals whose experience deviates from the norm in such a way as to make them less likely to answer the questions in the conventional way. This of course includes, in an American-normed test, all those who are not middle-class, American-born, raised in the English language, and/or white.

When intelligence is defined as factorial along cross-culturally-determined and well-demarcated lines, as with MI, it becomes clear that certain subtests are more applicable than others to any particular domain. Subtests are chosen first because of their theoretical, contextual and cross-cultural validity, and are only then validated psychometrically. A subtest such as Comprehension on the WISC-R, with its obvious culture loading (with questions like "What is the thing to do when you see a robbery taking place?"), would be unlikely to be considered useful in any of the MI domains. The theoretical underpinnings of the MI profile predispose it to greater culture-fairness than has been the case with IQ.

MI theory leads to a broader identification and programming policy in the field of gifted education, one which is more likely to include those children whose exceptionally high intelligence deviates from the norm in its domain of focus, for whatever reasons of family background, individual development or innate potential. The possibility arises, with the framework provided by this theory, of finding a way for gifted educators to encourage the development of previously unrecognized or underutilized individual resources, leading to accomplishment and fulfillment on a personal level, as well as to great social benefits and enrichment.

> The theoretical underpinnings of the MI profile predispose it to greater culture-fairness than has been the case with IQ.

I would like to suggest that on the basis of the findings and recommendations discussed above, there is sufficient support in the cognitive science literature to consider Multiple Intelligence a viable construct of intelligence, a theory worthy of further investigation and consideration. It appears that MI, by virtue of its integrative possibilities and theoretical breadth, may have much to offer the field of gifted education.

REFERENCES

Baltes, P.B., Nesselroade, J. R., & Cornelius, S.W. (1978). Multivariate antecedents of structural change in development: A simulation of cumulative environmental patters. *Multivariate Behavioral Research, 13*, 127–152.

Bamberger, J. (1982). Growing up prodigies: The mid-life crisis. In D. H. Feldman (Ed.), *Developmental approaches to giftedness and creativity* (pp. 61–77). San Francisco: Jossey-Bass.

Bamberger, J. (1986). Cognitive issues in the development of musically gifted children. In R. J. Sternberg & J. E. Davidson (Eds.), *Conceptions of giftedness* (pp. 388–413). New York: Cambridge University Press.

Benbow, C. P. (in press). Sex differences in mathematical reasoning ability in intellectually talented preadolescents: Their nature, effects and possible causes. *Behavioral and Brain Sciences.*

Benbow C. P., & Stanley, J. C. (Eds.). (1983). *Academic precocity: Aspects of its development.* Baltimore: Johns Hopkins University Press.

Berliner, D. C. (1985). How is adaptive education like water in Arizona? In M. C. Wang & H. J. Walberg (Eds.), *Adapting instruction to individual differences.* Berkeley, CA: McCutchan.

Block, J. H. (1984). *Sex role identity and ego development.* San Francisco: Jossey-Bass.

Bruner, J. (1985). Narrative and paradigmatic modes of thought. In E. Eisner (Ed.), *Learning and teaching the ways of knowing: Eighty-fourth yearbook of the National Society for the Study of Education* (pp. 97–115). Chicago: University of Chicago Press.

Burt, C. L. (1975). *The gifted child.* New York: Wiley.

Case, R. (1986). The new stage theories in intellectual development: Why we need them; what they assert. In M. Perlmutter (Ed.), *Perspectives on intellectual development: The Minnesota Symposium on Child Psychology,* vol. 19. Hillsdale. NJ: Erlbaum.

Chi, M. T. H. (1978). Knowledge structures and memory development. In R. S. Siegler (Ed.), *Children's thinking: What develops?* (pp. 73–96). Hillsdale, NJ: Erlbaum.

Chi, M. T. H. (1981). Knowledge development and memory performance. In M. Friedman, J. P. Das, & N. O'Connor (Eds.), *Intelligence and learning* (pp. 221–231). New York: Plenum.

Chi, M. T. H. (1985). Changing conceptions of sources of memory development. *Human Development, 28,* 50–56.

Cole, M., & Means, B. (1981). *Comparative studies of how people think.* Cambridge, MA: Harvard University Press.

Ericsson, K. A., Chase, W. G., & Faloon, S. (1980). Acquisition of a memory skill. *Science, 208,* 1181–1182.

Feldman, D. H. (1986). Giftedness as a developmentalist sees it. In R. J. Sternberg & J. E. Davidson (Eds.), *Conceptions of giftedness* (pp. 285–305). New York: Cambridge University Press.

Feldman, D. H., & Gardner, H. (1987). Project Spectrum. Third annual report submitted to the Spencer Foundation. Harvard Project Zero; Tufts University.

Ford, M. E. (1982). Social cognition and social competence in adolescence. *Developmental Psychology, 18,* (3), 323–340.

Frederiksen, N. (1986). Toward a broader conception of human intelligence. *American Psychologist, 41,* 4, 445–452.

Gardner, H. (1982). *Art, mind & brain: A cognitive approach to creativity.* New York: Basic Books.

Gardner, H. (1983). *Frames of mind: The theory of multiple intelligence*. New York: Basic Books.

Gilligan, C. (1982). *In a different voice: Psychological theory and women's development*. Cambridge, MA: Harvard University Press.

Glaser, R. (1985). Cognition and adaptive education. In M. C. Wang & H. J. Walberg (Eds.), *Adapting instruction to individual differences*: Berkeley, CA: McCutchan.

Horowitz, F. D. (1987). A developmental view of giftedness. *Gifted Child Quarterly, 31*, 4, 165–168.

Jackson, N.E., & Butterfield, E. C. (1986). A conception of giftedness designed to promote research. In R. J. Sternberg & J. E. Davidson (Eds.), *Conceptions of giftedness* (pp. 151–181). New York: Cambridge University Press.

Kaufmann, F. A. (1981). The 1964–1968 Presidential Scholars: A follow-up study. *Exceptional Children, 48*, 2, 164–168.

Keating, D. P. (1978). A search for social intelligence. *Journal of Educational Psychology, 70*, 218–223.

Keating, D. P. (1980). Four faces of creativity: The continuing plight of the educationally underserved. *Gifted Child Quarterly, 24*(2), 56–61.

Keating, D. P., & Bobbitt, B. L. (1978). Individual and developmental differences in cognitive-processing components of mental ability. *Child Development, 49*, 155–167.

Keating, D. P., & Clark, L. V. (1980). Development of physical and social reasoning in adolescence. *Developmental Psychology, 16*(1), 23–30.

Keating, D. P., List, J. A., & Merriman, W. E. (1985). Cognitive processing and cognitive ability: A multivariate validity investigation. *Intelligence, 9*, 149–170.

Keating, D. P., & MacLean, D. J. (1987). Cognitive processing, cognitive ability and development: A reconsideration. In P. A. Vernon, *Speed of information-processing and intelligence*. Norwood, NJ: Ablex.

Marr, D. B., & Sternberg, R. J. (1987). The role of mental speed in intelligence: A triarchic perspective. In P. A. Vernon, *Speed of information-processing and intelligence*. Norwood, NJ: Ablex.

Porath, M. (1988). Synchrony and asynchrony in the cognitive development of gifted children. Paper presented at the tenth biennial Conference on Human Development, Charleston, S. C. March.

Rabinowitz, M., & Glaser, R. (1985). Cognitive structure and process in highly competent performance. In F. D. Horowitz & M. O'Brien (Eds.), *The gifted and talented: Developmental perspectives*. Washington, D.C.: American Psychological Association.

Renzulli, J. S. (1978). What makes giftedness? Reexamining a definition. *Phi Delta Kappan, 60*, 180–184, 261.

Siegler, R. S. (1986). Unities across domains in children's strategy choices. In M. Perlmutter (Ed.), *Perspectives on intellectual development: The Minnesota Symposium on Child Psychology*, vol. 19. Hillsdale, NJ: Erlbaum.

Spearman, C. (1927). *The ability of man.* New York: MacMillan.

Stanley, J. C., & Benbow, C. P. (1986). Youths who reason exceptionally well mathematically. In R. J. Sternberg & J. E. Davidson (Eds.), *Conceptions of giftedness* (pp. 361–387). New York: Cambridge University Press.

Sternberg, R. J. (1985). *Beyond IQ: A triarchic theory of human intelligence.* New York: Cambridge University Press.

Sternberg, R. J. (1986). A triarchic theory of intellectual giftedness. In R. J. Sternberg & J. E. Davidson (Eds.), *Conceptions of giftedness,* (pp. 223–243). New York: Cambridge University Press.

Sternberg, R. J., Conway, B. E., Ketron, J. L., & Bernstein, M. (1981). People's conceptions of intelligence. *Journal of Personality and Social Psychology, 41,* 37–55.

Sternberg, R. J., & Davidson, J. E. (1985). Insight on the gifted. *Educational Psychologist, 18,* 51–57.

Sternberg, R. J., & Smith, C. (1985). Social intelligence and decoding skills in nonverbal communication. *Social Cognition, 3*(2), 168–192.

Sternberg, R. J., & Wagner, R. K. (Eds.). (1986). *Practical intelligence.* New York: Cambridge University Press.

Thurstone, L. L. (1938). *Primary mental abilities.* Chicago: University of Chicago Press.

Torrance, E. P. (1977). Creatively gifted and disadvantaged gifted students. In J. C. Stanley, W. C. George, & C. H. Solano (Eds.), *The gifted and the creative: A fifty-year perspective.* Baltimore: Johns-Hopkins University Press.

Turnure, J. E. (1986). Stages in cognitive development: Comments on Case's paper. In M. Perlmutter (Ed.), *Perspectives on intellectual development: The Minnesota Symposium on Child Psychology.* Hillsdale, NJ: Erlbaum.

Walters, J. M., & Gardner, H. (1985). The development and education of intelligences. In F. R. Link (Ed.), *Essays on the intellect.* Alexandria, VA: Association for Supervision and Curriculum Development.

Walters, J. M., & Gardner, H. (1986). The theory of multiple intelligences: Some issues and answers. In R. J. Sternberg & R. K. Wagner (Eds.), *Practical intelligence.* New York: Cambridge University Press.

Zukier, H. (1986). The paradigmatic and narrative modes in goal-guided inference. In R. M. Sorrentino & E. T. Higgins (Eds.), *Motivation and cognition.* New York: The Guilford Press.

Special Applications

Implementing the theory of multiple intelligences is a creative process. Each one who applies the theory interprets it according to his or her particular style. In this final section, four innovative applications of multiple intelligences theory are explored. From setting goals to developing curriculum and creating alternate assessments, the expanded notion of intelligence as seven frames of mind is creating an impressive display of educational fireworks.

In "Using Multiple Intelligences to Set Goals," Launa Ellison explains how her fourth grade fall conferences help students develop goals for the year in all of the seven intelligences. Her goal-setting design incorporates a "checking time" in February to see how students are progressing with their goals and includes parents in the process.

Thomas Armstrong contributes to this section with an article on seven ways to develop curriculum. In "Multiple Intelligences: Seven Ways to Approach Curriculum," Armstrong tells stories of his own classroom encounters and concludes with a blueprint for the future, using the multiple intelligences to ensure success for all children.

In "Multiple Technologies for Multiple Intelligences," Dee Dickinson promotes the use of multimedia applications in the classroom as a way of exploring and expanding students' intelligences. The author categorizes various technologies according to the intelligence they help develop and explains how the applications "can help educators to address these multiple intelligences." Dickinson's survey is an excellent starting point for incorporating technological applications into the development of the seven frames of mind.

The final piece, by Mara Krechevsky, promotes the multiple intelligences as an assessment tool. "Evaluating young children's strengths in many domains, not just language and logic" is the focus of Krechevsky's article, "Project Spectrum: An Innovative Assessment Alternative." In reading about number games, art portfolios, and creative and athletic performances, it becomes clear that Gardner's theory is at the root of the authentic assessment movement. The principles of blurring the line between curriculum and assessment, embedding assessment in meaningful, real-world activities, using measures that are "intelligence fair," emphasizing children's strengths, and attending to the stylistic dimensions of performance, align with the goals of the global drive for broader assessments and more authentic measures.

Using Multiple Intelligences to Set Goals

by Launa Ellison

S tudents arrive on our doorsteps vastly different from one another.

Some students are self-confident. They are organized, alert, and capable. Some students slump low in their chairs, hoping to survive but feeling defeated.

Some children have many friends. They know how to solve interpersonal problems using "win-win" strategies. They respect others and cooperate. Other students do not.

Some children have a vast knowledge of the world. They have traveled and have benefited from extensive interaction with adults. Other children have only seen the world through the television set.

To meet the needs of such diverse students, our K–8 public school began individual "Goal-Setting Conferences." Over the last 10 years, we have found that goal setting gives credence to the many factors that affect learning, not just the "basic skills." In 1991, we reformatted our goal setting to reflect Gardner's theory of multiple intelligences, a system that suggests all humans can be intelligent in as many as seven ways.

> Over the last 10 years, we have found that goal setting gives credence to the many factors that affect learning, not just the "basic skills."

From *Educational Leadership,* vol. 50, no. 2, p. 69–72, October 1992. © 1992 by the Association for Supervision and Curriculum Development. Reprinted with permission.

As I began using our new goal-setting form, I sensed that parents had an increased respect for their child's abilities now that they held the status of "intelligence." The child who excelled at drawing was now valued as demonstrating Visual-Spatial Intelligence. The child who made friends easily and worked well in groups became respected for her Interpersonal Intelligence. The intelligence label validated the importance of the skill.

SEPTEMBER CONFERENCES

We begin our goal setting with conferences in September. These conferences provide me with the opportunity to learn about my students while establishing a warm, open relationship with parents. I encourage parents and students to verbalize what they feel is important to accomplish during the school year. My role during the conference is to listen and to ask questions.

> I encourage parents and students to verbalize what they feel is important to accomplish during the school year.

I begin with the student: "Have you thought about your goals for this school year?" Setting goals is a basic, lifelong skill. Goals guide and focus one's energy. Because our students have been involved in Goal-Setting Conferences since kindergarten, they often have very clear opinions regarding their own goals. On the other hand, some do not.

I ask parents, "What is your child really good at? What is important in his life?" I note the child's strengths.

I continue, "What is hard for your child? What are you concerned or frustrated with?" Parents are the resident experts on their children. They know a child's history and way of approaching the world. I learn a lot by listening to what is said—and unsaid.

THE GOAL-SETTING FORM

Our goal-setting form begins with Intrapersonal Intelligence (the capacity for understanding the self). Students' goals focus on their feelings, confidence, responsibility, and self-management. Intrapersonal Intelligence is crucial for school success.

Sue needs to figure out why she gets frustrated. Bonnie's goal is to relax and smile more. A 4th grader wants to "remember what assignments to get done." Andrew's parents want their son to "be proud of your work." Devin's goal is to "ask questions when I don't understand something."

The second goal area relates to Interpersonal Intelligence (the ability to understand others). Most students set goals of "making a lot of new friends," working well in cooperative groups, and solving interpersonal problems immediately rather than letting them fester. One student's goal was to learn the names of his classmates. To help him achieve this goal, I often asked him to pass out papers to the class. Other common goals relate to planning for cross-age mentoring with 1st and 2nd graders and peer tutoring within our classroom.

The conference form continues with goals related to Linguistic Intelligence. One child stated, "I want to be reading chapter books by the end of the year." Another needs to "pay attention to proofreading." A 5th grader wants to write "dynamic reports," and John wants to be faster at cursive writing.

Students tend to have very specific Logical-Mathematical goals. For instance, "I want to be really good at long division." "I want to feel comfortable about all fractions." "I want to learn negative numbers."

For Visual-Spatial goals, students often aim for achievements in geometry and art. One child wants to "make 3-D constructions." Another wants to "draw cats well" or "draw houses in perspective."

Bodily-Kinesthetic goals often include earning the Presidential Physical Fitness Award, a concrete achievement. One child wants to "run better so I don't get tired." Another hopes to "play hard in gym rather than hanging back."

Students' goals for Musical Intelligence often involve practicing an instrument: "I'm going to practice my flute 20 minutes every day." Another goal is "better cooperation during music class."

Our goal-setting form mentions two goals beyond Gardner's system. The World Understanding goal encompasses social studies and science information: "I want to study whales," or "I want to know all the countries of the world." In a section titled Other Goals in Your Life, students write statements like, "I'm going to keep my room clean," and "I want to be a lunchroom helper."

CHECKING IN

February brings a second round of conferences to review progress toward the original goals. I begin by asking the student for self-evaluation. "How do you feel you are doing on remembering the assignments?" "Do you feel you are learning hard enough math?" "Are you able to work through group problems more than you were earlier in the year?" Our February conference reaffirms, refocuses, and celebrates. I also redirect goal statements, since I now have a better understanding of my student's abilities and learning styles.

> As students internalize the many forms of intelligent behavior, they broaden their respect for the diversity of abilities within our classroom.

Throughout the year, I refer to the concept of multiple intelligences in class. When I read aloud to my students, I discuss the type of intelligence the novel's characters seem to possess. As students create 3-D geometric shapes, I discuss Visual-Spatial Intelligence. I play Native American flute or Spanish guitar music as background during journal or work time, and then I discuss Musical Intelligence. I refer to the wide variety of intelligent behaviors that world cultures value. As students internalize the many forms of intelligent behavior, they broaden their respect for the diversity of abilities within our classroom.

VALUING GOALS

While the goal-setting process is important, remembering the goals and consciously working toward success are also crucial. I help students rewrite each of their goals into affirmation statements. In their journals, they write and draw about imagined successes relating to their goals. Two-time Olympic pentathlete Marilyn King describes the process: "To accomplish any goal, you must have a crystal clear image of that goal and keep it uppermost in your mind. We know that by maintaining that image, the 'how-to' steps necessary for the realization of that goal will begin to emerge spontaneously. If you cannot imagine the goal, the 'how-to' steps will never emerge, and you'll never do it. Clearly the first step to any achievement is to dare to imagine that you can do it" (1988, p. 15).

The goal-setting form is an important part of our student assessment and an important aspect in building a positive relationship with parents. Our documentation of student growth includes portfolios, collections of significant student work, students' successes, comments, and photographs of presentations, plays, and three-dimensional creations. The portfolios contain students' self-evaluations as well as learning style assessments. Drawings, writing, and summative computer printouts on math computational skills are also included. Parents are invited to Achievement Days to examine the portfolios. Not only do parents and children thoroughly enjoy this personal focus time, but parents also get to see how goal setting has affected their children's education.

Individual goal-setting conferences require precious teacher time in September and February, but the benefits significantly outweigh the effort. Goal setting has proved to be an excellent system in our school and has been adopted by others.

Individual goal setting helps us honor student differences and plan for the wide range of diverse needs. And by using Gardner's multiple intelligences, all areas of growth become the domain for school learning and all kinds of excellence are celebrated.

REFERENCES

Armstrong, T. (1987). *In Their Own Way*. Los Angeles: Jeremy Tarcher.

Gardner, H. (1983). *Frames of Mind*. New York: Basic Books.

King, M. (Winter 1988). "Ordinary Olympians." *In Context* 18:14–15.

Lazear, D. (1991). *Seven Ways of Knowing*. Palatine, IL: IRI/Skylight Publishing.

Lazear, D. (1992). *Seven Ways of Teaching*. Palatine, IL: IRI/Skylight Publishing.

Multiple Intelligences: Seven Ways to Approach Curriculum

by Thomas Armstrong

I don't remember how I learned to tell time. So, when I was asked by a Wisconsin school district to develop a multiple intelligences way of teaching time to a group of 1st graders, I was initially stymied. My thoughts went back to my own teaching experience as a learning disability specialist. My students' workbooks on telling time had them drawing in the large and small hands on pictures of clocks. Boorr-ing! If we wanted to get a little more experiential, the special education office furnished cardboard clock faces. Students were supposed to get "hands on" experience by pushing the little hands around these faux clocks. Not very inspiring.

> The theory of multiple intelligences consistently amazes me with its ability to serve as a template in constructing strategies for student success.

Fortunately, I had a new model of learning—the theory of multiple intelligences—to help me in my quest. Developed a little over 10 years ago by Howard Gardner, professor of education at Harvard University, the theory of multiple intelligences consistently amazes me with its ability to serve as a template in constructing strategies for student success. The intelligences, briefly described, are:

- **Linguistic:** the intelligence of words.
- **Logical-mathematical:** the intelligence of numbers and reasoning.

From *Educational Leadership*, vol. 52, no. 3, p. 26–28, November 1994. © 1994 by the Association for Supervision and Curriculum Development. Reprinted with permission.

- **Spatial:** the intelligence of pictures and images.
- **Musical:** the intelligence of tone, rhythm, and timbre.
- **Bodily-Kinesthetic:** the intelligence of the whole body and the hands.
- **Interpersonal:** the intelligence of social understanding.
- **Intrapersonal:** the intelligence of self-knowledge.

At times, I almost think of Gardner as an archeologist who has discovered the Rosetta stone of learning. One can use this model to teach virtually anything, from the "schwa" sound to the rain forest and back. The master code of this learning style model is simple: for whatever you wish to teach, link your instructional objective to *words, numbers* or *logic, pictures, music, the body, social interaction,* and/or *personal experience.* If you can create activities that combine these intelligences in unique ways, so much the better!

> **One can use this model to teach virtually anything, from the "schwa" sound to the rain forest and back.**

A STORY OF TIME

When I marched into that 1st grade classroom in Wisconsin to teach "time," I had no worksheets or tiny cardboard clock faces in my briefcase. Instead, I began by telling them a story about a Land of No Time and how confusing it was for people there (they were always missing appointments). The King and Queen sent a group of adventurers in quest of time because it was rumored that a Land of Time existed beyond the horizon. After many exciting adventures, the group finally arrived. They knew they'd arrived because there were clocks and watches everywhere! They met with the King and Queen of Time and were told to contact a family who lived up on a hill on the outskirts of Times City; an Irish family named (appropriately enough) the O'Clocks! They had 12 children. The youngest was named One, the next in age Two, and so on down the line. And twice a day, each child would climb up onto the highest point in the land and shout a little rhyme. This is what One O'Clock's rhyme sounded like:

My name's One O'Clock
I tell time
Listen while I sing
My timely little chime!
BONG!

Well, the adventurers were excited when they heard and saw this. They convinced the O'Clock family to come to the Land of No Time and set its home up on the highest point in the kingdom. Now everyone in the land had a reference point, for all they had to do was look up every hour and hear one of the kids sing a "timely little chime."

After hearing this story, students got up one at a time and stood in front of a huge handless plywood clock face five feet high and acted out the role of one of the O'Clocks. At this point I mentioned that each of the O'Clock children had one huge hand and one tiny hand. So with my assistance, each child made a different time with his or her back to the clock and "hands" pointing to the appropriate numbers while they sang their special rhyme.

After we all gathered around a circle, I told them that the Land of *New* Time (as it was now called) celebrated the O'Clocks' arrival by having a special "clock dance" every year. Twelve students sat in an inner circle, each one holding up a number from 1 to 12, while students got inside the circle and created a time of day using their hands and/or feet. Everyone danced around the clock to the tune of Bill Haley's "Rock Around the Clock." Then students went to their desks to write stories of the tale illustrated by clock faces showing different times. After they were finished, they returned to the circle and shared their pictures and words.

All of this took about an hour and a half. During this time, students used their whole bodies, their musical voices, their logical (number-counting) minds, their artistic selves, their co-operative spirit, and their own linguistic and personal intelligences to create images of telling time. The possibilities for extending this brief lesson into a more extensive curriculum was positively mindboggling. Students could put on a play of the story (interpersonal/bodily-kinesthetic), invent their own special time pieces (bodily-kinesthetic/spatial), make up their own time songs or raps (musical/linguistic), keep a personal journal of special times in their day (intrapersonal/linguistic), and explore other ways of telling time historically or cross culturally. This kind of approach to the curriculum begins to make worksheets with clock faces sound like educational malpractice!

A BLUEPRINT FOR THE FUTURE

Of course, some educators may think that this learning philosophy works fine with younger kids but that when students reach middle or high school age, they need to put these frills aside and get serious about learning. Unfortunately, this narrow perception of learning helps contribute to the alienation of adolescents. Children do not leave their multiple intelligences behind once they reach puberty. If anything, the intelligences become even more intense (especially bodily-kinesthetic and the personal intelligences).

> Children do not leave their multiple intelligences behind once they reach puberty.

Consequently, students should be learning their algebra, ancient history, government, chemistry, literature, and more through multiple intelligences. In algebra, students should be talking about the unknowns (the "x's") in their own lives. In chemistry, they should be learning Boyle's law by puffing some air into their mouths (gas in a chamber) and then seeing the pressure go up when they put all the air into one side, where it occupies a smaller volume (Boyle's law: volume is inversely proportional to pressure). They should be role-playing literature. They should be interviewing, surveying, building, dramatizing, rapping, cooperating, computing, problem solving, sketching, and learning in a thousand other ways. Why? Because these are the activities that go on in the real world.

If we could travel the world and look at the many ways in which different cultures show their capabilities, we'd probably observe thousands of different intelligences. The theory of multiple intelligences makes things a little simpler for us. By chunking the broad range of human abilities into seven basic intelligences, we now have a map for making sense out of the many ways in which children learn, and a blueprint for ensuring their success in school and in life.

READING LIST

Armstrong, T. (1987). *In Their Own Way: Discovering and Encouraging Your Child's Personal Learning Style.* New York: Tarcher/Putnam. An introduction to the theory of multiple intelligences for parents, especially those with kids who've had school difficulties.

Armstrong, T. (1993). *7 Kinds of Smart: Identifying and Developing Your Many Intelligences.* New York: Plume. This book focuses on using multiple intelligences as a tool for personal growth. Designed for the adult learner.

Armstrong, T. (1994). *Multiple Intelligences in the Classroom.* Alexandria, Va.: ASCD. A nuts-and-bolts guide to multiple intelligences covering subjects such as lesson planning, teaching strategies, classroom management, activity centers, thematic instruction, assessment, special education, cognitive skills, and cultural diversity.

Campbell, L., B. Campbell, and D. Dickinson. (1992). *Teaching and Learning Through Multiple Intelligences.* Tucson, Ariz.: Zephyr Press. Includes lots of strategies for activating the neglected intelligences: musical, spatial, bodily-kinesthetic, intrapersonal, and interpersonal.

Gardner, H. (1987). *Frames of Mind.* New York: Basic Books. The "bible" of multiple intelligences. Use it as a reference guide and as a means of supporting your classroom practice with solid theory.

Lazear, D. (1991). *Seven Ways of Knowing: Teaching for Multiple Intelligences.* Palatine, Ill.: IRI/Skylight Publishing. A teacher-friendly handbook full of ideas for helping students develop their multiple intelligences.

Multiple Technologies for Multiple Intelligences

by Dee Dickinson

I t is essential to help all students master basic skills and knowledge, but it is also essential to offer them opportunities for rich, creative experiences and opportunities to apply what they have learned in other contexts as well as in the classroom. Clearly, no one approach alone can meet the needs of all students. We must begin to integrate the most effective ways to teach and learn, drawn from all of history, including the present.

Modifying learning environments—especially with the help of multimedia technology—can vastly improve learning and even the very development of intelligence. People come equipped with the most complex form of technology on the face of the earth—the brain. How we learn has a great deal to do with how complex our neural connections become as we grow.

> **Modifying learning environments—especially with the help of multimedia technology—can vastly improve learning and even the very development of intelligence.**

According to researchers such as Marian Diamond, neurophysiologist at the University of California at Berkeley and author of *Enriching Heredity*, our raw "intelligence"—the complexity of our neural connections—depends not just on what nature bequeaths to us genetically, but also on how positive, nurturing, and stimulating a learning environment we have grown up in. Animal studies, for example, have revealed that animals with a wider variety of "toys" in their environments de-

From *The Electronic School*, vol. 14, no. 9, p. 8–12, September 1992. © 1992 by the National School Boards Association. Reprinted with permission.

velop more complex neural connections than those who have few such stimuli. Recent studies of the human brain corroborate that finding.

In addition to providing an interesting variety of materials and topics for stimulation, educators know that interactivity is a key element of a positive, nurturing, and stimulating learning environment. All ages learn best when they have many opportunities to interact with their environments: responding to questions, posing questions, hypothesizing, experimenting, failing, and trying again in a positive setting where it is safe to take risks.

> With multimedia, educators are acquiring new tools to address the individuality of special education students *and* regular students.

Educators who have learned to use devices such as videodiscs, CD-ROM, hypermedia, and the latest multimedia computers also know that these technologies create extraordinary opportunities to bring a degree of interactivity to the learning environment that is rarely achieved with more traditional learning materials. Information technology literally exists for the exploration and expansion of intelligence, through communication and the promotion of higher-order thinking.

Think about it: Huge data bases of information, accessible by on-line telecommunications, provide a wealth of "toys" to "stack up" as learners build towers of knowledge. Hypermedia, which allows learners to jump from one concept, image, or sound to another while investigating a topic, adds interactivity. And the latest multimedia systems pull all the resources together for easy exploration.

An additional aspect of multimedia systems makes them especially important: their ability to address the widely varying learning styles of different students. Conscientious educators have longed for centuries to treat every student as an individual, with individual backgrounds, aptitudes, and needs. Usually, however, only special education students get an individualized education plan that addresses their "differentness," facilitating learning through whatever means possible. With multimedia, educators are acquiring new tools to address the individuality of special education students *and* regular students.

Howard Gardner, a professor of education at Harvard University and author of *Frames of Mind* (New York: Basic Books, 1983), has developed a theory of seven or more "multiple intelligences" that are of equal importance in human beings. These separate intelligences develop at different times and in different ways in different individuals. Teachers find these different types of intelligence are synergistic: When one changes, others might be affected. And, Gardner writes, "the ways in which intelligences combine and blend are as varied as the faces and the personalities of individuals." Many of the current strategies used to expand human development are based on his theory.

Multimedia technology, and sometimes even "lower-tech" technology applications, can help educators to address these multiple intelligences. Following are Gardner's multiple intelligences, along with some of the multimedia applications educators can use to help their students develop those intelligences:

VERBAL/LINGUISTIC INTELLIGENCE: the ability to think, communicate, and create through words both in speech and in writing. Here are a few of the applications that help develop this kind of intelligence:

• IBM EduQuest's "Writing to Read" offers a rich opportunity to combine many kinds of creative, hands-on tasks using a variety of materials and work at a computer. It enables first- and second-graders to experience success in writing long before their fine motor skills enable them to spell out by hand what their minds are imagining.

• Wings for Learning/Sunburst's "Muppet Slate" helps youngsters produce texts illustrated with graphics that are a delight for children to produce and read.

• Standard word processing software stimulates learners to interact more closely with their work, as it makes it easier to make multiple revisions without retyping the complete text. And to help children develop their speaking skills, how about the standard audiotape player/recorder or camcorder as technology that provides immediate feedback to help users of all ages learn to tell a good story?

• Telecommunications programs such as National Geographic Kids Network stimulate writing by connecting children with their peers nationwide. And Apple's, "HyperCard," IBM's

"LinkWay," and other multimedia software and hardware make possible the creation of multimedia term papers that are far beyond what a learner could do without the technology.

Technology can also help children with multiple handicaps and "different abilities" to communicate, learn, and express themselves in creative ways. Students who cannot move may talk into a computer that writes as they speak. Others who can move but cannot speak may work with computers that "say" what the students type. Those who suffer from delayed speech may be helped by a "Wolf" board produced by Adamlab with overlays of pictures or words that identify themselves vocally when touched.

> Technology can also help children with multiple handicaps and "different abilities" to communicate, learn, and express themselves in creative ways.

New worlds of possibilities open for handicapped students with the use of technology such as LTJ Design's "Wee Talk" and Microflip's "Full Talk" for the deaf; flexible "Smart Keyboards" that fit the body shapes of handicapped users and are developed by Arjan Khalsa for Unicorn; "touch screens" that let the physically handicapped enter computer commands with ease; and EduQuest programmer Frank McKiel's "talking mouse" for the blind. Additional EduQuest software applications include "Speech Viewer" and "Phone Communicator" for the hearing impaired, "Screen Reader" and "Voice Type" for the visually impaired, and "THINKable" for those who need special help developing cognitive skills.

LOGICAL/MATHEMATICAL INTELLIGENCE: not just the ability to memorize and perform mathematical operations or algorithms, but also the ability to think mathematically, logically, and analytically and to apply that understanding to problem solving. Many software programs that deal with this area go far beyond the original drill-and-practice programs, which were simply workbooks programmed into computers. For example:

• Wings for Learning/Sunburst's "King's Rule" and "Safari Search" computer software develop mathematical and logical thinking through challenging, visual/spatial tasks.

• Brøderbund's "Geometry, Physics & Calculus" computer software develops higher-order mathematical thinking by making abstract ideas concrete.

• Videodiscovery's multimedia videodiscs "The Physics of Auto Collisions" and "The Tacoma Narrows Bridge Collapse" graphically illustrate physics concepts.

Other kinds of programs, such as Stanley Pogrow's HOTS (Higher Order Thinking Skills) learning system, develop logical and analytical skills by combining Socratic thinking in small groups with individual work at computers. HOTS is an excellent example of merging the best of ancient and new approaches, plus the most effective human and technological processes.

VISUAL/SPATIAL INTELLIGENCE: the ability to understand the world through what we see and imagine and to express ideas through the graphic arts. Technology is especially effective at bringing visual images into the classroom, not only for group presentation but also in individual learning.

Sometimes the effect of imagery is subtle. Accelerated learning methods that take a holistic approach to learning use charts, diagrams, and pictures on classroom walls to illustrate the topic of the day, even when no reference is made to them in discussion. This visual reinforcement of learning produces impressive results with students.

"Paint" programs are technological palettes that let students who are unskilled with paper and brush nevertheless create art on computer screens. Some argue that such technology is a crutch that bypasses "real" art learning, but I've seen it boost students to success and spark an interest in going back to the beginning, doing the hard word, and becoming off-screen artists as well.

A few programs worth noting:

• "Guernica," a multimedia program produced by EduQuest, is an exhaustive data base of information and interpretation of Picasso's great painting, available in random access to students at any level of ability or sophistication.

• "Illuminated Books and Manuscripts," also by Edu-Quest, supplies multimedia data bases, including Tennyson's poem "Ulysses" and Martin Luther King's "Letter from a Birmingham Jail."

• Scholastic's "Hyperscreen" and "Slide Show" computer software add visual imagery to oral presentations of both teachers and students. Desktop publishing, using word processing and printing for professional-looking text and graphics, enables even very young students to write, revise, illustrate, and publish poems, stories, and even books. What a motivation to continue writing.

Students can use camcorders to create their own documentaries as occasional alternatives to written reports. Teachers using VCRs can go beyond simple passive/receptive learning. For example, they can develop anticipatory thinking in students by stopping a video midway for discussion about what might happen next or by beginning the video part-way through and discussing what might have led to a particular situation.

Virtual reality, a burgeoning technology you can try in video arcades, lets users interact with seemingly real environments through electronic goggles and gloves. Medical students might practice operating on a human brain and architectural students could work out structural problems in virtual reality before they try the real thing. This exciting new technology will eventually reach K–12 classrooms as well.

A production of Shakespeare's "Macbeth" at Seattle's Repertory Theater suggests an exciting possibility for yet another form of electronically generated imagery. The ghost of the character Banquo appeared on stage in holographic form—quite ghostlike indeed. Some schools already are experimenting with holographic productions.

BODILY/KINESTHETIC INTELLIGENCE: the ability to learn through physical coordination and dexterity and the ability to express oneself through physical activities. This type of intelligence is highly developed in football players, ballet dancers, and surgeons, but we all can enhance the ability to learn and solve problems through physical movement or the use of manipulative materials. Multimedia technologies can also contribute to the process. Teachers of wiggly youngsters and bored-looking high school seniors—especially many "at-risk" students—will appreciate new methods of addressing their students' need to learn by moving.

Popular computer games such as "Pong" and "Breakout" led a Russian mathematician, Alexei Pajitnov, to develop an exciting educational program called "Tetris," available on Nintendo systems and, on disk, from Spectrum Holobyte. This highly interactive technology challenges fine-motor coordination even as it develops skills in logical thinking and mastery over abstractions—and, on top of all that, gives the learner an instant evaluation of skill.

> Teachers of wiggly youngsters and bored-looking high school seniors...will appreciate new methods of addressing their students' need to learn by moving.

Some programs offer ways to connect the computer to such items as Lego blocks with gears, wheels, and motors. An example is "Lego Logo," from LCSI/Logo Computer Systems, which lets students manipulate Lego-brand toy building blocks by computer using the simple Logo programming language. Using such programs, students can invent machines and program computers to make the machines work. Clearly, this process not only exercises higher-order thinking skills, but also helps students take responsibility for their own learning.

Similarly, Brøderbund's "Science Tool Kit" assists students in conducting physical or scientific experiments, using computer technology to document and analyze data.

Finally, consider "electronic field trips"—programs that allow students to interact electronically with a scientist who is exploring the depths of the Mediterranean or the inside of a volcano or some other interesting site. One school in the Midwest recently took a "field trip" to Puget Sound, where students were able to talk to a diver exploring marine life. At the program's conclusion, they could see and touch a real sea cucumber that was flown to them for the occasion.

MUSICAL INTELLIGENCE: the ability to understand, appreciate, perform, and create music by voice or instruments or in dance. Most educators know the value of mnemonic methods in memorizing key concepts—such as the song we used to learn the alphabet and have never forgotten. Technology applications that help develop students' musical intelligence can be equally valuable. For example, students can hum a tune into synthesizers such as the EPS 16+ from Ensoniq or the SZ-1 from Casio and make it sound like any instrument they choose, accompanied by a full rhythm section.

The Musical Instrument Digital Interface system, better known as MIDI, makes it possible to make music on an electronic keyboard, which can be made to sound like any instrument and then can be orchestrated electronically. Pygraphics' "Music Writer" and Activision's "Music Studio" are computer software programs that do the same. Just as the word processor enhances writing skills, synthesizers exercise and develop musical intelligence by giving students an early feeling of control and competence.

> **Synthesizers exercise and develop musical intelligence by giving students an early feeling of control and competence.**

"Menulay's Musicland" software from Computer Systems Research Institute can be used with children as young as three, who compose music by drawing colored shapes on a musical staff and then see their work translated into musical notation. A computer can then play back their compositions.

Multimedia programs such as Voyager's interactive videodisc of Beethoven's Ninth Symphony let students understand music on many different levels; listening to it, seeing the score as it is played, hearing individual instruments played alone, reviewing biographical material about the composer, and gaining access to information about the music's historical and cultural backgrounds.

Other multimedia music programs include Warner New Media's "Music Exploratorium" and the University of Delaware's "Videodisc Music Series." Such programs lead not only to learning and appreciating music but also to the development of musical thinking and understanding on deeper levels.

INTERPERSONAL INTELLIGENCE: the ability to work cooperatively with other people and to apply a variety of skills to communicate with and understand others. Studies show that groups of students working together on computers make much greater progress than when individual students work alone at the machines. Such cooperative-learning exercises develop interpersonal intelligence in supportive and stimulating ways.

Interpersonal skills also can be enhanced through electronic networks that link learners with peers in other parts of the school, community, or the world. One such network is National Geographic Kids Network, which puts students on-line with each other and with practicing scientists to do scientific experiments and share their data and analysis. Other networks include these:

> **Interpersonal skills also can be enhanced through electronic networks that link learners with peers in other parts of the school, community, or the world.**

• The Global Education Model in Yorktown Heights, N.Y., which links 41,000 students in grades K–12 with students in the Netherlands, Spain, and Indonesia to exchange information and ideas.

• The Albuquerque Public Schools network, which links 600 users in 120 schools through a districtwide electronic mail network.

• The Pacific Northwest Center, which links Washington State's innovative "Schools for the 21st Century" model schools.

• Internet, a network of more than 5,000 networks, which reaches more than 3.5 million people, interconnecting supercomputers, mainframes, workstations, personal computers, and even laptop computers and pocket radios along the way.

In addition, the Copen Family Fund in New York has fostered the development of a number of computer networks, such as I*EARN, which links five U.S. sites with 15 foreign countries. The fund is piloting on-line, low-cost computer conferences.

For educators, who often suffer from isolation in traditional school settings, telecommunications networks provide an important professional resource and support system. The new America Tomorrow on-line network, for example, links leaders in education, business, and communities and offers up-to-the-minute education news and resources related to school restructuring.

Finally, some schools are using "Lumaphones," by Teleclass International, to link Spanish language students to their native Spanish-speaking peers in Puerto Rico, transmitting photographic images as well as voice, offering rich opportunities for improving cultural understanding as well as language learning. Video telephones that came to the market in 1992 enable additional links of this kind.

INTRAPERSONAL INTELLIGENCE: the ability to understand, bring to consciousness, and express one's own inner world of thoughts and emotions. Multimedia technology can offer students the means to explore and better understand their inner worlds and can help teachers turn classrooms into centers of student-directed inquiry. Technology offers tools for thinking more deeply, pursuing curiosity, and exploring and expanding intelligence as students build "mental models" with which they can visualize connections between ideas on any topic. Students can jump back and forth at will between detail and overview, allowing them to exercise and develop both analytical and global thinking strategies and enhancing their understanding of their own thoughts and feelings.

> Technology offers tools for thinking more deeply, pursuing curiosity, and exploring and expanding intelligence...

Computer programs such as Ceres' "Inspiration" are "thought processors" that use text and graphics to help their users capture ideas and visualize the relationships between them.

Research by Allen Tough at the Ontario Institute for Studies in Education indicates that individual learning projects account for about 80 percent of all learning. Individual growth plans, created collaboratively by students, teachers, and parents, can encourage the development of intrapersonal intelligence. Technology supports such plans with electronic records, videotaped interviews, and multimedia portfolios of student work.

Intelligent tutoring systems track students' preferred learning styles and provide information in ways that are compatible with students' strengths or that help to develop weaker areas. At the same time, they help students become conscious of the ways they learn. Despite the clear benefits of using technology in the classroom, only about a third of the teachers in the United States have had as much as eight hours of training in technology use. The increasing availability of technology will mean little unless schools of education provide effective training and unless teachers have access to ongoing opportunities for staff development. Telephones, computers, and modems should be standard equipment in every classroom to make it easier for teachers to work together and to take advantage of the innumerable data bases, networks, and software available.

Teachers must become competent users of technology if school systems are to keep up with the rapid change in every field of knowledge and if students are to be equipped to undertake nearly any kind of work or profession. Indeed, the intelligent use of technology is now indispensable for creating a true, collaborative world of learning.

MULTIMEDIA SOURCES

Adamlab, 3350 Van Born Road, Wayne, Mich., 48184, (313) 467-1415

Apple Computer, Inc., 20525 Mariani Ave., Cupertino, Calif., 95014, (408) 996-1010

Brøderbund Software, 500 Redwood Blvd., P.O. Box 6121, Novato, Calif., 94948-6121, (415) 382-4400

Casio, 570 Mt. Pleasant Ave., Dover, N.J., 07801, (201) 361-5400

Ceres, 2920 S.W. Dolph Court, Suite 3, Portland, Ore., 97219, (800) 877-4292

Computer Systems Research Institute, Attn: Martin Lamb, University of Toronto, 6 Kings College Road, Toronto M5S 1A1, Ontario, Canada

Ensoniq, 155 Great Valley Pkwy., P.O. Box 3023, Malvern, Pa., 19355, (800) 553-5151

HOTS Project, College of Education, University of Arizona, Tucson, Ariz., 85721, (602) 621-1305

IBM EduQuest, P.O. Box 2150, Atlanta, Ga., 30055, (800) 426-3327

LCSI/Logo Computer Systems, P.O. Box 162, Highgate Springs, Vt., 05460, (800) 321-5646

LTJ Designs, 4207 Ambler Drive, Kensington, Md., 20895, (301) 496-4991

Microflip, 11211 Petworth Lane, Glenn Dale, Md., 20769, (301) 262-6020

National Geographic Society, Educational Services, P.O. Box 98018, Washington, D.C., 20090, (800) 368-2728

Nintendo, 4820 150th Ave. N.E., Redmond, Wash., 98052, (800) 633-3236

Pygraphics, P.O. Box 639, Grapevine, Texas, 76051, (800) 222-7536

Scholastic Software, 730 Broadway, New York, N.Y., 10003, (800) 541-5513

Spectrum Holobyte, 2061 Challenger Drive, Alameda, Calif., 94501, (510) 522-3584

Unicorn Educational Software, 6000 S. Eastern Ave., Las Vegas, Nev., 89119, (702) 597-0818

Videodiscovery Inc., 1700 Westlake Ave. N., Suite 600, Seattle, Wash., 98109-3012, (800) 548-3472

Voyager Company, 1351 Pacific Coast Highway, Santa Monica, Calif., 90401, (800) 446-2001

Warner New Media, 3500 W. Olive Ave., Burbank, Calif., 91505, (818) 955-9999

Wings for Learning/Sunburst, P.O. Box 660002, Scotts Valley, Calif., 95067, (800) 321-7511

Project Spectrum: An Innovative Assessment Alternative

by Mara Krechevsky

I t's free choice time in the afternoon 4-year-olds' classroom at the Eliot-Pearson Children's School in Medford, Massachusetts. The class is participating in Project Spectrum, an innovative approach to assessment in early childhood. Hallie, not quite 4 years of age, is once again roaming from activity to activity, finding it difficult to concentrate on a task for longer than five minutes at a time. Her ever-patient teacher first tries engaging her in the art table project, then in experimenting with the siphons at the water table, and finally in playing hospital at the dramatic play area, all to little avail. Hallie is easily distracted; she becomes sillier as the hour wears on, making increasingly poor eye contact with the teacher and speaking in nonsense words.

With 20 minutes left until group time, Hallie's turn comes up for the week's Spectrum activity: the assembly task. This task involves taking apart and reassembling two food grinders. Successful completion of the activity depends on a combination of fine motor skills with visual-spatial and problem-solving abilities. Hallie's eyes light up expectantly upon seeing the first grinder, and she immediately touches the main fastener, which loosens the handle and inner mechanism. Within minutes, the grinder is completely disassembled, and Hallie begins to put the pieces back together, carefully figuring out the correct direction in which to turn each screw. She adopts a trial-and-error ap-

From *Educational Leadership*, vol. 48, no. 5, p. 43–48, February 1991. © 1991 by the Association for Supervision and Curriculum Development. Reprinted with permission.

proach, her feet swinging excitedly up and down from her chair whenever she succeeds. She remains focused, persistent, and methodical throughout—correcting her own mistakes, oblivious to the rest of the class.

This anecdote illustrates the power of the Spectrum approach to assessment. Spectrum began in 1984 at Harvard and Tufts Universities as an attempt to reconceptualize the traditional linguistic and logical/mathematical bases of intelligence. Our first four years of research centered on identifying young children's distinctive cognitive and stylistic profiles. In addition to assessing linguistic and mathematical abilities, the Spectrum assessment battery examines mechanical, spatial, bodily, musical, social, and scientific abilities as well (see fig. 1). In a political climate that places increasing pressure on educators to extend formal instruction downward and embrace a narrow view of scholastic readiness, Spectrum offers a developmentally appropriate alternative based on a broad view of the mind.

> Spectrum offers a developmentally appropriate alternative based on a broad view of the mind.

A RICH CLASSROOM ENVIRONMENT

The theoretical foundation of the project stems from Howard Gardner's (1983) theory of multiple intelligences and David Feldman's (1980) theory of development in non-universal domains. Although many early childhood educators still think in terms of children's progressing through broad, undifferentiated stages of universal development, Spectrum was designed to recognize variation in both children and areas of activity. Thus, the Spectrum model identifies domain-specific strengths in areas often not included in many Piagetian or neo-Piagetian approaches to education. Spectrum is based on the assumption that every child has the potential to develop strength in one or several content areas and that it is the responsibility of the educational system to discover and nurture these proclivities. Rather than building around a test, the Spectrum approach is centered on a wide range of rich activities; assessment comes about as part-and-parcel of the child's involvement over time in these activities.

As Figure 1 indicates, the Spectrum measures range from relatively structured and targeted tasks (for example, in the number and music domains) to less structured measures and observations (for example, in the science and social domains). These measures form one part of a rich classroom environment that is equipped with engaging materials, games, puzzles, and learning areas. The learning areas enable children to make initial explorations of materials related to the domains assessed by Spectrum, as well as offering follow-up activities. For example, after the storytelling task, children can be asked to create their own storyboards at the art area. The assessment activities are administered throughout the school year. Documentation takes a variety of forms, from score sheets and observation checklists to portfolios and tape recordings.

Fig. 1. Areas of Cognitive Ability Examined in Project Spectrum

Numbers

Dinosaur Game: Measures a child's understanding of number concepts, counting skills, ability to adhere to rules, and use of strategy.

Bus Game: Assesses a child's ability to create a useful notation system, perform mental calculations, and organize number information for one or more variables.

Science

Assembly Activity: Measures a child's mechanical ability. Successful completion of the activity depends on fine motor skills and visual-spatial, observational, and problem-solving abilities.

Treasure Hunt Game: Assesses a child's ability to make logical inferences. The child is asked to organize information to discover the rule governing the placement of various treasures.

Water Activity: Assesses a child's ability to generate hypotheses based on his or her observations and to conduct simple experiments.

Discovery Area: Includes year-round activities that elicit a child's observations, appreciation, and understanding of natural phenomena.

Music

Music Production Activity: Measures a child's ability to maintain accurate pitch and rhythm while singing and his or her ability to recall a song's musical properties.

Music Perception Activity: Assesses a child's ability to discriminate pitch. The activity consists of song recognition, error recognition, and pitch discrimination.

Language

Storyboard Activity: Measures a range of language skills including complexity of vocabulary and sentence structure, use of connectors, use of descriptive language and dialogue, and ability to pursue a storyline.

Reporting Activity: Assesses a child's ability to describe an event he or she has experienced with regard to the following criteria: ability to report content accurately, level of detail, sentence structure, and vocabulary.

Visual Arts

Art Portfolios: The contents of a child's art portfolio are reviewed twice a year and assessed on criteria that include use of lines and shapes, color, space, detail, and representation and design. Children also participate in three structured drawing activities. The drawings are assessed on criteria similar to those used in the portfolio assessment.

Movement

Creative Movement: The ongoing movement curriculum focuses on children's abilities in five areas of dance and creative movement: sensitivity to rhythm, expressiveness, body control, generation of movement ideas, and responsiveness to music.

Athletic Movement: An obstacle course focuses on the types of skills found in many different sports such as coordination, timing, balance, and power.

Social

Classroom Model Activity: Assesses a child's ability to observe and analyze social events and experiences in his or her classroom.

Peer Interaction Checklist: A behavioral checklist is used to assess the behaviors in which children engage when interacting with peers. Different patterns of behavior yield distinctive social roles such as facilitator and leader.

A LOOK AT SPECTRUM'S FACETS

Distinctive features of the Spectrum assessment system include:

1. **Blurring the line between curriculum and assessment.** By gathering information over time in the child's own environment, Spectrum effectively blurs the traditional division between curriculum and assessment. For example, teachers collect children's artwork in portfolios and observe bodily-kinesthetic abilities through a biweekly creative movement session. The traditional test setting of a small room with an unfamiliar exam-

iner administering timed and standardized instruments, in the Spectrum view, provides too narrow and skewed a view of the child. In the Spectrum tasks, children's skills are integrated, rather than isolated. Thus, as we saw earlier, the assembly activity engages Hallie in an applied and meaningful task presented as part of her preschool curriculum.

2. **Embedding assessment in meaningful, real-world activities.** Rather than just focusing on skills useful in the school context, Spectrum uses the concept of adult *endstates* to focus its assessments on abilities relevant to achieving significant and rewarding adult roles. Examples of endstates include *naturalist, salesperson, singer, dancer,* and *social worker.* Thus, in the language domain, Spectrum examines a child's ability to tell stories or provide a descriptive account of an experience—valuable skills for novelists and journalists—rather than his or her ability to repeat a series of sentences. For Hallie, the applicable endstate is *mechanic.* In contrast to many standardized assessments, which might have Hallie copy shapes or block patterns, Spectrum provides her with a real machine to work on. This grounding of assessments in real-world activities ensures that the areas addressed are likely to be meaningful to the child, the teacher, and the child's family.

> Spectrum uses the concept of adult *endstates* to focus its assessments on abilities relevant to achieving significant and rewarding adult roles.

3. **Using measures that are "intelligence-fair."** Rather than viewing all abilities through the window of language and logic, as most standardized tests do, Spectrum attempts to tap abilities directly, via their own particular medium. In the above anecdote, Hallie works directly with simple mechanical objects, rather than answering questions about how machines work. The music perception and production tasks of the assessment employ Montessori bells and simple songs, while the movement activities elicit both athletic and creative movement.

4. **Emphasizing children's strengths.** In contrast to many educational approaches, particularly those used with children at risk for school failure, the Spectrum assessment approach seeks to identify children's areas of strength and to construct their education as much as possible around those domains of compe-

tence. Giving children experience in their areas of strength might not only increase their sense of self-esteem but suggest ways to address areas that are not as strong. For example, to boost Hallie's language skills, she could be asked to dictate instructions for disassembling a grinder or to tell a story about a machine she might invent.

> Giving children experience in their areas of strength might not only increase their sense of self-esteem but suggest ways to address areas that are not as strong.

5. **Attending to the stylistic dimensions of performance.** In order to capture fully a child's approach to a task, we soon discovered it was important to look not only at a child's cognitive skills but at certain stylistic features as well. "Working styles" describe how a child interacts with the materials of a domain, such as his or her persistence, attention to detail, and level of confidence (see fig. 2). While some children exhibit the same working style across domains, others have styles that are much more content-specific. Such information has important implications for designing educational interventions. In Hallie's case, she revealed the capacity to become extremely focused and reflective when working in her area of strength.

In the Spectrum approach, all of the information collected on a child is compiled at year's end into a "Spectrum Profile"; a short description, written in nontechnical prose, of the child's participation in the project's activities. The report addresses each child's areas of strength, either relative to himself or herself or to the child's peer group. Because of our belief that psychologists spend too much time ranking children and not enough time trying to help them, we also give concrete suggestions for follow-up activities that can be carried out at home or in the community. A "Parent Activities Handbook" suggests home activities that use inexpensive and easily acquired materials (for example, different ways to grow seeds, measuring and counting games, and so on).

Fig. 2. Stylistic Features Examined in Project Spectrum

Child is:
- easily engaged/reluctant to engage in activity
- confident/tentative
- playful/serious
- focused/distractible
- persistent/frustrated by task
- reflective about own work/impulsive
- apt to work slowly/apt to work quickly

Child:
- responds to visual/auditory/kinesthetic cues
- demonstrates planful approach
- brings personal agenda/strength to task
- finds humor in content area
- uses materials in unexpected ways
- shows pride in accomplishment
- shows attention to detail/is observant
- is curious about materials
- shows concern over "correct" answer
- focuses on interaction with adult
- transforms task/material

EARLY RESEARCH RESULTS

Hallie's class was one of two Eliot-Pearson preschool classrooms that participated in the initial phase of Spectrum research. This phase focused on assessing individual children's cognitive and stylistic strengths. Preliminary results from the two classrooms suggest that the Spectrum system does indeed identify distinctive intellectual profiles in young children[1] (for a full report, see Gardner and Hatch 1989, Krechevsky and Gardner 1990). We also found some evidence that a child's strength in one area might facilitate performance in another. For example, one child demonstrated exceptional storytelling ability, yet generally refused to participate in creative movement. However, she moved with unusual expressiveness when presented with storyboard props as a stimulus during one of the movement sessions.

With regard to working styles, most children seem to exhibit domain-specific configurations. Many were reflective and attentive to detail only in their areas of strength. However, some children demonstrated a more general working style, which at times worked to their disadvantage. For example, one boy approached every activity with his own agenda of ideas. Although in the less structured environment of the class he conducted many compelling experiments to test his hypotheses, he was unable to adjust to more structured task situations.

> With regard to working styles, most children seem to exhibit domain-specific configurations.

Preliminary follow-up data on children in the original Spectrum class indicate that strengths and working styles remained roughly constant one or two years later. Sometimes the particular combination of a child's areas of strength and working style determined whether or not a strength would reemerge. One girl, who in preschool constantly sought the positive regard of her peers, spent a lot of time at the writing table because her language abilities were advanced for her age group. However, because she was not the most able in her group the following year, she devoted the majority of her free time to art activities. Thus, the language abilities identified earlier were less likely to resurface and develop.

Responses from parents indicated that the areas where they were most surprised to learn of strengths included music perception, mechanical ability, and creative movement. A number of parents in the follow-up found it very useful to have a written profile to which they could compare more recent views of their child. The area parents were most likely to encourage at the one-year follow-up was drama, perhaps because they saw it as an especially effective way to combine ability in the language, social, and movement domains.

Currently, the Spectrum approach is being modified for use with children in kindergarten and 1st grade and for children who are more at risk for school failure. A broad-based Spectrum curriculum is being implemented in selected 1st grade classrooms with a large at-risk population in Somerville, Massachusetts. Children are being encouraged to develop their areas of strength in an apprentice-type model and to bring these strengths to bear on the established curricular goals of the 1st grade. We are administering pre- and post-tests to determine change in children's academic achievement, self-esteem, attitude toward school, and school adjustment.

THEIR PLACE IN THE SUN

It may be important at this point to outline the disadvantages and the advantages of Spectrum. First, a pluralized model of intelligence runs the risk that achievement-oriented parents will push their children in 15 areas, instead of a few. Second, parents and teachers may be tempted to track a child prematurely into pursuing his or her area(s) of strength. Finally, parents outside the mainstream culture may not be as concerned with their children's performance in domains not valued by the traditional culture.

Nevertheless, the approach offers a number of benefits. The Spectrum battery exposes children to more domains than are typically included in early childhood assessments or curriculums. Spectrum also actively involves children in the assessment process. They collect their work for the art portfolios and tape their own stories and songs. Time is also set aside for children to reflect on the activities in general. The Spectrum approach can be used on many levels: as assessment, as curriculum, or as a powerful philosophical framework through which to view children and their particular sets of strengths and working styles. In fact, the approach is as much a framework and set of ideas as it is a discrete program. Spectrum is currently being adapted for a variety of purposes by both researchers and practitioners in the field.[2] Because the approach takes individual differences seriously, it enables teachers to accommodate diverse populations and to individualize their curriculums. Moreover, because of its provision of many ways to demonstrate excellence, including ways that go beyond conventional scholastic success, Spectrum may be particularly suited for at-risk children. At best, the Spectrum approach promises to increase the chances for all children to find their place in the sun.

Author's note: The work described in this article was supported by generous grants from the William T. Grant Foundation, the Rockefeller Brothers Fund, and the Spencer Foundation.

NOTES

1. Because of the small sample size, the results reported in this article should be regarded as tentative.

2. We encourage these efforts and are interested in hearing from people who have tried to implement Spectrum. However, for reasons of logistics and limited resources, at present we cannot provide much in the way of support.

REFERENCES

Feldman, D. H. (1980). *Beyond Universals in Cognitive Development.* Norwood, N.J.: Ablex.

Gardner, H. (1983). *Frames of Mind: The Theory of Multiple Intelligences.* New York: Basic Books.

Gardner, H., and T. Hatch. (November 1989). "Multiple Intelligences Go to School: Educational Implications of the Theory of Multiple Intelligences." *Educational Researcher 18*, 8:4–10.

Krechevsky, M., and H. Gardner. (1990). "The Emergence and Nurturance of Multiple Intelligences: The Project Spectrum Approach." In *Encouraging the Development of Exceptional Skills and Talents*, edited by M.J.A. Howe. Leicester, U.K.: The British Psychological Society.

Authors

Jacqueline Anglin is a professor of Education and Human Sciences and the director of Faculty Grants and Research at Berry College, Mount Berry, Georgia.

Thomas Armstrong is the author of *Seven Kinds of Smart, Multiple Intelligences in the Classroom, Awakening Your Child's Natural Genius*, and *In Their Own Way*. He is director of Armstrong Creative Services in Cloverdale, California.

Tina Blythe is an educational researcher at Harvard Project Zero, Harvard Graduate School of Education.

Patricia J. Bolanos is the principal at Key Elementary School in Indianapolis, Indiana.

Bruce Campbell is a classroom teacher who has successfully bridged MI theory to practice. He is also a nationally recognized speaker and author on multiple intelligences, best known for his 1994 book, *The Multiple Intelligences Handbook: Lesson Plans and More....*

Dee Dickinson is CEO and founder of New Horizons for Learning, a Seattle-based international education network that bases its conferences on Howard Gardner's multiple intelligences theory.

Launa Ellison is a teacher in the Minneapolis public schools. She is the editor of the "Consortium for Whole Brain Learning" newsletter and author of *Seeing with Magic Glasses*.

Kathy Faggella teaches language arts, science, and art to children at the Norwalk Seaport Association in Norwalk, Connecticut. She has authored many books for teachers and children.

David E. Fernie is associate professor of Early and Middle Childhood Education at Ohio State University. His research interests include children's play and the ethnographic study of classrooms for young children.

Howard Gardner is professor of education and codirector of Harvard Project Zero, Harvard Graduate School of Education, research psychologist at the Boston Veterans Administration Medical Center, and adjunct professor of Neurology at the Boston University School of Medicine. He has authored and coauthored many books, articles, and papers on the theory of multiple intelligences.

Thomas Hatch is a project director at Harvard Project Zero, Harvard Graduate School of Education.

Janet Horowitz, a former teacher, is an educational psychologist and author of many education-related books.

Robert J. Kirschenbaum is an adjunct professor with the University of Phoenix and a school psychologist.

Mindy Kornhaber is a research coordinator at Harvard Project Zero, Harvard Graduate School of Education, and coauthor with Howard Gardner and Warren Wake of *Intelligence: Multiple Perspectives* (forthcoming).

Mara Krechevsky is an educational researcher at Harvard Project Zero, Harvard Graduate School of Education, and director of Project Spectrum.

Dona Matthews teaches courses on gifted education and various other education-related aspects of exceptional development at the University of Toronto, and has a private assessment/counseling practice focusing primarily on giftedness.

Joseph Walters is codirector of Harvard Project Zero, Harvard Graduate School of Education. He is currently involved in projects to implement student portfolios in five schools in Massachusetts and to evaluate the Aesthetic Education Institutes, programs that bring artists into classrooms across the country.

Noel White is an educational researcher at Harvard Project Zero, Harvard Graduate School of Education.

cknowledgments

Grateful acknowledgment is made to the following authors and agents for their permission to reprint copyrighted materials.

Section 1
Prufrock Press for "An Interview with Howard Gardner" by Robert J. Kirschenbaum. From *Gifted Child Today,* vol. 13, no. 6, p. 26–32, November/December 1990. Copyright © 1990 by Prufrock Press. Reprinted with permission. All rights reserved.

The National Council of Teachers of English (NCTE), David E. Fernie, and Harvard Project Zero for "Profile: Howard Gardner" by David E. Fernie. From *Language Arts,* vol. 69, no. 3, p. 220–27, March 1992. Copyright © 1992 by NCTE. Reprinted with permission. All rights reserved.

The Mid-Western Educational Research Association for "Reflections on 'The Unschooled Mind': An Interview with Howard Gardner" by Jacqueline Anglin. From *Mid-Western Educational Researcher,* vol. 6, no. 1, p. 18–20, Winter 1993. Copyright © 1993 by Mid-Western Educational Research Association. Reprinted with permission. All rights reserved.

Section 2
Harvard Project Zero for "The Development and Education of Intelligences" by Joseph Walters and Howard Gardner. A position paper from Harvard University, September 1984. Copyright © 1984 by Harvard Project Zero. Reprinted with permission. All rights reserved.

Section 3

The American Association of School Administrators (AASA) for "From Theory to Practice: Indianapolis' Key School Applies Howard Gardner's Multiple Intelligences Theory to the Classroom" by Patricia J. Bolanos. From *The School Administrator*, vol. 51, no. 1, p. 30–31, January 1994. Copyright © 1994 by AASA. Reprinted with permission. All rights reserved.

Section 4
Scholastic Inc. for "Different Child, Different Style: Seven Ways to Reach and Teach All Children" by Kathy Faggella and Janet Horowitz. From *Instructor*, vol. 100, no. 2, p. 49–54, September 1990. Copyright © 1990 by Scholastic Inc. Reprinted with permission. All rights reserved.

The National Association of Elementary School Principals (NAESP) for "Learning Differences—Not Disabilities" by Thomas Armstrong. From *Principal*, vol. 68, no. 1, p. 30–31, September 1988. Copyright © 1988 by NAESP. Reprinted with permission. All rights reserved.

Dona Matthews and *Roeper Review*, P. O. Box 329, Bloomfield Hills, MI 48303, for "Gardner's Multiple Intelligence Theory: An Evaluation of Relevant Research Literature and a Consideration of Its Application to Gifted Education" by Dona Matthews. From *Roeper Review*, vol. 11, no. 2, p. 100–104, October 1988. Copyright © 1988 by *Roeper Review*. Reprinted with permission. All rights reserved.

Section 5
The Association for Supervision and Curriculum Development (ASCD) and Launa Ellison for "Using Multiple Intelligences to Set Goals" by Launa Ellison. From *Educational Leadership*, vol. 50, no. 2, p. 69–72, October 1992. Copyright © 1992 by ASCD. Reprinted with permission. All rights reserved.

The Association for Supervision and Curriculum Development (ASCD) and Thomas Armstrong for "Multiple Intelligences: Seven Ways to Approach Curriculum" by Thomas Armstrong. From *Educational Leadership*, vol. 52, no. 3, p. 26–28, Novem-

Index

Training and Publishing Inc.

We Prepare Your Teachers Today
for the Classrooms of Tomorrow

Learn from Our Books and from Our Authors!

Ignite Learning in Your School or District.

SkyLight's team of classroom-experienced consultants can help you foster systemic change for increased student achievement.

Professional development is a process, not an event. SkyLight's seasoned practitioners drive the creation of our on-site professional development programs, graduate courses, research-based publications, interactive video courses, teacher-friendly training materials, and online resources—call SkyLight Training and Publishing Inc. today.

SkyLight specializes in three professional development areas.

Specialty #

Best Practices

We **model** the best practices that result in improved student performance and guided applications.

Specialty #

Making the Innovations Last

We help set up **support** systems that make innovations part of everyday practice in the long-term systemic improvement of your school or district.

Specialty #

How to Assess the Results

We prepare your school leaders to encourage and **assess** teacher growth, **measure** student achievement, and **evaluate** program success.

Contact the SkyLight team and begin a process toward long-term results.

Training and Publishing Inc.

2626 S. Clearbrook Dr., Arlington Heights, IL 60005
800-348-4474 • 847-290-6600 • FAX 847-290-6609

There are

one-story intellects,

two-story intellects, and three-story

intellects with skylights. All fact collectors, who

have no aim beyond their facts, are one-story men. Two-story men

compare, reason, generalize, using the labors of the fact collectors as

well as their own. Three-story men idealize, imagine,

predict—their best illumination comes from

above, through the skylight.

—*Oliver Wendell*

Holmes

TRAINING AND PUBLISHING, INC.